Science Experiences
for the
Early Childhood Years

Science Experiences for the Early Childhood Years

Jean Durgin Harlan

Ohio University

CHARLES E. MERRILL PUBLISHING COMPANY

A Bell & Howell Company

Columbus, Ohio

Published by
Charles E. Merrill Publishing Company
A *Bell & Howell Company*
Columbus, Ohio 43216

This book was set in Caledonia and Futura.
The Production Editor was Linda Lowell.
The cover was designed by Will Chenoweth.

Illustrations by Anne Clark Culbert
Photographs by John T. Harlan

ISBN: 0-675-08649-3

Library of Congress Catalog Card Number: 75-25420

7 8—83 82 81 80 79

Printed in the United States of America

For my children,
Betsy, Anne, John, Susan, and Julie,
and my mother,
who have taught me

Preface

"Wow! I just invented electricity!" That was Russell rejoicing. Russell was almost five. He had just spent ten absorbed minutes figuring out how to add a knife switch to the simple circuit he had completed. When the tiny bulb lighted, the glow of pride on Russell's face was brighter by far. Galvani and others preceded Russell in the invention of electricity, but he truly did discover electricity for himself.

When we present science experiences in the early childhood years we are not introducing new activities to children. We are merely *defining* a process they began at birth: making sense of their world with the intellectual processes currently available to them. If we define carefully, we can help children perform their self-imposed learning tasks more efficiently. We can also help them feel more secure as they find causes for events that worry them. In addition, we can help them become confident problem solvers by supporting their search for understanding.

The goals of this teaching framework, therefore, extend beyond the immediate acquisition of useful science information. They extend to strengthening the means of, and the motivation for, a lifetime of learning.

Acknowledgments

For their help in reading and criticizing this material, I am grateful to Lane Butler Nudd and Carolyn Quattrocki. Scientific accuracy was checked by Dr. Laurence Larson, Dr. William Romoser, Dr. Myron Sturgeon, and Dr. Louis Wright, all associated with Ohio University. Helpful insights were given by Dr. Wayne Aspey, Nancy Hultz, Polly Gagliano, Dr. Shirley Slater, Alice Lockard, and Lee Kliesch. Louise Frink, Lynn Aspey, Dr. Ernest Stricklin, and especially Dr. Mary-Lyell Rogers gave me needed encouragement and support. In addition, the four- and five-year-old discoverers from the Ohio University Nursery Child Care Center contributed significantly to this writing. I thank them all.

Contents

PART ONE   **The Rationale**

1 THE FRAMEWORK   **3**

2 SCIENCE PARTICIPANTS: CHILDREN, TEACHERS, AND   **7**
  PARENTS

3 IMPLEMENTING THE FRAMEWORK   **13**

PART TWO   **Concepts, Experiences, and
                 Reinforcements**

4 WHAT IS AIR?   **23**

5 WHAT IS WATER?   **41**

6 THE EFFECTS OF MAGNETISM   **61**

7 THE EFFECTS OF GRAVITY   **73**

8 SIMPLE MACHINES   **85**

9 SOUND   **105**

10 LIGHT   **121**

11 STATIC AND CURRENT ELECTRICITY   **135**

12   ROCKS AND MINERALS   149

13   PLANT LIFE   165

14   ANIMAL LIFE   191

APPENDIX 1   219

APPENDIX 2   221

INDEX   225

PART
ONE

The Rationale

1

The Framework

Recently leading science scholars in the United States collaborated to improve the design of elementary school science curricula. They rejected the formal expository teaching of science facts in favor of the more effective mode of guided discovery learning and called for active involvement with real materials in accordance with the precepts of Jean Piaget. This mode has much in common with the self-motivated approach traditionally used in good preschools and, more recently, adapted for integrated open classrooms.

Some early childhood educators believe that giving younger children opportunities to freely explore classroom materials provides adequate experiential foundations for future science learnings. Others agree with Robert Gagné's conviction that unguided discovery learning makes concept acquisition a slow process. This view is supported by cognition research findings that show:

Children learn more effectively when events and objects are verbally labeled for them.[1]

Presenting concepts to young children in a variety of contexts facilitates learning.[2]

Children's attention is alerted, and exploratory behavior is challenged by something just a bit different from what has already been experienced.[3]

This framework incorporates these findings in order to engage and reward children's curiosity and to encourage their competence as learners. The framework also suggests ways in which children may retain central ideas in their play

3

and creative fun. This approach strengthens recall of concepts by revealing their usefulness in everyday events.

The Areas of Investigation

Topics have been chosen according to the criteria of appeal for young children, functional value in the child's immediate surroundings, and easy translation to inexpensive materials for experimentation. The suggested activities can be adapted to fit the needs of specific groups of children and the possibilities or limitations of varied classroom circumstances.

Children's health and safety considerations are included wherever they fit well in topic areas. Affective values are also brought out in each of the chosen topics.

There is no intent to design a formal curriculum according to fixed rates of intellectual achievement, nor does the list of concepts exhaust the possible ideas that can be presented well to young children. Topics are suggested in the light of Jerome Bruner's challenge that "any subject can be taught effectively in some intellectually honest form to any child at any stage of development." [4]

Activities and Reinforcements

Concepts are built slowly from many simple facts or instances that can be generalized into a unifying idea. Therefore many related science experiences for exploring each topic area are suggested here. Within each topic area the suggested experiences are sequenced so that each provides foundation learnings for experiences that follow. For the sake of brevity, the activity directions are stated to show one way of guiding the children's experiences toward concept formation.

Science activities lose much of their value to children if they are offered as isolated events. When, over a period of time, a variety of interesting things-to-do reflects a science concept, deeper meaning is added. As Bruner points out, "Unless detail is placed into a structural pattern, it is rapidly forgotten." [5] Thus the intent of this learning framework is to create a system for reinforcing conceptual gains.

Primary Reinforcements

As a primary way of reinforcing the concepts and giving them functional meaning, varied activities are suggested for integrating the topics with other aspects of the school program. Stories, poems, finger-plays, improvised or familiar songs, art projects, creative movement, field trips, food experiences, thinking games, math activities, and dramatic play themes are shaped as potential sources of science learning transfer and reinforcement. The effect is diagrammed in figure 1.

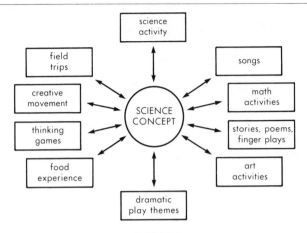

FIGURE 1

Secondary Reinforcements

Two important secondary methods of reinforcing concepts are less direct, since they depend upon the teacher's ability to capture the opportune moments to apply them. They are: (1) keeping concepts alive by applying them and (2) helping children relate new information to already acquired concepts.

Children can be greatly helped in thinking through such relationships by themselves if the topics to be linked are presented sequentially whenever possible. The understandings from one set of activities can then lead directly or transfer indirectly to those that follow. As topics are developed some general suggestions will be made for continuing these conceptual concerns and accommodating new information to already established concepts. These secondary reinforcements surround the primary reinforcement model as depicted in figure 2.

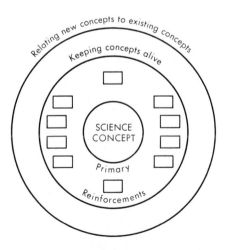

FIGURE 2

Objectives for Science Experiences

The broad objectives underlying the learning experiences in this book focus as much upon the child's feelings and his approach to learning as they do upon the acquisition of information. Observations of the basic harmony in physical and natural world relationships build feelings of security and confidence in children. Reducing fear of the unknown leads to feelings of mastery and strength. Support for curiosity promotes problem-solving ability and offers an avenue for learning how to learn. The reward of acquiring information through questioning and trial leads to new questions and new ways of relating the learnings to other ideas.

We do not know enough about the learning style unique to each young child to make accurate evaluations of his or her classroom experiences. Sometimes the teacher is not even the recipient of indications that something has been learned. That feedback may spill out to a parent at home during a sleepy bedtime conversation. Or perhaps the learning is applied nonverbally weeks after the classroom experience has taken place. Success in having children state facts may reflect the children's desire to please the teacher more than their comprehension of ideas. For these reasons the learning objectives included in the science experiences do not specify criteria for measuring learning outcomes.

The learning objectives are stated at the awareness level. Preoperational thinkers are acquiring the beginnings of concepts from their experiences. Concepts are stated abstractly in this book for the sake of the teacher's understanding. Young children are not expected to fully absorb all concepts in their abstract form.

NOTES

1. A. R. Jensen, "Learning in the preschool years," *Journal of Nursery Education* 18 (1963): 133-39.

2. G. Razran, "The observable unconscious and the inferable conscious in current Soviet psychophysiology: interoceptive conditioning, semantic conditioning and the orienting reflex," *Psychological Review* 68 (1961): 126-27.

3. Jerome Kagan, "Attention and psychological change in the young child," *Science* 170 (1970): 826-32.

4. Jerome S. Bruner, *The Process of Education* (Cambridge: Harvard University Press, 1960), p. 12. Reprinted by permission of the publisher.

5. Ibid., p. 24.

2

Science Participants: Children, Teachers, and Parents

The Children

Jean Piaget believes that, at some point between the second and the seventh years, a marked shift occurs in the child's thinking. This shift can be observed in the child's approach to manipulative materials: from the exploratory handling of the younger child to the definite organization visible in the older child's style.

Compare the ways that three-year-olds and four-year-olds might explore a basket filled with assorted bottle caps. The three-year-olds are likely to take pleasure in the sheer handling of the caps in sensorimotor ways: heaping them, turning them to inspect shape and composition, clicking two caps together like castanets, plunging their hands into the pile, possessing them!

The older children might briefly repeat those earlier forms of exploring bottle cap potential, then spontaneously settle into more sophisticated maneuvers. They will notice distinguishing characteristics such as the color, or the printing; perhaps some will even recognize different brand names, thanks to the diligent teaching of television advertisers. Methodically the caps will be sorted into like classes, often to the accompaniment of oral mediating cues . . . "a funny *A* one . . . a curly *C* one . . . another funny *A* one . . . a 7 one." The groups of like caps might be patterned into clusters, lined up, or stacked for counting and comparing with another child's assortment. These exploratory styles arise on the child's own initiative, according to his own classifying logic. They depend upon having had opportunities to explore, so an older child whose experiences have been very limited might approach materials as the experienced three-year-old would.

Differences can also be seen in the problem-solving ability of experienced three- and four-year-olds. The younger child's thinking seems to be drawn to one part of a problem at a time. He or she is likely to be lured away from the central idea in a problem by details that seem irrelevant to an older child. When he compares the weight of a large red cup of sand with that of a small blue cup of sand, he may base his conclusion upon the color difference rather than size. He may be firmly convinced that the first cup of sand is heavier because it is red.

Piaget points out that the quality of problem-solving ability changes gradually in the early childhood years. The child of five or six may reach an accurate conclusion to a problem without being able to explain the reasoning involved. These characteristic ways of thinking do not deny the usefulness of early science experiences. More mature reasoning ability will develop as a result of having had problems to think about. Abundant experiences provide foundations for future intellectual growth.

Developmental differences in orientation to materials and problems fall within Erik Erikson's description of the sense of initiative that dominates the four-year-old personality. In Erikson's view the child of this age is eager for new experience and new information. The child's emerging reasoning powers blend with his developing imagination, leading him to ask searching questions. His budding behavior control system allows him to slow his activity long enough to become immersed in dealing with something that captures his attention. Such qualities make this an ideal time to explore the regularities, relationships, and wonders of the world close at hand.

Some adults feel that the charming innocence of childhood is lost when opportunities for accurate cause-effect learning are offered. These people have forgotten their own childhood longings to feel grown-up. The writings of Maria Montessori stress the importance of the sense of mastery to the learning child. Those of us who have recently brought a difficult bit of understanding under our control, or mastered a new skill, can appreciate how much this deep satisfaction contributes to a child's self-esteem. To the young child, knowing means growing.

The Teachers

Any teacher who is capable of maintaining a classroom atmosphere of warmth, acceptance, and nurturance has the basic qualifications for presenting science concepts to young children. *Little can be taught when a close rapport between children and teacher is missing.*

A second necessary quality for early science teaching is an authentic interest in finding out. This means a willingness to help children find answers to their questions; a willingness to re-examine ideas in order to convey them with clarity; and a willingness to learn along with children.

The teacher's own interest in finding out sustains the children's ready curiosity. It can revive curiosity in children who have been belittled for asking questions, and it can rebuild curiosity that has atrophied in an unstimulating environment. When the teacher's own sense of wonder is alive and active, curiosity behavior is modeled for the children. This important attitude has a place in the science-teaching framework as a secondary reinforcement, as indicated in figure 3.

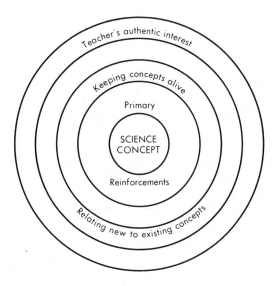

FIGURE 3

How much academic background is required for good early science teaching? Actually the number and variety of science courses under the teacher's belt are less important than is their effectiveness. Too many people have been discouraged by science courses that have emphasized memorizing facts rather than understanding and applying useful principles. Anyone who has turned a doorknob, boiled a pot of water, sharpened a pencil, slipped on a patch of ice, or hummed a tune has applied science.

Recognizing that everyday events have roots in scientific principles is a reassuring base from which to venture into discovery experiences with young children. The teacher who sees the functional aspects of science can then reverse the process: first providing activities that help children discover underlying principles, then helping children find that the principles really work in daily life. *This is purposeful science. It can be offered by teachers who are not science specialists.* Most teachers already use informal awareness activities to broaden their children's perception of the world. The science viewpoint just goes a step beyond appreciating the sensory aspects of the commonplace, to seeking the structure that *underlies* the commonplace and relating it to other structures.

Try this simple exercise. It will demonstrate two things: the awesome complexity and delicate harmony in the designs of nature, and the number of different ways that a commonplace event can be probed for meaning. However please note that it is not advisable to cluster so many concepts into a single experience for young children.

Release a single drop of water from an eyedropper onto a stiff feather. Take a close look at the result. Enjoy it for a moment. Did anything happen to the feather? To the drop of water? What would this mean to a bird out in a rainstorm? Look at the construction of the feather through a magnifying glass. Separate some segments of the feather. Put a drop of water on this portion. Does the drop retain its perfect shape? Look through the drop of water. Does it have a magnifying effect? Why? Will the same things happen with a different drop of water? A different feather? What do you predict? Try it. Was your prediction accurate?

The open-endedness of this exercise and the lack of correct answers at the bottom of the page may make some people uncomfortable. But raising questions and triggering new ideas are significant aspects of the scientific process. Correct answers of the past may become obsolete when someone questions the accepted. Recognizing this will help teachers allow and encourage children to ask questions, seek answers, and reach conclusions for themselves with only a light guiding touch from an adult.

Children can gain much from simple experiences with inexpensive materials provided by a willing, interested teacher. However teachers need time to gather materials, plan, and try experiences themselves. They also should be able to tolerate messiness, risk new enterprises, and profit from mistakes. These efforts and abilities are well rewarded in both personal growth for the teacher, and in the pleasure of sharing the sense of achievement and mastery that children find through their science discoveries.

The Parents

All parents have information about the world that can be passed on to their children—to their mutual benefit. Jim's dad, who was perpetually "on welfare," let his son scrub tires and wipe grease off bolts for him as he salvaged parts from the derelict cars that stood in their front yard. As a consequence Jim was able to make contributions to class discussions about simple machines, after weeks of virtually silent presence in school.

Michael's dad was a businessman who loved to feed his four-year-old son's hunger for information. Their Saturday walks often led them to laboratories where adults allowed Michael to see what they were doing. Michael then shared detailed, accurate information with his classmates about such things as the function of chlorophyll in leaves, the reactions of litmus paper, and the powers of the microscope.

The link between our school study of sound and her daddy's professional interests as an automobile salesman resulted in this report from Michelle. "I told Daddy 'bout bi-ber-ations when we was drivin' home, 'nen he told me 'bout 'em too, and we feeled that yella car shakin'."

Unfortunately far too many parents are unaware of the pleasures and potentials of this natural teaching role. Teachers can do much to help fathers and mothers undertake this partnership in education. To do so requires good communication between home and school.

Teachers can notify parents about the science activities under way in school, or about science-related exhibits and field trip possibilities so that they can participate with their children. Teachers may also suggest supportive ways for parents to respond to their children's indications of interest. This support can strongly reinforce the classroom experiences. Teachers can make a list or display of common cast-off materials that parents can send to school to serve as raw materials for science. The flow of information can be maintained through newsletters, parent meetings, home visits, or during informal chats as children are picked up at school.

Parents who have special skills and knowledge about science-related topics may be invited to share their resources with the class. Alisa's mother played her flute and piccolo for a group of children who were learning about vibrating air columns and variations in the pitch of sounds. She also brought a set of soft drink bottles filled to marked levels with water so that the children could play "Yankee Doodle" on the water chimes. She confided, "Alisa tells me that now I'm not just a music mommy but a science mommy, too." The reinforcing influence of parental support completes the framework, as shown in figure 4.

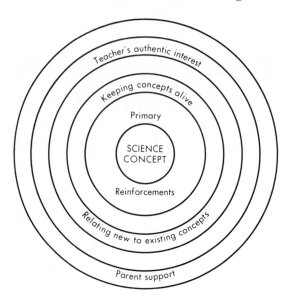

FIGURE 4

3

Implementing the Framework

Ideally science teaching can occur at any time or place. When a child calls, "Come over here, I want to smell ya' somepin'," the adult comes and sniffs, thereby enhancing the child's satisfaction in finding something worthwhile. If the teacher goes on to help the child relate his discovery to something that he already knows, or if the adult asks a question that leads to further exploration, the child's spirit of inquiry grows. A flourishing scientific attitude, one which is completely portable and ready for use at a moment's notice, is an important asset for teachers of young children.

Phenomena must be noticed before they can become objects of scientific inquiry. Young children can be fantastic noticers of significant minutia that adults callously overlook, like a sparkling bit of something embedded in the playground cement, or the iridescent sheen of a beetle's back. A response of "Let's try to find out more about that" from the teacher capitalizes on child-instigated scientific inquiry.

The thoroughly pursued incidental approach to science is an ideal teaching strategy. However few of us can manage it in the day-by-day dynamics of working with real children in ordinary classrooms. Nor can casual exploration of this sort be depended upon to include all of the science concepts that children can absorb and use. Random incidents are rarely sufficient to help children link important ideas together and fit them into other situations that have meaning in their lives. To do this adequately takes planning and preparation.

The activities described in this framework should not be presented separately in a desultory fashion. They should be unified episodes that may last from several days to several weeks. The term *episodes* is used instead of the familiar term *units*, because the latter implies that an area of study can be completed. An episode suggests a portion of a continuous chain of learning that develops throughout life.

Fluctuating Interest in Knowing

It would be unrealistic to assume that the spontaneous desire to know will consistently lead all children in a group to take part in every science activity made available to them. It would certainly abuse the developmental goal of encouraging autonomous decision making to require the whole group to engage in each science event that the teacher presents. Our knowledge of the uniqueness of individual development should make it clear that each child brings different capacities and motivation into learning situations.

Subtle directives from parents can strongly influence the choices children make in school. Direct or indirect messages like, "be careful with those good clothes . . . boys don't cook . . . girls are afraid of spiders and worms," can be powerful inhibitors to children who are unsure of their affection rating with their parents. The directives may curb a child's interest in trying new experiences.

Children also may have needs that may take precedence over the desire to find out. The child who is lonely at home may be very reluctant to pass up any chance to play with special school friends. He may choose a science activity only when his friends make the choice. Children who are tired, hungry, or feeling under par may not be able to summon enough interest to observe what is happening at the science table.

If a child consistently spurns science activities, it would be well to think about possible causes and consider ways to make participation easier for him. The teacher may simply need to ask for that child's help while organizing materials for the day's science activity. Children usually take a proprietary interest in a project that they have helped to prepare. However, when a science topic becomes a central theme threading through many parts of the school program, even the children who do little active exploring will become aware of the concepts being presented.

Drawing Attention to Science Activities

Good classrooms are alive with interesting activities for children. If a science activity should appear unheralded in a little-used corner of the room, it may not be noticed by busy children. To insure attention, both direct and indirect means can be used to whet children's appetites for a learning opportunity.

Direct Focusing

Many teachers use group meetings to describe activities which children may engage in during a self-chosen period. An enthusiastic discussion of the science project, one that includes the children's own recounting of what they already know about the topic under consideration, will usually suffice to alert children to an interesting project.

It might be desirable to build interest in a new topic by using it as the object of a spur-of-the-moment thinking game. The teacher may hold up a closed hand and say, "There is a tiny tool tucked into my hand that some children will use at the science table today. It's made of plastic and rubber . . . you can squeeze one end of it . . . right now it has air inside of it. . . ."

At other times the less said, the greater the enticement becomes. A feeling box containing an unexplained object of science interest can be passed around as a clue to the day's activity. A piece of science equipment might be introduced by slowly, carefully lifting it out of its carton for the children to see and speculate about.

Indirect Focusing

Teachers need to weigh the probable pulling power of the plans made for each day. One project can be doomed to neglect if many other attractive ones are offered at the same time. Not too many children will choose to find out something new about air if they are simultaneously offered opportunities to make gingerbread and to use a fresh supply of scrap lumber at the workbench. It might be feasible to shift events in the daily schedule so that physically active choices could be available at one time, and quieter activities could be grouped for another period.

Finding a location that both invites children's participation, yet controls distractions, and varying the location to fit the requirements of the activity can also be interest-building factors. Science is very popular on the days when it takes place under a blanket-covered table! However the best method of indirectly focusing children's thinking on science ideas goes deeper than the mechanics of arranging intriguing learning situations. It develops through the teacher's efforts to keep the science experiences relevant for the children.

Sharing Explorations With Children

Piaget's precept, "Telling is not teaching," is difficult for many of us to follow. While we respect the child's right to his or her own way of investigating, we may find it difficult to resist the temptation to hurry him along to "discover" what we already know. *We must be careful not to smother a child's tender spark of inquiry with a heavy blanket of directions and facts.* We really let children down when we fail to encourage their potential for creative thinking and problem solving.

The teacher should try to minimize intervention with children's explorations. Yet a helping hand may be needed when a child has been fumbling unsuccessfully with materials and seems about ready to give up. A tactful offer to help hold down a wire, over which the child is trying to tighten a screw, can be appropriate if it permits the child to achieve a success.

Fred Rogers, on his television program, "Mister Rogers' Neighborhood," offers inspiration to teachers of young children. When he presents ideas and materials for children to think about, he is relaxed, sincere, and patient. He seems to fade into the background, so that the child's involvement with the ideas takes precedence over the act of instruction. Compare his subtle technique with the teaching style used in commercial children's programs, or even "Sesame Street." In those programs the personality of the program "star" dominates the learning situation, drawing a disproportionate amount of the child's attention to the teacher rather than to that which could be learned.

When sitting down to share an experience with the children, the teacher should consider it a learning opportunity for everyone. It will be that if the teacher observes the children as they work, and listens closely to what the experience means to them.

Adapting Activities to Program Needs

As the school year progresses, emerging patterns of emotional climates seem to affect children's interest and ability to concentrate. For instance, in a child care center, where many of the children might spend eight to ten hours a day together, the Friday atmosphere tends to be marked by weariness. Monday may be a tense day after children have been cooped up for the weekend in small apartments or mobile homes, especially during a period of bad weather. The likelihood of such prevailing moods would dictate a slower tempo and more relaxed activities on those days. It would be desirable in such situations to confine new science explorations to the middle of the week.

Most of the activities suggested here are suitable for small group involvement; others may be enjoyed by the whole class together. The degree of adult supervision required will vary with the children's abilities to use materials and carry out directives independently. Some experiments permit children to achieve satisfactory conclusions on their own; others call for the stimulus of questions or bits of information to be supplied by the teacher.

Selecting Topics

Many elements will govern the choice of topics to be presented to a class, among them are: the teacher's interests and the children's appetites for science; the amount of freedom in planning available to the teachers; and the philosophy of the school. Public school teachers must also comply with mandatory state regulations for subject matter time allocations. Once the topics are selected, they should be presented as completely as possible to make the best use of children's time and interests. Skimming through suggested activities to touch lightly on many topics will not build lasting concepts.

Adapting Experiences for Younger Children

While the activities in this framework were planned for children four years of age and older, many of the experiences can be adapted for younger preschool children. Two-year-olds can enjoy simple sensory explorations such as feeling air as they move it with paper fans, spinning pinwheels, or swinging streamers on a breezy day; feeling rock textures and weights; touching ice, then touching the water it melts into; watching, then moving like a goldfish; tasting raw fruits and vegetables that have grown from plants; listening to loud and soft sounds; or gazing through transparent color paddles to see surroundings in a new light.

Three-year-olds might be expected to engage in similar activities, taking in greater detail. They will be able to direct deeper attention to such things as exploring new dimensions with a magnifying glass. This group can enjoy some of the classifying experiences on a beginning level: sorting rocks from objects that are not rocks; things that float from those that do not float; and objects that are attracted by a magnet from objects that are not attracted.

Younger children need clearly defined steps in order to gain from science activities. For instance, the seeds in a planting experience should be large and easy to see. A fine, dark lettuce seed is hard to distinguish from a bit of dirt, and a child may not be sure of what he has actually done after planting it. A large, pale bean or pumpkin seed that is obviously different from the soil would be a better choice.

Very young children can be very easily side-tracked in their reasoning by what they observe. To keep the objective of an experience evident to them, avoid using materials with irrelevant, distracting details. For instance, if size comparisons are to be made with measuring cups, use cups of the same color and shape to help children focus on size. Younger children will still be exploring materials with their mouths as well as with their fingers. *Nonfood materials must not be small enough to swallow.* Such foods as peanuts and popcorn should not be given to children too young to chew them well. As a matter of course, adults should closely supervise any activity for very young children.

Adapting for Disadvantaged Children

Groups of disadvantaged or inexperienced children may need more preliminary experience to become acquainted with new materials. They also benefit from having activities presented in smaller steps than some of those which will be described. For example, an inexperienced child enjoyed planting a seed in an eggshell. Then he concluded happily, "Now I will grow an egg!" He had so little information about eggs that he was unaware that the growth potential had been emptied from the shell, that eggs only grow inside female animals. His teacher could help him focus on seed growth by using a different type of container in another seed-planting attempt. She could also clarify his misconception and expand his information about eggs by planning a food activity in which eggs are opened. Incidentally, many children are bothered by the thought that using eggs as food prevents a chick from growing. The teacher should comment while breaking the eggs that only those eggs made by a mother hen and a father rooster together will grow into a baby chick. The eggs made only by a mother hen will not grow into chicks. People use those eggs for food.

Children who have not been allowed to play with water are unlikely to give their attention to a learning experience that uses water as a material. They will concentrate on dabbling in the water. If this happens with your group, give them some water-play opportunities. Let them enjoy getting acquainted with water before trying the learning activity again.

Adapting for Early Elementary Classrooms

In early elementary grades that are organized as open classrooms, in part or entirely, small group activities can be set up for self-selection by children. In other classrooms they can be offered as enrichment activities for children when other work has been completed, or as committee work which is followed by a report to the whole class. Printed instructions can be used increasingly to reduce the amount of teacher involvement as children's reading skills develop.

Self-selection is a valid strategy in any learning situation. Piaget emphasizes that self-motivated activity leads to the best learning. It also enables the learner to provide for himself the match between what he already knows, and the fresh intellectual challenge he seeks.

Gaining from Our Mistakes

Many of the materials and activities in this text have been revised as a result of trial-and-error encounters with the logic of young minds. On one occasion, children in my class were given matching plastic vials, some capped, some uncapped, to use in a buoyancy experience. Then five-year-old Greg explained why his capped, empty vial floated on the water, while his uncapped vial sank. According to Greg, the cap held up the first vial! To my dismay, he verified his conclusion by removing the plastic cap and floating it on the water. How confusing! According to *my* plan, he should have noticed that the capped vial was filled with air, hence, it was lightweight; the uncapped vial filled with water, hence, it was heavy. It took a while for my supposedly flexible, adult thinking to find a way back to the objective of the experiment. "Greg, you had a good idea about the cap. It does float by itself. Let's see what happens if we put the cap on the container full of water. Now let's put the same kind of cap on the empty-looking container and watch them again." Tuning in to the child's logic makes teaching an exciting learning process for the teacher.

Always try the experiences before presenting them to children, then record the results and the questions that come to mind. If your children have difficulties with an activity it may be possible that further changes are necessary. Remember that an unexpected outcome is not a failure if one learns how *not* to repeat it.

Moving Ahead

Students and teachers who are ready to go beyond the suggestions in this book could investigate the new elementary school science curricula. One of those programs, Elementary Science Study, has made separate unit guidebooks available commercially. Information can be obtained from the Education Development Center, 55 Chapel Street, Newton, Massachusetts 02160. Inquire there, also, about subscribing to the *ESS Newsletter*. The monthly publication, *Science and Children*, is another source of science-teaching stimulus. The teaching framework in this book will achieve its greatest effectiveness when it stimulates teachers to generate their own ideas for presenting science experiences to the groups of children they know best.

References

Bruner, Jerome. *The Process of Education.* Cambridge: Harvard University Press, 1961.

Erikson, Erik. *Childhood and Society.* New York: W. W. Norton, 1964.

Flavell, J. *The Developmental Psychology of Jean Piaget.* Princeton, N.J.: Van Nostrand, 1973.

Gagné, Robert M. "Varieties of Learning and the Concept of Discovery." In L. S. Shulman and E. R. Keislar, eds., *Learning by Discovery: A Critical Appraisal.* Chicago: Rand McNally, 1966.

Holt, John. *How Children Learn.* New York: Dell, 1972.

Hunt, J. McV. *Intelligence and Experience.* New York: Ronald Press, 1961.

Landreth, Catherine. *Early Childhood: Behavior and Learning.* New York: Alfred A. Knopf, 1967.

Montessori, Maria. *The Montessori Method.* New York: Schoken, 1964.

Pitcher, Evelyn G.; Lasher, Miriam; Feinburg, Sylvia; and Braun, Linda. *Helping Young Children Learn.* Columbus, Ohio: Charles E. Merrill, 1974.

PART
TWO

Concepts,
Experiences,
and
Reinforcements

4

What is Air?

Children become acquainted with hundreds of substances through their sensory encounters. They are intrigued by an invisible, ever-present substance that is not directly encountered by the senses until it affects something tangible. The activities in this learning episode are designed to reveal these concepts:

AIR IS ALMOST EVERYWHERE
AIR IS REAL (IT TAKES UP SPACE)
AIR PRESSES ON EVERYTHING ON ALL SIDES
MOVING AIR PUSHES THINGS
AIR SLOWS MOVING OBJECTS

In the experiences that follow children can find air in empty-looking containers and become aware of breathing air. They can feel air enclosed in something, see how it occupies spaces, and note how air pushes on everything. Also, they can enjoy making things for moving air to push.

Introduce the topic of air to children by holding up your hands, cupped together, suggesting that, "There is something important inside my hands. You may peek in, but you won't be able to see what it is. This important stuff is *invisible!* We'll be finding out more about it."

Concept: Air is Almost Everywhere

1. What Comes Out of an Empty-Looking Can?

LEARNING OBJECTIVE: To develop a beginning awareness that air is present almost everywhere, even if unseen.

MATERIALS:

Empty tin can, #303

Nail, hammer

Dishpan

Water

Plastic aprons for participants

Splash catcher (Inflatable wading pool is fine. Use on floor, inflated to confine spills. Put pan of water in center of the pool. Children stay outside the pool.)

SMALL GROUP ACTIVITIES:

1. Ask children to check contents of the can. Is anything in it?
2. Punch a hole in the bottom with a hammer and nail. Let a child do it, if possible.
3. "If there is something in the can, could we push it out through this hole? Let's see."
4. Invert can, slowly push it into the water. Invite a child to hold his hand just above the nail hole. What does he feel being pushed out of the hole, a stream of air? "Was there something real in that empty-looking can . . . something real that we can't see?"
5. Let the children experiment.

2. Can We Really Empty an Open Container?

LEARNING OBJECTIVE: To extend a beginning awareness that air is present almost everywhere, even if unseen.

MATERIALS:

Empty clear plastic shampoo bottles or tubes, uncapped

Downy feathers, milkweed fluff, or bits of tissue paper

SMALL GROUP ACTIVITIES:

1. Ask children to check contents of bottles or tubes. Do they look empty?
2. "Point the bottle top toward your chin, squeeze it. Do you feel something? What? See if you can squeeze all the air out. Keep trying."
3. Offer a feather to each child. "If your bottle is really empty, nothing will come out to push the feather from your hand. See what happens if you point the bottle toward the feather." (This can be lively unless limits are set for a feather-blowing space.)

3. Is There Air Inside Us?

LEARNING OBJECTIVE: To become aware of breathing air.

Whole Group Activity: Needed: a paper tissue for each child.

Suggest that all the children take a deep breath, shut their lips tightly, and pinch their nostrils shut as long as they can. "What happened? Why did you let go of your noses?

Did your body need something so much that you had to let go? Can you get along without air for very long? Let's try again."

"Our bodies need the part of air called oxygen. We need to breathe air into our bodies about every six seconds, because it is used up so quickly inside of us." Guide the discussion to bring out the idea that all living things must have air to stay alive. Discuss the danger of climbing into boxes with heavy doors that cannot be opened from the inside.

Give each child an unfolded tissue to hold near his nose and mouth. "Let's see what happens to the tissue when you bring air into your body; when you push the old air out. Try it with your lips closed; with your lips opened a bit. Are there two ways for the air to come in and out? Let's see if we can tell where the air is going inside our bodies." Ask children to take turns lying on the floor, or putting heads on the table so others can watch their chests go up and down as they breathe.

Note: read Whistle For Willie, by Ezra Jack Keats, and The Dragon In The Clock Box, by Jean M. Craige (see pages 34–35). Comment about breathing air and box-play safety.

Concept: Air is Real (It Takes Up Space)

1. Can We Feel the Air Inside a Bag?

LEARNING OBJECTIVE: To develop a beginning awareness that air has substance.

MATERIALS:

Plastic sandwich bags (Not fold-top kind)*

Drinking straws

Masking tape

Covered wire closures

GETTING READY:

Prepare a blowing bag for each child participating: gather top of the bag to form a neck. Insert straw in neck, secure neck of bag to straw with tape.

SMALL GROUP ACTIVITIES:

1. Ask, "Is the table real? How can you tell? If your eyes were closed, could you still tell that the table is real? Is feeling something a good way to know that it is real?"
2. Let children blow into the prepared bags. "What are you blowing into the bag? Can you see it inside the bag? Is it real? Can you feel it?"
3. Tie with wire closure if children want to keep a full bag of air to feel.

*Balloons may be used instead of the sandwich bag and straws. However the more transparent the container of air, the more apparent the concept that invisible air is taking up space inside the bag. We can feel air inside a container, we can see the container enlarge, but we cannot see the air. Children should leave the plastic bags at school so that younger children at home will not pick up the idea of playing with plastic bags.

2. Can a Glassful of Air Push Water Away?

LEARNING OBJECTIVE: To extend the awareness that air has substance.

MATERIALS:

Clear plastic bowl (corn popper dome is fine) or 5" deep glass mixer bowl, if it can be safely used

Pitcher of water

Cork

Clear plastic tumbler

Splash catcher, aprons

GETTING READY:

Inflate wading pool splash catcher. Put bowl in the center.

SMALL GROUP ACTIVITIES:

1. Put cork in the bowl. "The cork is touching the bowl now. What will happen if we pour water into the bowl? . . . Let's see."
2. Half fill the bowl with water. "Is the cork touching the bottom of the bowl now?"
3. "Can someone put the cork back on the bottom?" Let children try to do this. "Will it stay if you let go?"
4. See if something in the tumbler will push water away so that the cork can stay on the bottom of the bowl. Invert tumbler, push straight down to the bottom. "What is inside the glass that could push the water away? Do you see anything?"
5. Let the children experiment.

Group Discussion: Ask the children to catch some air in their cupped hands. "Poke your nose into your hands. Can you smell the air? Peek in. Can you see it? Can you hear it? Try to taste it." (Children love to hang their tongues out for research purposes.) Ask those who have experimented how they know that air is real. Children are proud of their new information, and are willing to repeat a discussion like this one. Next time, let a hand puppet be the skeptic who doesn't believe that invisible things can be real. The children will be happy to convince him otherwise.

3. Can Air in a Bag Push Something Over?

LEARNING OBJECTIVE: To extend the awareness that air has substance.

MATERIALS:

Sturdy, 8" x 12" paper bag

Wire twist closure, or masking tape

Bicycle tire pump, or bellows-type air mattress pump

Heavy book or block

GETTING READY:

Gather bag top into a neck, fasten with a wire closure or tape.

SMALL GROUP ACTIVITIES:

1. Demonstrate the pump, if children don't know what it is. Look at air intake hole, where air comes in to be pushed out by the pump. (Remove intake valve cap from bellows pump.) Feel air being pushed out.
2. "Do you think a bag full of air could push that book over? How could we find out?"
3. Insert end of pump hose into the bag. Tighten the closure, or simply hold bag firmly to hose while children take turns pumping air into it, pushing the book over. "Is air really doing that? Is it real stuff, even though we can't see it?"

Put bag on floor, stand
book upright on it. Put
pump near the bag.

   Note: Children love to demonstrate how strong they are. Using the pump is a good
medium for this self-concept enhancement.

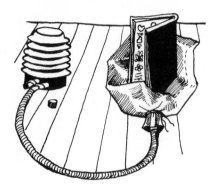

FIGURE 5

Read: *The Ball That Wouldn't Bounce* by Mel Cebulash (page 34).

Concept: Air Presses on Everything on All Sides

1. Can Air Keep Water in a Tube, a Straw?

LEARNING OBJECTIVE: To notice the effects of air pressure on liquids in a small tube.

MATERIALS:

Baster (kitchen tool)

Medicine droppers (plastic
or thick glass tubes are
safest)

Small containers of water
for each child

Pint jar half full of water

Sponge, pan, newspapers,
or splash catcher for cleanup

Drinking straws, cut in half

SMALL GROUP ACTIVITY:

1. Examine baster with children. Is the tube empty?
   Squeeze bulb to feel what comes out.
2. Put baster in jar of water. "What do you see
   when I push air out of the baster? Watch the tube
   when I slowly let go of the rubber bulb on top.
   What is happening?"
3. Hold up the filled baster. "Is water running out
   now? Why not? Is something we can't see pushing
   on the baster to keep the water in it?"
4. Squeeze bulb to release the water. Repeat step 2
   with baster *not quite* in the water. Does it fill with
   water or air? Let children experiment with droppers
   and containers of water.*

5. "Now let's try the same thing with straws."
Insert a straw in water. Put index fingers over top
and bottom of straw to lift it from the water. Keep
finger on top, remove finger from bottom. Most of
the water will stay in the straw. Why?
(Air keeps it in.)

6. "Nothing can get into the straw from the top with
my finger on it. Watch as I let some air push into
the straw." Remove finger from top. Water is
pushed out of the straw. Let children experiment.

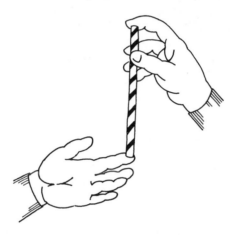

FIGURE 6

*Note: Some children may be satisfied that a dropper is filled with water if drops just
cling to the outside. Help them hold the dropper tube in the water *while* releasing the bulb.

Concept: Moving Air Pushes Things

Introduction: Ask the children to wave their hands back and forth in front of their faces.
"What do you feel on your skin? You feel air now because it is moving. You didn't notice
it when it wasn't moving." Explain that we feel air moving against us in the same way
whether we are moving when the air is still, or whether air is moving by itself as wind
when we are still.

1. Does Moving Air Push on Us?

LEARNING OBJECTIVE: To experience the pushing effects of moving air.

MATERIALS: OUTDOOR ACTIVITY:

Sheets of newspaper   Give children sheets of paper outside. "Will paper
Used adding machine tape   stick to you as you stand here? See what happens when

Nice to have:
  Pinwheels
  Kites

you run as fast as you can. Do you have to hold the paper to press it to yourself? What held it there?"
Let children enjoy running with paper tape streaming behind them. Try pinwheels standing still and running. Try the kite on a calm day, on a windy day.

Listen to "What Makes The Weather," sung by Tom Glazer in *Now We Know (Songs to Learn By).* (Music references are listed in Appendix 1.)

2. Can We Make a Glider Drift on Moving Air?

LEARNING OBJECTIVE: To notice that moving air can carry a glider launched by a child.

MATERIALS:

A sheet of typing paper for each child

GETTING READY:

Draw a lengthwise line down the center of the paper.

Draw parallel lines 1½" from the center line.

Draw a line ¾" from the bottom across the paper.

SMALL GROUP ACTIVITY:

1. Show the children how to fold up ¾" from the bottom of the paper. Continue to fold this amount 4 times.
2. With the cuff on the outside, crease the paper and the folded cuff lengthwise on center line. Now fold back each side on the lines 1½" from the centerfold, making wings. You're finished!
3. Launch glider with cuff in front, holding center, as shown. If the glider always nosedives, reduce the weight of the front end by unfolding one fold of the cuff. Also try to push the glider straight ahead!

FIGURE 7

Note: Primary children may want to make more elaborate gliders. See *How To Have Fun Making Paper Airplanes*, by the editors of *Creative.*

Concept: Air Slows Moving Objects

Group Discussion: Show the children a piece of typing paper and a small solid object like a rock or a wooden spool. "If I hold these two things up as high as I can reach and then let go of them, what will happen to them? . . . Yes, they will fall. Do you think that both things will fall in just the same way? Let's find out." Repeat the action as needed to allow the children to carefully observe and report. "Which one fell more slowly? Can you think of anything beneath the paper that might have pushed against it and slowed its fall?" Mention that everything that moves above ground, or above water must push air aside as it moves. Big things push more air aside than do small things.

1. What Does a Parachute Do?

LEARNING OBJECTIVE: To compare the ways air slows the fall of a weight with and without a parachute.

MATERIALS:

For each child:

1 wooden thread spool, or stringing bead*

12″ square of closely woven, light fabric.

4 feet light string

Extra wooden spool

Large needle

*The spool must be heavier than the fabric. Tie on metal washers or nuts if more weight is needed.

GETTING READY:

Sew a 12″ piece of string to each corner of fabric.

Hold parachute by strings, fabric corners even, as shown in figure 8. Knot strings together 7″ from corners.

Tie spool to string ends.

SMALL GROUP ACTIVITY:

1. Allow children to help make parachutes if they can tie. Younger children can crayon designs on fabric before strings are tied.
2. If a safe stairway is nearby, let one child go up, reach through banisters to drop the extra spool and parachute. Compare results.
3. Fold parachute fabric, wind with the strings and spool. Let children throw them as high as they can into the air outdoors. Add weight to the spool if parachutes fail to open well.

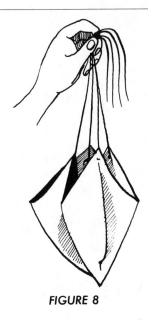

FIGURE 8

Concept: Warm Air Expands

1. Will Heat Make Cold Air Get Bigger?

LEARNING OBJECTIVE: To observe the expansion effect of air that has been warmed.

Introduction: "If you should blow up this balloon, how would it change? Yes, it would get bigger. A word for that is *expand*. What would make the balloon expand? Air. The air you blow into a balloon makes the balloon expand. There is one thing that can make the air itself expand: heat. Let's find out what will happen if we heat a bottleful of cold air."

MATERIALS:

Plastic bottle, about
1 pint size

Small balloon

Pitcher of *hot* water

Saucepan (old-style steam radiator can be the heat source. Put bottle *near* it, not directly on it.)

Refrigerator freezer (or a windowsill in freezing weather)

SMALL GROUP ACTIVITY:

1. Remove bottle cap. "What is in the empty-looking bottle? Yes, air. Is there much air in this balloon? No, it hasn't been blown up."
2. "Let's stretch the neck of the balloon over the bottle top. Now let's make the air inside the bottle very cold." Leave bottle in the freezer till air is cold (balloon will be slightly sucked into bottle as cold air contracts).
3. Immediately put bottle in pan. Pour hot water over bottle. "Watch closely while we warm the air inside the bottle." (Air should expand enough to push into the balloon, causing it to stand up quite suddenly.) Try it again.

Group Discussion: Children will enjoy talking about this experiment. Mention what happens to toy balloons that are left outdoors on a hot day. Show a picture of a hot air balloon carrying a passenger.

Primary Reinforcements

Music

1. After children have finished clapping the rhythm of a song they enjoy singing, compare two styles of clapping. Listen to the sound made by clapping with palms open and flat, then to the sound made by clapping with slightly cupped hands. What is caught between the cupped hands to change the sound?

2. Sing this air song with appropriate tasting and looking gestures to add fun:

Air Song
(To the tune of "Goober Peas")

Math Experience

Sing "Ten Blue Bottles of Air-on-the-Chair" as a flannel board counting song (see next page). Cut out ten simple blue felt bottle shapes. Try to let one child put up the bottle shapes to begin the song; let another child remove one bottle shape for each verse as the song progresses down to "no blue bottles of air-on-the-chair."

Stories and References for Children

Cebulash, Mel. *The Ball That Wouldn't Bounce.* New York: Scholastic Book Services, 1972. A cast-off basketball needs some air before it will bounce.

Craige, Jean M. *The Dragon in the Clock Box.* New York: W. W. Norton, 1962. Joshua provides air for his newly hatched pretend baby dragon.

Ten Blue Bottles of Air-on-the-Chair

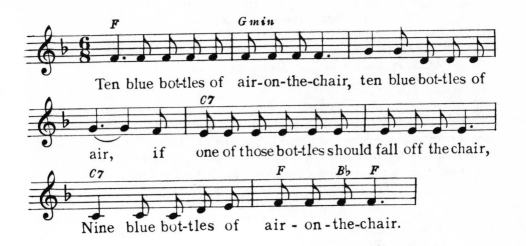

Ten blue bot-tles of air-on-the-chair, ten blue bot-tles of air, if one of those bot-tles should fall off the chair, Nine blue bot-tles of air - on - the-chair.

Creative, Editors of. *How to Have Fun Making Paper Airplanes.* Pleasantville, N.Y.: Reader's Digest Services, 1974.

Ets, Marie Hall. *Gilberto and the Wind.* New York: Viking Press, 1963.

Keats, Ezra Jack. *Whistle for Willie.* New York: Viking Press, 1964. Peter hides in a box that he can get out of easily. He also learns how to blow air out from his lips as a whistle.

Marino, Dorothy. *Edward and the Boxes.* New York: J. B. Lippincott, 1957. Ask children to think about providing air for the animals in the boxes.

Milne, A. A. *Winnie-The-Pooh.* New York: E. P. Dutton, 1961, chapter 1. Read this after children have made parachutes. Ask whether a small balloon could really slow Pooh's fall.

Mizumura, Lazue. *I See the Winds.* New York: Thomas Crowell, 1966.

Nodset, Joan L. *Who Took the Farmer's Hat?* New York: Scholastic Book Services, 1970. Moving air is the culprit.

Podendorf, Illa. *The True Book of Science Experiments.* Chicago: Childrens Press, 1972.

Rey, H. A. *Curious George Gets a Medal.* New York: Scholastic Book Services, 1957. George drifts to earth under a parachute after a space flight.

Scarry, Richard. *Great Big Air Book.* New York: Random House, 1971. The air we breathe, flight principles, parachutes, moving air and its uses, pollution, and the absence of air on the moon are all part of this learning-while-laughing book.

Selsam, Millicent. *Plenty of Fish.* New York: Harper & Brothers, 1960. Willie discovers that fish and people get air in different ways. An amusing story.

Tresselt, Alvin. *Follow the Wind.* New York: Lothrop, Lee & Shepard, 1950.

Poems (References found in Appendix 1)

The wind is a favorite topic in poems for children.
In *Poems Children Will Sit Still For,* by de Regniers:
"Who Has Seen the Wind" by Christina Rossetti.
"Wind Song" by Lillian Moore.
In *Now We Are Six,* by A. A. Milne:
"Wind On the Hill"
In *Poems to Grow On,* by Jean Thompson:
"The Kite" by Harry Behn.

Fingerplays

Seeds with silky wings are scattered by moving air. (See page 169.) Recall the milkweed blowing that children may have enjoyed in plant life experiences, or try to find a milkweed pod to open outdoors now if it is a new idea.

Baby Seeds

In a milkweed cradle	(cup hands)
Snug and warm	
Baby seeds are hiding	(make yourself small)
Safe from harm.	
Open wide the cradle	(open hands)
Hold it high.	
Come Mr. Wind	(blow in the hands)
Help them to fly.	

—Author unknown

Art Activities

1. EASEL PAINTING. Cut newsprint into the shapes of things that move on the air: birds; balloons (tape a dangling string to the back); butterflies; kite shapes.

2. COLLAGE. Use air-borne nature materials: feathers to represent birds; milkweed fluff and seeds; maple tree seeds. Cut some actual air bubbles from sheets of plastic packing material to glue on them.

3. Make paper fans to move air. They may be accordian-pleated sheets of paper which the children decorate, or they may be small paper plates stapled to popsicle sticks.

4. Make simple gliders to decorate with crayon designs.

5. Use air pressure with medicine droppers as an art medium. Let children make designs by dropping diluted food coloring onto absorbent paper with the droppers. A fleeting, fascinating art form—snow painting—also makes use of droppers and food coloring. Gather a big bucket of snow. Store it on the window-ledge. Quickly pack individual plastic meat trays with snow, ready to receive the drops of color. Have another bucket ready for the sloshy end results.

6. Do blow painting with plastic straws. Children can use straws and air pressure to pick up tempera paint from jars and drop it onto smooth surfaced paper. The puddles of paint are then changed in shape by blowing on them through the straws.

Dramatic Play

1. SERVICE STATION. Contrive a gasoline pump from an oblong carton and a length of garden hose. Help the children create a car with chairs, hollow blocks, and a paper-plate steering wheel—or a real one. Add an old inner tube and a bicycle tire pump for the repairman to inflate. A ring of keys and pliers add fun.

2. BOAT. Help the children create a block and plank boat, with two planks angled together to form a prow. Let them blow up a plastic ring, or pump up the inner tube, for a life preserver.

3. PLANE. Angled planks form the nose of the plane, hollow blocks form the tail and sides, two more planks stretch out to form the wings. Children who have flown can contribute ideas about oxygen and air to the play.

4. HOUSEKEEPING PLAY. Try to borrow a child-size inflatable chair to add interest to this play. Let the children beat up a detergent suds "soufflé" at the sink with a wire whisk or egg beaters. Comment on the amount of air their strong muscles are beating into the dish.

Other Air-related Play

1. Blow soap bubbles, using straws in cups of water and detergent. For younger children use baby shampoo, which won't irritate eyes, instead of detergent.

2. Let children take turns pumping up a sturdy air mattress to use as a tumbling mat for somersaults.

3. Pump up an inner tube to use across the seats of two facing chairs as a target for foam ball tossing.

Food Experience

If an electric mixer is available, make whipped milk topping. State that the beater is stirring many tiny air bubbles into the mixture. Watch it change and expand.

Combine: ½ cup instant dry skim milk
½ cup COLD water

Beat at highest speed for four minutes.

Add: 2 Tbls. sugar
½ tsp. vanilla

Beat at highest speed until mixture stands in peaks, about four minutes longer. Serve a mound of whipped milk to each child. Edible science is impressive. Children really remember that air was part of the tidbit they enjoyed eating.

Thinking Games

CLASSIFYING GAME. Find pictures of things that move with the help of air (sailboats, planes, kites, balloons, birds, bats, butterflies, and so forth) and pictures of things that move without the help of air (trains, steamships, motor boats, caterpillar tractors, roller skates, and so on). Mount the pictures on cardboard and put them in a box with *yes* and *no* marked inside the lid and the bottom section, respectively. Use the pictures as a game with the whole class, or as a quiet table game for a few children. (Pictures of cars and other things using inflated tires could be classified either way. Air does not push a car along, but a car with a flat tire certainly won't go very far. Let the children decide the issue after discussing it.)

Field Trips

1. AIRPORT VISIT. If this should be possible, keep the science focus simple. There will be too many exciting things to see to make lengthy explanations of flight principles bearable for the children. Be sure that any adult who offers a guided tour of the facility understands this.

2. SERVICE STATION VISIT. Make arrangements with the station manager beforehand to have a demonstration of the tire changer, and to allow children to feel air from the tire pump. This can be done in connection with a study of simple machines, if the station is too far away to warrant two trips.

Creative Movement

1. Let children pretend to be balloons that are blown into large shapes. Suggest that they make themselves into flat, limp shapes on the floor. "Now I'm blowing, and blowing, and blowing some more. And you are getting bigger and bigger." When the shapes have been stretched as large as they can be, suggest that you will pretend to prick each imaginary balloon shape. Each shape collapses into a limp piece of rubber on the floor as the air goes out of it.

2. After trying the warm air expansion experiment, its concept can be added to the balloon movement.

3. Children can move like birds or butterflies soaring on moving air. They might enjoy holding a feather in each hand to become a bird with outstretched-arm wings.

4. The library may have a record-lending service including an RCA Victor Dance-A-Story record by Anne Lief Barlin entitled, *Balloons.* (Reference listed on page 219.) It will offer an example to those who are new to creative movement, indicating how spoken ideas guide the movement.

5. Some excellent ideas for related creative movement can be found in, *Creative Movement for the Developing Child,* by Clare Cherry. (Reference listed on page 220.)

Secondary Reinforcements

Keeping Concepts Alive

1. Make casual comments or inquiries about the function or presence of air when suitable opportunities arise. When outdoors with a class, observe planes or birds flying overhead, or leaves, seeds, or litter blowing past.

Suggest that children fill their mouths with a giant air bubble when the class needs to walk quietly through school corridors. Puff up your own cheeks to model this funny way to stay quiet. It's more positive than saying, "Be quiet!" Air takes up talking space.

2. Use medicine droppers to water tiny seedlings, give moisture to insects in jars, and for art projects. If necessary, remind children to push the air out of the dropper while it is still in the liquid. Can they see the air bubbling into the liquid?

3. If you need to open a vacuum-sealed container, such as using a punch-type opener with a can of juice, let the children listen closely for the hiss of air rushing into the can. When using the bellows-type step pump, show the rubber cap on the air intake valve. Push the air out so the bellows are flat. Remove the cap so that air rushes in with a hiss, and the bellows expand dramatically.

Relating New Concepts to Existing Concepts

1. Relate water concepts to air when investigating evaporation. Water droplets, or vapor, become part of the air. Speak of fog and clouds as very wet air. Moving air, the sun, and water combine to make different kinds of weather.

2. Relate plant propagation (seed scattering) to moving air.

3. Relate sound to air concepts. Sound travels through air; moving air causes some things to vibrate and make sounds; air vibrates when enclosed in a column like a flute or a whistle.

Involving Parents

A newsletter to parents can suggest ways to support and add to the air experiences at school. When families are out together, they can watch for soaring birds, planes, and clouds being pushed along by moving air. They can point out how air is used in their homes to keep people comfortable: heated in winter; passed through coolers in summer. Notify parents if there are exhibits in your area where children can see model or real gliders, small planes, windmills, or weathervanes.

References

Blough, Glenn. *After the Sun Goes Down*. New York: McGraw-Hill, 1956. Describes night-gliding animals in the woods.

Bonsall, George. *How and Why Wonder Book of Weather*. New York: Wonder Books, 1960.

Freeman, Mae. *A Book of Real Science*. New York: Scholastic Book Services, 1966.

————. *When Air Moves*. New York: McGraw-Hill, 1968.

Keen, Martin. *How and Why Wonder Book of Science Experiments*. New York: Wonder Books, 1962.

Piltz, Albert. *What is Air?* Chicago: Benefit Press, 1960.

Pine, Tillie S. *Air All Around*. New York: McGraw-Hill, 1960.

Schneider, Herman and Nina. *Let's Find Out*. New York: William Scott, 1946.

Wyler, Rose and Ames, Gerald. *Prove It*. New York: Scholastic Book Services, 1963.

5

What is Water?

All living things require water to survive. Water is also splendid for pouring, splashing, and spraying. Most children enjoy learning about this vital part of our environment. The experiences in this chapter will explore these concepts:

WATER HAS WEIGHT
WATER'S WEIGHT HELPS THINGS FLOAT
WATER GOES INTO SOME THINGS: NOT OTHERS
SOME THINGS DISAPPEAR IN WATER, SOME DO NOT
WATER GOES INTO THE AIR
WATER CAN CHANGE FORMS REVERSIBLY
THE SURFACE OF STILL WATER PULLS TOGETHER

It is hard to imagine sparkling, transparent water as having weight. Once children recognize that water does have substance, they understand more readily how water can hold things up.

In the following experiments children experience the weight of water; note that water is heavier than air; and explore buoyancy. Other experiences deal with water absorption and repellency; objects that dissolve in water; evaporation; condensation; freezing; melting; and surface tension of water.

Concept: Water Has Weight

1. Does Water Feel Heavy?

LEARNING OBJECTIVE: To experience firsthand that water has weight.

MATERIALS:

Outdoors when its warm:

Small wading pool

Gallon bucket

Two quart pitcher, or
½ gallon milk cartons

Water

For indoor use add:

Rubber boots

Plastic smock

GETTING READY:

If outdoors, have children
remove shoes and socks, roll
up trouser legs.

If indoors, have children
wear boots and smock.

SMALL GROUP ACTIVITY:

1. Pass pitcher of water for children to dabble
   fingers in. "Do you think this clear-looking water
   could be heavy? Let's find out."
2. Let children take turns standing in the pool to hold
   the empty bucket.
3. Let other children pour water into the bucket till
   it becomes too hard to hold. Conclusions about
   the weight of water are easily formed and
   communicated in this direct investigation.

2. Do Things Weigh the Same Dry and Damp?

LEARNING OBJECTIVE: To notice that the weight of a material increases when water is added to it.

MATERIALS:

Part 1

Inexpensive postage or calorie
counting scale

Matching set of small cups:
film canisters, spray can tops,
etc.

Small pitchers or half-pint
milk cartons

Water

Sponges, newspapers

Part 2

Tiny scoops

Sand, cornmeal

Pan for wet sand

SMALL GROUP ACTIVITY:

1. Put an empty cup on the scale. "What does a
   scale do? Let's see what happens if we pour water
   in the cup. What does it mean when the pointer
   moves down? Does a cup of water weigh more
   than a cup of air?"
2. Put dry sand in two matching cups. Weigh each to
   be sure that they are equal.
3. "Will you pour a little water in the sand cup
   on the scale now? Where is the pointer now?
   Why did it move from 2 to 3?" Check weight of
   other sand cup again to verify the change in damp
   sand weight.
4. Show how to record dry and wet weight on the
   chart.
5. Let children measure, weigh, and add water.
   Some may wish to try each set of cups to see if
   results will be the same.

GETTING READY:

Spread newspaper on table.

Cover postal rate finder, etc., with masking tape, so the indicator only points to ounce numerals.

Make a simple chart for children to keep weight records of dry and wet material.

Read the chart results to the whole class afterward. What was added to the damp sand that made it heavier?

Concept: Water's Weight Helps Things Float

1. Will Some Things Float, Some Sink?

LEARNING OBJECTIVE: To discover which objects, among a collection varying in dimension and weight, will be supported by water; which will not.

MATERIALS:

Dishpans of water

Small wading pool

Plastic aprons

Assorted objects: rocks, sticks, bath toys, corks, washers. Try to find like objects of different materials: ping-pong ball/golf ball; toy plastic key/metal key

Old kitchen scale, postage scale, or balance

Two trays

GETTING READY:

Place pans of water in the wading pool.
Tape card marked *float* to one tray; *sink* to other.

SMALL GROUP ACTIVITY:

1. Let children enjoy relaxed play with the materials.
2. "Does the water hold some things up on top? All things? Why did this ball stay on top and that ball sink down?"
3. Encourage children to weigh objects on the scale to confirm that similar objects can differ in weight; can act differently in water.
4. Put out *sink* and *float* trays. Suggest classifying objects, placing in correct trays.

2. Can Air Help Some Things Float?

LEARNING OBJECTIVE: To discover whether air inside an object helps the object float on water.

MATERIALS:

Dishpans of water

Small wading pool

Plastic aprons

Foot-long pieces of clear garden hose

2 corks to fit each hose

Many small plastic bottles, prescription vials *with caps*

GETTING READY:

Fit corks securely into hose ends.

Place pans of water in the dry wading pool.

SMALL GROUP ACTIVITY:

1. Remove one cork from a hose. Submerge it in water. Let it fill *almost* to top with water. Replace cork. "Are two kinds of stuff in the hose now? Is air or water on top? Which will be on top if the hose is turned upside down? On its side? Try it to find out." Allow time for experimenting.
2. Drop two capped bottles on the water. "What will happen if you take the cap off one bottle? Will it still float? Find out. What is in the bottle with the cap on it?"

READ: *The Story About Ping*, by Marjorie Flack.

Concept: Water Goes into Some Things: Not Others

1. Which Things Will Absorb Water?

LEARNING OBJECTIVE: To discover which materials among a collection will absorb water and which will repel water.

MATERIALS:

Part 1

Plastic aprons

Dropper-top medicine bottle for each child

Tiny funnel and baster

Plastic meat trays

Test materials: sponges, wood, cotton, paper towels, tissues, dried clay, stones

SMALL GROUP ACTIVITY:

Part 1

1. "What happens when you put drops of water on different things on your tray?" Listen to the children's ideas. Supply the term *absorb*.
2. Give a small cube of dry sponge to each child. Put in a dry place. "Watch closely, something will change fast." Squeeze water from baster onto sponge.

Part 2

6" squares of old cotton fabric

Plastic sheeting or rubberized fabric pieces

Waxed paper, scraps of leather

Smooth feathers

Spray bottle

Water

Part 2

1. Move from child to child with a piece of plastic, dry fabric, and the spray bottle.
2. Drape cloth over child's arm. Spray with water. "What do you feel?" Repeat with plastic. "Which material would you want for a raincoat? Why?" (This firsthand experience with water repellency intrigues children.)
3. Give each child a feather to hold while you carefully place *one drop* of water on the feather. Listen to the responses. Talk about birds staying

GETTING READY:

Let children fill bottles
with water.

Arrange a tray of test
materials for each child.

dry in the rain. Let children experiment with water
drops, feathers, and leather scraps.

READ: *Wet and Dry*, by Seymour Simon.

Group Experiences: 1. Put some dried beans into a plastic screwtop jar. Mark the level
of beans with a wax pencil. (Use less than half a jar of beans.) Let each child squeeze a dry
bean and put it in the jar. How did it feel? Pour in water to cover the beans. Cap the jar.
Set aside a few dry beans for comparison. Next day check the amount of space the beans
take up in the jar. What happened? Where is the water? Compare soaked and dry beans.

2. Weigh a dry sponge on a kitchen scale. Drop it in a bowl of water. Ask children
for predictions about the weight of the wet sponge. Reweigh the sponge. Let the children
decide what made the weight difference. Squeeze the water out over a dry bowl. Weigh
it again.

3. Use the term *absorb* whenever a spill must be wiped up from now on. Let the children use the sponge to absorb spills. They feel more in control of the situation if they can
undo what they have done accidentally.

Concept: Some Things Disappear in Water, Some Do Not

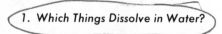

1. Which Things Dissolve in Water?

LEARNING OBJECTIVE: To discover which materials among a collection will dissolve in water and
which will not.

MATERIALS:

Muffin pans and plastic ice
cube trays with separated
molds, or plastic prescription
vials

Pitcher of water

Assorted dry materials: salt,
sand, cornstarch, flour, fine
gravel, seeds, cornmeal, etc.

Spoons for dry materials

Salad oil

Small screw-top bottle

SMALL GROUP ACTIVITY:

1. "See what happens when you put a little salt in
   one of your pans of water. Stir it. Can you see it?
   Feel it? Where is it?"
2. "Dip a finger in the pan. Taste the water. Is it salty?
   Yes, the salt is still there, but it is in such tiny bits
   now, we can't see it. It *dissolved* in the water."
3. "Try the other materials, put each in its own pan of
   water. Find out which ones dissolve."
4. Half fill the bottle with water. Add some oil.
   Cap securely. Let the children shake it. Does it
   seem to dissolve? Let it stand a while. Where is the
   oil now?

Plastic aprons

Newspaper

Sponge

Sticks for stirring

Cleanup bucket

GETTING READY:

Spread newspapers on work
table.

Half fill pans with water

Note: There seems to be a direct relationship between the amount of mess, and the amount of interest that children show in a science activity!

Group Experience: Mix some sand, dirt, and gravel with water in a pint jar. Let it stand undisturbed for a day or more. Check the jar. Is the water still muddy looking? Did the sand and dirt really dissolve? Which is on the bottom?

Concept: Water Goes into the Air

---

1. Will Warm Air, Moving Air, Take up Water?

LEARNING OBJECTIVE: To observe the results of air taking up water and to participate in hastening the process.

MATERIALS:

Two trays

Pans of water

Paper towels

Blackboard or other dark,
smooth surface

Cardboard or paper fans

Hand-held hair dryer

Paper

GETTING READY:

Check safety of the dryer cord
position.

Let children make folded
paper fans.

If possible use the hair dryer

SMALL GROUP ACTIVITY:

1. "If we wet some towels, squeeze them, and spread them out on these trays, what will happen to them? Let's see." Put one tray in a sunny or warm place, the other in a cool, darker place. Check them in half an hour.

2. Meanwhile show children the hair dryer, feel warm air coming from it. "What do you feel? This warm air can help us think about what is happening to the towels."

3. Let children dip a finger in water, then trace their names on the blackboard. "Take turns blowing the warm air on your wet name. Watch closely to see what happens to the water. . . . Where could it be? Only air touched it. The water has gone into the air in such tiny drops that we can't see it any more. When air takes up water, the water *evaporates.*"

close to floor level to
minimize tripping on the cord
or dropping the dryer.

4. "Try blowing on your wet name. Fold a paper fan and wave it near your name to make a breeze. Does the water go into the air? Let's see what happened to the paper towels. Did the water evaporate from both sets of towels? From the towels in the sunny place?"

READ: *The Rain Puddle,* by Adelaide Holl.

Group Experience: Early in the morning put measured amounts of water into three pie pans. Place pans where children can see, but not tip them over. Have one in the sunlight, one in the shade, one close to a heat source. Check several times during the day to note changes. If the weather is humid, you may need to continue to check the next day. What happened?

Concept: Water Can Change Forms Reversibly

1. Will Temperature Change Make Water Change?

LEARNING OBJECTIVE: To observe how changes in temperature transform water from liquid to
  solid and from solid to liquid.

MATERIALS:

Water

Two identical shallow plastic bowls. (Not ice cube trays. In some parts of the country children may believe that ice is formed only in cube shapes.)

Access to a freezing compartment or, better yet, to freezing weather.

SMALL GROUP ACTIVITY:

1. Early in the morning let children fill bowls almost to the top with water. Help them deliver one bowl to the freezer or to the near-zero outdoor location. Leave the other bowl in the room out of spilling range, for an hour or more.
2. "Will both bowls of water stay the same, or will one change? Let's check."
3. Bring ice back to the room when it is solid. Turn it out onto a pie pan for all to see.
4. "What will happen if we leave the bowl of water in the cold place? Let's find out." Repeat the activity if children request it.*
5. Bring snowballs or icicles indoors to melt in a pan, when possible.

READ: *The Snowy Day, by Ezra Jack Keats.*

*Some children may have had enough experience with water and ice to accurately predict reversibility of this change in water form. The transformation from water to vapor through temperature change is less familiar. Both forms of reversibility may need repeating several times to begin to clarify cause and effect ideas for less experienced children.

2. Can Water Change to Vapor; Vapor Change to Water?

LEARNING OBJECTIVE: To observe how changes in temperature transform water from liquid to vapor and from vapor to liquid.

MATERIALS:

Vaporizer, baby bottle warmer, or facial sauna heating unit

Rectangular cake pan

Blocks, bricks, or books

Ice cubes

Water

GETTING READY:

Arrange two stacks of blocks on either side of the heating unit, high enough to support the pan above the boiling water.

Check water heating unit cord and locate it with child safety in mind—where it can't possibly be tripped over.

Do not let children do this without close adult supervision of the heating unit.

SMALL GROUP ACTIVITY:

1. Show children the heating unit. "I will plug this in, then add water that will get *very hot*. It will change to invisible droplets called vapor. It will look like a pretty cloud, but it will be *burning hot! It must not be touched!*"
2. Connect the unit, add water in the amount stated on the unit label. "This hot vapor is steam. Clouds and fog are vapor, too, but they aren't as hot. Clouds, fog, and steam are all very wet air."
3. Let children fill the pan with ice. Place the pan over boiling water, resting it on block stacks. "Let's cool the wet air to see what happens."
4. Watch the underside of the pan to see vapor droplets turn cold, then condense into fat, heavy drops of water. It's raining!

Go slowly with this. Listen to children's ideas. Don't expect them to verbalize everything that happened. Do again, if possible.

FIGURE 9

Comment that the tiny droplets of water in clouds, fog, or steam are so little that they can float in the air. When droplets come together in cold air, they become too heavy to float. They fall down as raindrops.

READ: *Georgie and the Noisy Ghost*, by Robert Bright.

Group Activity: Ask the children to breathe slowly into their cupped hands. Does their breath feel warm or cold when it comes from their bodies? Pass out small mirrors or foil pans for children to exhale on. Are these surfaces cool? Ask for predictions about the outcome of breathing onto the cool mirror or metal. Find out what happens. Can the children see results? "How does the cloudy place feel? Is it wet or dry? Try it again. Feel the cloudy place, then feel a place that wasn't breathed on. Why do we feel wetness?"

Concept: The Surface of Still Water Pulls Together

1. Are Drops of Water Curved?

LEARNING OBJECTIVE: To notice the curved form taken by drops of water and the adhesion property of water drops.

MATERIALS:

Water

Tiny funnel

Small bottles

Medicine droppers

Baster

Waxed paper or formica-topped table

Plastic aprons

Spoons, popsicle sticks

Sponge to *absorb* spills

GETTING READY:

Fill individual bottles with water. Children like to do this with a tiny funnel and small pitcher. Let them try to help.

SMALL GROUP ACTIVITY:

1. Give each child a square of waxed paper. "What will happen if a bit of water is squeezed from the dropper onto the paper. Find out. Did it make a flat splash or a rounded drop? Watch closely to see the water pull into drops."
2. Suggest seeing what happens when many drops are made close to each other; when drops are made with the baster.
3. Talk about the outside edges of the drops pulling together to make an invisible "skin." This "skin" is not very strong.
4. Suggest gently dipping the spoon handle or stick into a big drop, *watching closely.* Does the water cling for a bit as the spoon is slowly pulled away?

2. Can Surface Tension Hold Some Weight?

LEARNING OBJECTIVE: To explore the nature of surface tension.

MATERIALS:

Clear glass or plastic jar, about 4" diameter

SMALL GROUP ACTIVITY:

1. Fill one or two jars almost to top with water.

Water

Syringe-type baster

Plastic aprons

Sponge and newspapers to *absorb* spills

Bucket for cleanup

Talcum powder, pepper, uncooked spaghetti, aluminum foil, waxed paper

2. While children watch with heads close to the table, slowly add drops of water from the baster until the jar is full. Ask, "What might happen if more drops are added?" Find out, drop by drop. Did the surface pull more drops into a curve of invisible "skin"?

3. Hold a piece of spaghetti with thumb and forefinger. Gently rest it on the surface. Now push it through the "skin" vertically. What happens? (Only dry pieces rest on the "skin.")

3. Does Soap Break Water's Surface Tension?

LEARNING OBJECTIVE: To cause surface tension to dissipate, using soap.

MATERIALS:

SMALL GROUP ACTIVITY:

Pepper or talcum powder

Pitcher of water

Small jar

Spoon

Slivers of soap

Shallow foil pans

Liquid detergent

Plastic aprons

Newspaper, bucket, sponge for cleanup

1. "If we stir pepper (talcum) and water together in this jar, will they mix? Find out."
2. "Will they mix if we gently sprinkle pepper on top of the water? Try it with the pans of water."
3. "What could be keeping it on top of the water?" (surface tension)
4. "Let's see what happens when we touch that invisible 'skin' with a bit of soap."
5. Let the children experiment, changing water as needed. Try adding a few drops of detergent instead of soap. What happens?

GETTING READY:

Pour 1" of water in foil pans

Half-fill jar with water

Find directions for making a "soap power" boat, using the soap/surface-tension reaction in: *Fun In The Making*, a Department of Health, Education and Welfare Publication.

Primary Reinforcements

Music (See Appendix 1 for numerical references in parentheses)

1. It's fun to be vigorously involved in singing, "Row, Row, Row Your Boat," (2) joining hands and touching feet with a partner to pull back and forth. It's good to recall that water holds boats up, also.

2. Sing "The Eency Beency Spider," (1) after the evaporation experiences with an adaptation in lyrics. Change: "and dried up all the rain," to "and evaporated the rain." Look for rain spouts near the school which children may watch after a rain.

3. Sing the old nursery song, "One Misty, Moisty Morning." (4)

Misty Moisty was the morn, Rainy was the weather.
When I met an old man, Dressed all in leather.

After experimenting with absorption and repellency discuss with the children whether the old man was dry inside his leather clothes.

4. Sing this song after experimenting with forms of water:

(To the tune of "Twinkle, Twinkle, Little Star")
Water, water from the stream
When it boils it turns to steam.

Water, water is so nice;
Freeze it cold, it turns to ice.

Cool the steam; warm the ice
It's water again, clear and nice.

Math Experiences

1. Encourage the children to count aloud the number of stirs each child takes as drink mixes or jello are dissolved. Let the children be the clock watchers to remind you when the jello should be solidified. If you have a play clock, set the hands to the appointed time. The children will have a means of checking the hand position of the real clock.

2. Let the children record the weight of materials being compared in dry and wet states. A discussion of the results could bring in more-than, less-than comparisons. "Are four ounces more than two ounces?"

3. Provide a set of Mary Ann measuring cups; 4 ounce, 8 ounce, and 16 ounce plastic bottles; or three sizes of paper milk cartons for casual use by children playing with water. Ask how many small containers of water it takes to fill a bottle or carton this size, and so on.

Stories and References for Children

Bright, Robert. *Georgie and the Noisy Ghost*. New York: Scholastic Book Services, 1972.
    Georgie engineers a rescue for his family who are adrift at sea in a thick fog.

Flack, Marjorie. *The Story About Ping*. New York: The Viking Press, Seafarer Ed.,
    1970. In this classic story, a barrel tied to his back keeps a houseboat boy afloat
    after he tumbles into the Yangtze River.

Holl, Adelaide. *The Rain Puddle*. New York: Lothrop, Lee and Shepard, 1965. Evaporation of a puddle confuses some already befuddled animals.

Keats, Ezra Jack. *The Snowy Day*. New York: Viking Press, 1962. What happens to the snowball in Peter's pocket?

Koch, Dorothy. *Let It Rain*. New York: Holiday House, 1959. This pleasant story leads into discussions of water repellency, absorption, and surface tension. (Skip the page showing children sawing wood on a chair seat and hammering nails on a table.)

Milgrom, Harry. *ABC Science Experiments*. New York: Macmillan Co., 1970. Several water experiments are included in this picture book for very young children.

Milne, A. A. *Winnie the Pooh*. New York: E. P. Dutton, 1961, chapter 9, "In Which Pooh is Entirely Surrounded by Water." Pooh and Christopher Robin use unorthodox means of floating through flood waters.

Rey, H. A. *Curious George Rides a Bike*. New York: Scholastic Book Services, 1973. George forgets to deliver newspapers, because he is so absorbed in making newspaper boats and floating his fleet downstream.

Rosenfeld, Sam. *A Drop Of Water*. Irvington-on-Hudson, N.Y.: Harvey House, 1970. An appealing story tracing a drop of water from its place on a rock through the water cycle and back.

Schulevitz, Uri. *Rain, Rain, Rivers*. New York: Farrar, Straus, and Giroux, 1969. A simple story illustrating that children, birds, and plants benefit from rain.

Simon, Seymour. *Wet and Dry*. New York: McGraw-Hill, 1969. This is an appealing book of water experiments designed for very young children.

Tresselt, Alvin. *Hide and Seek Fog*. New York: Lothrop, Lee and Shepard Company, 1965.

Poems (References found in Appendix 1)

Three poems about the weather in the collection, *Poems Children Will Sit Still For*, by deRegniers, Moore, and White, reinforce some of the water experiences. They are:

"Dragon Smoke," by Lilian Moore
  (Describes condensation of breath moisture)
"Weather," by Eve Merriam
"Galoshes," by Rhoda Bacmeister

Now We Are Six, by A. A. Milne, has a raindrop-watching poem, "Waiting at the Window."
Poems To Grow On, by Jean Thompson, includes "The Snowflake," by Walter de la Mare.

Fingerplays

Here is a fingerplay about evaporation:

In soapy water   (scrubbing motion)
I wash my clothes,
I hang them out to dry.   (pantomime)
The sun it shines   (hands form circle)
The wind it blows,   (wave arms, sway)
The wetness goes into the sky.

Art Activities

1. MIXING PAINT. Children enjoy discovering that their tempera paint is a mixture of water and a powdered pigment medium. If it can be conveniently arranged, allow well-covered children a chance to help prepare paint. An efficient blending tool for the job is a French wire whisk. Put the correct proportion of water in a wide-mouth jar, add dry tempera, and rotate the whisk briskly for a few seconds to make smooth paint.

2. ICE CUBE PAINTING. Use finger paint and glossy paper, but do not wet the paper as you would to prepare for finger painting. Instead offer the children ice cubes with which to spread and dilute the paint, while making designs. Children who have watched ice melt like to apply the effect in something they create. (*Suggested by Lillian Dean.*)

3. RAIN COLLAGE. Children can create a rain scene by swirling glue on paper, then sprinkling confetti or computer punchouts over the sticky areas. Pictures of plants cut from seed catalogs can be added to the collage as things that benefit from the rain. Whenever wet paintings are hung up to dry, use the term *evaporate*.

Dramatic Play

1. INDOOR CAMPING. Devise a partial tent by securing a blanket over a climbing box, or arrange it lean-to fashion from a high shelf to the floor. Make a fishing pond by placing a dishpan of water in an empty wading pool. Provide a stick and string fish pole. Tie a cork about six inches from the end as a bobber above water, and a metal washer on the end of the string as a sinker.

2. HOUSEKEEPING PLAY. Wash doll clothes. If possible hang some to dry in the sunshine, some in a shady location, and some indoors. Compare drying times.

3. INDOOR WATER PLAY. Place two or three dishpans of water inside an empty wading pool. Provide plastic or metal pitchers, plastic funnels, and lengths of tubing for play. Mark several plastic baby bottles with tape and numerals to indicate 2, 4, and 6 ounce levels to which the bottles can be filled with water.

4. OUTDOOR WARM WEATHER WATER PLAY. Barefooted children can transfer water from buckets to the wading pool, using a plastic hand pump from the automotive supply section of a variety store. Try putting a bucket on a pile of hollow blocks next to the wading pool for experimentation with a garden-hose syphon. See page 58. READ: *Curious George Rides a Bicycle*, by H. A. Rey. Then help children make newspaper boats to float in the wading pool, following the techniques George uses in the story.

5. BUBBLE MAKING. Choose some of these ways to have fun with surface tension:

> Use commercial bubble solutions and ring-tipped wands to wave or blow bubbles. Replenish the solution with a concentrated mixture of liquid detergent and water. If available, try the commercial set of giant rings and multiple bubble template. Use these outdoors.

> Provide straws and cans of detergent/water solution for children to blow *into*. This is easier for children who aren't able to cope with blowing bubbles into the air.

> Try fat drinking straws as pipes for blowing detergent/water solution bubbles into the air. Show the children how to dip the end of the straw into the solution to let a film collect across the bottom of the straw. Suggest holding the straw slightly downward to avoid dripping solution into the mouth.

> Try using soft plastic funnels to blow giant bubbles. (Have several ready, and be prepared to wash mouthpieces before sharing turns.) Put the funnel upside down into a bowl of detergent solution. Gently blow a few bubbles into the bowl to allow a film of solution to coat the inside of the funnel. Lift out the funnel and softly blow a beautiful bubble!

Talk with the children about how the outside edges of the soap film pulled together like a balloon around the air. The soap or detergent mixture made a stretchier, stronger skin than the water makes alone.

Food Experiences

Children put many of the water concepts to use when they dissolve powdered drink mixes; boil water to dissolve jello and melt ice cubes to thicken it; and freeze fruit juice popsicles. Cooking rice for lunch offers both water absorption and volume measurement experiences. Popping corn is an exciting edible way to illustrate a property of water: high temperature changes water to steam. Children are surprised and pleased to learn that moisture inside the kernels of corn changes to steam so fast that it pops the kernel open. The steam is very evident in a plastic-domed corn popper.

Thinking Games

Invent a story mixup to tell that includes references to water concepts. Illustrate the story with mounted pictures cut from magazines or catalogs. When the concept is referred to, let it be in the form of an obvious misstatement for the children to catch and correct. Perhaps it could be a camping story where "the children could hardly wait to cool off by skating on the lake in the summer sunshine . . . John and Anne filled the boat with heavy rocks to help it float on the water . . . Dad put the teakettle in the ice box to boil the water for soup."

Creative Movement

1. BUBBLES. Add a soap bubble movement stimulus to your collection of emergency ideas: ideas to use when you have a group of children ready to do something that isn't quite ready for the children! Tell the children that you will blow imaginary bubbles to them to catch. "Here's a high one . . . catch this one

on your elbow . . . your shoulder . . . your chin. Don't let this one touch the ground . . . catch this one on a fingertip and blow it back to me . . . pretend that your hands are made of soap film. Blow into them till they can't stretch any more and they pop."

2. SNOWMEN. Guide the children as they roll imaginary snowmen, rolling slower and slower as the ball gets larger. "Let's make a smaller ball for a chest . . . now a smaller ball for a head . . . lift them into place. Oh! there it goes . . . snowballs this size are very heavy. Now, be the snowman yourself, all curvy and cold and tall. But wait, the sun is beginning to shine and warm the air. Oh! What's happening to your arms, your body. . . ." Continue with your suggestions, and the children's responses till the snowman is a puddle that will soon evaporate and vanish without a trace.

3. Take the children on an imaginary trip to a lake in summer where they can pretend to float on their backs and tummies while the water holds them up. They can invent ways to swim, dive, and row a boat. "Now it's winter and we can't swim, but it's so cold that we can. . . ."

Secondary Reinforcements

Keeping Concepts Alive

1. Discuss evaporation whenever clothes have to be dried at school—after play in the snow or a fall into a puddle. It's especially reassuring to a child who is worried about staying neat to know that an accidental stain can be washed out, that the moisture will evaporate and the garment will look fine again. When children come to school in raincoats and boots, look for drops of water still on the outside of the garments, evidence that these materials don't absorb water.

2. Examine puddles in the playground after a rain. Try to mark the outline of the puddle size with stones when it is at its fullest level. This will make it easier for the children to make comparisons from day to day as they watch for changes in the puddle. They will remind you if you should happen to forget the puddle-checking ritual. Those in the Temperate Zone might be able to see the puddle freeze and thaw as well as evaporate. Cold air caused the water to freeze.

3. Watch the clouds when a rain is forecast. Talk about the tiny droplets in the clouds forming into heavier drops when the clouds get cold.

Relating New Concepts to Existing Concepts

Some of the relationships between air and water can be observed in caring for classroom fish and plant life, some can be effectively demonstrated with simple experiments:

1. Children can see evidence of *air in water* when they watch a covered jar of water that has been allowed to stand in the room. Rows of tiny air bubbles will appear on the sides of the jar. Read the story, *Plenty of Fish,* by Millicent

Selsam. In it, Willie learns that fish must have air to live, and that water takes in air. He discovers that fish have their own way of getting the air they need from the water. Point out the safety fact that children cannot get air from the water when they swim. They must learn how to breathe, how to let the water hold them up, and how to use their arms and legs to move along when they swim.

2. The evaporation-condensation cycle can be observed in daily caring for classroom plants. A terrarium lets children see the condensation of moisture on the cover glass. When children water the other plants in the room, ask them occasionally whether the terrarium plants need to be watered every day. Why not? Check to see that the plants are growing well with infrequent sprinklings of water.

3. Plant dependence upon water can be seen quite well in thin-leafed plants that have gone without water for a weekend. An avocado plant droops dramatically, then recuperates within an hour or so after a good watering.

4. Air pressure can be used to empty the aquarium, to drain water from a large waterplay tub, or to provide outdoor waterplay. Make a syphon by completely filling approximately a yard of tubing with water, pinching the ends together to keep air from entering the tube. Place one end of the tube in the water, one in the bucket below. The water will drain into the bucket, unless air entered the tube. Explain that air presses on the surface of the aquarium water, pushing water up the tube. Read about the boy who empties his fishbowl this way in *The True Book of Science Experiments,* by Illa Podendorf.

Involving Parents

There are many opportunities for parents to point out examples of water and water/air concepts at home: moisture condensing on mirrors and windows at bath time; steamy kitchen windows when dinner is cooking; water dripping from air-conditioning units or dehumidifiers; and the "smoke" of moisture condensation that emits from clothes dryer vents in cold weather. All of these amplify the classroom experiences.

Parents are the best supervisors of the field trips that extend water learnings in the most concrete ways: the swimming pool and beach visits. There children can stride through shallow water to test its weight and substance. With encouraging parents standing by, children can learn that the buoyancy principles work to support their own floating bodies.

References

Bonsall, George. *How and Why Wonder Book of Weather*. New York: Wonder Books, 1960.

Dempsey, Michael, and Sheehan, Angela, eds. *Water*. New York: World Publishing, The Danbury Press, 1970.

Keen, Martin. *How and Why Wonder Book of Science Experiments*. New York: Wonder Books, 1962.

Leavitt, Jerome, and Huntsberger, John. *Fun-time Terrariums and Aquariums*. Chicago: Children's Press, 1961.

Pine, Tillie, and Levine, Joseph. *Water All Around*. New York: Whittelsey House, McGraw-Hill, 1959. Dissolving, evaporation, condensation, clouds, snow, and frost experiments and descriptions.

Wyler, Rose. *First Book of Science Experiments*. New York: Franklin Watts, 1971.

Wyler, Rose, and Ames, Gerald. *Prove It*. New York: Scholastic Book Services, 1963. Water Experiments.

VISUAL AID

Air and Weather. The Instructor Primary Science Concept Charts. F. A. Owen Publishing, 1960. Simple posters illustrating air/water relationships.

PAMPHLET

Fun in the Making. Publication #OCD 73-31, Department of Health, Education and Welfare, 1973. Price: 55 cents. Superintendent of Documents, U.S. Government Printing Office, Washington, D.C. 20402

6

The Effects of
Magnetism

Magnets attract iron, steel, and the attention of young children! While magnetic attraction cannot be seen or felt, its effect can be seen and felt. Children can accept the reality of an invisible force when they can have fun putting that force to work. The concepts underlying the experiences in this chapter are:

MAGNETS PULL SOME THINGS, BUT NOT OTHERS
MAGNETS PULL THROUGH SOME MATERIALS
ONE MAGNET CAN BE USED TO MAKE ANOTHER MAGNET
MAGNETS ARE STRONGEST AT EACH END
EACH END OF A MAGNET ACTS DIFFERENTLY

Children can experiment with familiar objects to see what magnets will pull and what they will pull through; to make temporary magnets; and to discover how opposite magnetic poles affect each other.

Concept: Magnets Pull Some Things, But Not Others

1. What Will Magnets Pull?

LEARNING OBJECTIVE: To experience visually and tactually the effects of magnetic attraction and to apply the effects to sort iron or steel objects from nonferrous objects.

MATERIALS:

Magnets, assorted shapes and sizes

Small Styrofoam meat tray filled with test items for each child. (iron/steel suggestions: keys, key chains, bolts, screws, nails, paperclips, lipstick cases) (non-iron/steel items: pennies, brass fasteners, rubber bands, plastic, glass, wood, aluminum objects)

Two large trays or box covers

GETTING READY:

Have only magnets on the table when children gather. Count them together. (Tiny magnets are easily misplaced.)

Prepare a mixed collection of objects for each pair of children.

Tape a *yes* label on one tray, a *no* label on the other.

SMALL GROUP ACTIVITY:

1. Give each child a paper clip and a small magnet to try out. To see the effect well, slide magnet toward the clip on the table top. To *feel* the effect, hold clip in the palm of the hand.
2. "Do you think the magnet will pull everything to it? Let's find out with the things on the small trays."
3. After some exploration, suggest sorting objects pulled by the magnets from those that are not. Use the *yes* and *no* trays.
4. "Things on the yes tray do not look alike, but they are made of the same stuff." Children may note that all items are metal. You can use the specific terms, *iron* or *steel.* "Magnets pull only on iron or steel."
5. Let children swap items to explore again. Count magnets before putting them away.

Note: Good magnets can be purchased from school suppliers. Inexpensive magnets sold in packaged kits as toys are rarely strong enough for school use. An electric motor repair shop may be willing to give you old magnets removed from motors. (Remove your watch before using a very strong magnet.)

READ: *Mickey's Magnet,* by Franklyn Branley and Eleanor Vaughn.

Concept: Magnets Pull through Some Materials

---

1. Can Magnets Pull through Things Not Attracted?

LEARNING OBJECTIVE: To discover forms of nonferrous materials through which magnetism will pass.

MATERIALS:

Magnets*

Steel wool pad

SMALL GROUP ACTIVITY:

1. "Do you know what this (steel wool) is made from? Could a magnet help you find the answer?"
2. Tear off bits of steel wool. Give some to each

Iron and steel objects (Nails, washers, bolts, clips.)

Paper, cardboard, aluminum

Shoe box

Drinking glasses

Sand or dirt

Water

GETTING READY:

Put steel object in tumbler.
Put steel objects in box, cover with sand.
Put water in another tumbler, drop a washer in it.
Put water in a third tumbler, drop a washer in it.

child. "Can a magnet pick up steel that is covered with a piece of paper?" Find out. Try cardboard; aluminum. "Does magnetism pull through these things to pick up steel?"

3. Touch magnet to the outside of a dry tumbler. Does it attract the steel object inside the tumbler? Try different magnets, different objects.
4. Suggest dipping magnet into the sand-filled box; the tumbler of water. Can magnetism pass through materials which it does not attract?

* The thickness of the noniron material and the strength of the magnet are factors in the success of this experiment. A new "Magnik" from Creative Playthings will attract a paperclip through one's fingertip. A weak magnet will not attract a paperclip through cardboard.

Group Discussion: When the children try out various magnets, they will find that some work better than others. Talk about this with the whole group. Children can help keep magnets strong by remembering to put a steel "keeper bar" across both ends of a horseshoe magnet. They can also keep magnets strong by not jarring them.

Note: A child may believe that a keeper bar is also a magnet; one that just doesn't happen to work right when it is separated from the magnet. From the child's experience a plain bar of metal has no assigned function. Find a familiar iron or steel object to use as a temporary keeper bar. "Are children's scissors magnets? (no) Will a magnet attract them? (yes) Good, then we can leave this pair of scissors across the ends of the horseshoe magnet to keep it strong, while you experiment with the other keeper bar." Experience may clarify a child's ideas about the keeper bar, while verbal persuasion from an adult may not.

Concept: One Magnet Can Be Used to Make Another Magnet

---

1. Can We Make a Magnet?

LEARNING OBJECTIVE: To learn how to make a temporary magnet.

MATERIALS:

2" needles or straightened paper clips

SMALL GROUP ACTIVITY:

1. Let children use the magnet to determine if needles or clips are made of steel.

Strong magnet (bar, horseshoe)

Paperclips, steel wool, straight pins

2. "Try to pick up steel wool bits with the needles or clips. Are they magnetic?" (Not yet.)
3. Show children how to pull the needle *across one end* of the magnet *in one direction*. Count aloud about 25 strokes.
4. "Now try to attract steel wool with the needle. It should be magnetized. It has become a temporary *magnet.*"

Note: This is a good time to demonstrate how jarring a magnet weakens it. Hit the magnetized needle against something hard a few times. Now try to pick up some light steel object. The pull will be very weak.

Concept: Magnets Are Strongest at Each End

1. Which Parts of a Magnet Are Strongest?

LEARNING OBJECTIVE: To notice that the ends of a magnet act differently than the middle of the magnet.

MATERIALS:

Bits of steel wool

Paper clips, steel key chain or light switch pull chain

Horseshoe and bar magnets

GETTING READY:

Cut the steel wool into fine bits. (Did some of the steel cling to the scissor edges? The scissors became a temporary magnet.)

Open out the key chain full length.

SMALL GROUP ACTIVITY:

1. Hold curved end of the horseshoe magnet over steel wool. Is any steel attracted to the middle of this magnet? "Hold the *ends* of the magnet over the steel wool. Do the *ends* act differently than the middle?" Try with a bar magnet.
2. Touch the chain with both ends of a magnet. Does the whole chain cling to the magnet, or does the middle part dangle free? (chain should be longer than the bar magnet: 1″ bar magnet, 3″ key chain)
3. Dangle the key chain $\frac{1}{4}$″ to $\frac{1}{8}$″ above the center of a bar magnet. (The pull of a strong magnet will visibly curve the end of the chain toward one end.)

Concept: Each End of a Magnet Acts Differently

1. Are Magnets Alike on Both Ends?

LEARNING OBJECTIVE: To notice that each end of a magnet acts differently; that like ends of two magnets push away, unlike ends pull together.

MATERIALS:

2 strong bar magnets, or 2 horseshoe magnets

String

Nail polish or tape

GETTING READY:

If using lightweight magnets, tape the string to a table top or chair seat.

Tie the string to any horizontal bar or chair back that will allow a heavy magnet to swing freely.

SMALL GROUP ACTIVITY:

1. Tie the string to the center of a magnet, balancing it.
2. Let the magnet hang and swing freely. When it stops moving, one end of the bar, or one side of the horseshoe magnet, will be pointing North. Mark this end with tape or a dot of nail polish. Do the same for the second magnet. (This is also how a magnetic compass works. Some children may know about compasses already. Others may find directional discussion confusing at this point.)
3. Let the children hold a magnet in each hand, then try to touch like ends (North to North, South to South). Do they push each other away? Try to touch unlike ends. What happens?

Give children lots of time to explore the attraction and repulsion effect. With strong magnets, results are fascinating. This understanding will clarify the jumping effects of *Magniks* sold by Creative Playthings. To retain strength, make a point of storing bar magnets in pairs with opposite poles touching.

Note: In this instance, using the correct scientific term can create more confusion than clarity. The ends of magnets are called the north (seeking) pole and the south (seeking) pole. Adults find it confusing that the North *Geographic* Pole is not in quite the same location as the earth's North *Magnetic* Pole. Young children hold firmly to yet a different abstraction about the North Pole!

Primary Reinforcements

Math Experiences

1. MAGNET IN THE GRAB BAG. Half fill a large grocery bag with used bottle caps (a vending machine operator can keep you well supplied), or use 3 or 4 pounds of common nails instead. Tie a strong magnet to a stick with string, fishpole style. Let children take turns dipping the magnet into the bag, then counting aloud the number of caps they have pulled up. A numeral recognition version of this game can be played by cutting out colored paper fish, writing a numeral on each, and fastening a paper clip or safety pin to each fish.

2. Plastic numerals and counting shapes are made with magnets to use on coated steel bulletin boards. Use them to form sets of objects, labeled with corresponding numerals. Make a game of this by letting children draw the numerals from a paper bag, choose the corresponding quantity of objects, and place them on the bulletin board. You may have an old tin-coated steel baking sheet in your kitchen that would substitute well for the commercial steel bulletin board.

Music

Try singing the "Magnet Song."

Magnet Song

(To the tune of: "The Cat Came Back")

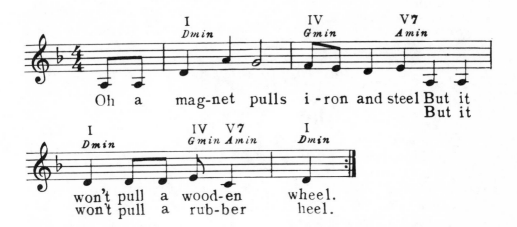

Oh a mag-net pulls i-ron and steel But it
But it

won't pull a wood-en wheel.
won't pull a rub-ber heel.

Sometime mention to children that we couldn't hear music from a record player, radio, television set, or tape recorder without magnets. Recording tape is coated with magnetized powdered iron, and the other four devices have magnets in their mechanism.

Stories and References for Children

Branley, Franklyn, and Vaughan, Eleanor. *Mickey's Magnet*. New York: Thomas Y. Crowell, 1956.

Freeman, Mae. *The Real Book of Magnets*. New York: Scholastic Book Services, 1967. A small bar magnet is taped to the inside cover of this book when it is ordered by mail.

Pine, Tillie, and Levine, Joseph. *Magnets and How to Use Them*. New York: Scholastic Book Services, 1963.

Podendorf, Illa. *The True Book of Science Experiments*. Chicago: Childrens Press, 1972.

Story Telling with Magnets

Tell a story featuring practical uses of magnetic gadgets that could also be props for the telling. A small magnet could save the day when father drops his keys down the register; when sister's box of bobby pins spills in her bubble bath; when someone upsets a box of pins; a glass jar of nails breaks on the garage floor. These and other calamities could be resolved with an upholsterer's tack hammer; a magnetic-holder flashlight; a paper clip or pin box with a magnetized top; or other magnetic equipment that may be available.

The effects of magnetism can be used throughout the school year as a story-telling device in three ways:

1. MAGNETICALLY DIRECTED PUPPETS. Hammer several tacks or a pronged steel caster to the bottom of small wooden dollhouse dolls. Put an open shoebox on its side to make a platform for the puppets. Make the puppets move with magnets held in each hand beneath the platform.

FIGURE 10

(Thread spools with button heads glued on, clothespin dolls with paperclip feet, or pipe cleaner dolls could also be used.) Children love using magnet puppets to retell familiar stories or to create their own plays.

2. PAPER DOLL STORIES. Cut out paper figures to illustrate a story. Tape paper clips or small safety pins to the backs. Invert a large grocery bag, plain or decorated, as a backdrop, and manipulate the paper figures with magnets held inside the bag.

3. MAGNETIC BULLETIN BOARD STORIES. Use fabric or paper figures as you would for a flannel-board story. Hold them in place with a shirt-button sized magnet. Try to fit one of the whimsical magnet insects into the story.

Art Activity

Make junk sculpture with iron or steel:

1. Prepare bottle caps and cocoa tin lids by punching two nail holes into each one.

2. Prepare sculpture bases using mounds of damp clay, chunks of Styrofoam, or cardboard fruit trays.

3. Put out a tray full of iron and steel discards: paper clips, nails, bottle caps, hairpins, pipe cleaners, cocoa tin lids, twist bag closures, washers, strips of screening, soft wire, and so on. Put out several magnets so that the children can test materials for magnetic attraction. Explain that the sculpture for today will be made only of iron or steel.

4. Show how wire can be threaded through the punched bottle caps; how

paperclips can be opened; and how wire pipe cleaners can be coiled around a finger to make interesting shapes.

Dramatic Play

AUTOMOBILE SERVICE. Tie a small magnet to a toy tow truck for children to use in hauling steel cars to the garage.

Table Games Using Magnets

1. NAME GAME. Print capital letters on separate small squares of paper. Put a staple through each square. Pile the squares into a small basket. Let the children fish for those letters contained in their names with a magnet tied to a stick on a string.

2. MAGNET CONSTRUCTION GAME BOX. Collect 3 or 4 small, strong magnets with keeper bars or nails to serve that purpose. Find iron and steel discard items similar to those suggested for the junk sculpture. Try to include steel key chains, notebook rings, old keys, and cocoa box lids. Children enjoy combining odd shapes that are held together by magnetic attraction. Try to find a "tin" cookie box for storing the game. The lid and the box can serve as bases for the constructions.

3. Many magnet games appear from time to time in variety stores. "Chain Reaction," "Tickle Bee," kissing dolls, and dancing animals sometimes can be found in mail order toy catalogs. Childcraft offers a set called "Magnasticks." Galt toys in England offers a sturdy magnetic construction set.

Thinking Game

I AM A MAGNET. Collect a tray of assorted objects: key, bottle cap, spool, stick, rock, nail, bolt, paper clip. Sit with the children in a circle on the floor. Place the tray in the center. Start off as the leader when introducing the game. Ask the child next to you to choose one of the objects to pretend to be. Say, "I am a great, strong magnet. What are you, Maria?" If Maria replies that she is a bottle cap, say: "Then we'll cling together," and hold her hand. Encourage Maria to say to the child next to her, "Josh, I'm a magnetized bottle cap. What are you?" If Josh decides to be a rock, Maria goes on to the next child until she finds someone to cling to. End the game with, "Now I am a teacher again and my pulling strength is gone."

Secondary Reinforcements

Keeping Concepts Alive

1. Point out magnets in use around the school whenever they come to your attention: refrigerator-door sealing strips, car seat-belt clasps, fancy buckles on children's belts, cupboard-door latches. For the latter example, it is a good idea

to suggest that children using those cupboards try to close them gently, without banging them so that the magnets won't lose their strength.

2. Make magnets a standard part of classroom cleanup equipment. Hang a magnet and keeper bar on a low peg near the workbench if you have one. Let the children use it on the floor, in workbench drawers, or on the workbench to gather up stray nails. Use it to sort out tiny nails from wooden shapes after children have worked with hammer-on design kits. Use the magnet to locate small steel cars that have become buried in the sandbox.

Relating New Concepts to Existing Concepts

1. When discussing the effect of magnetism passing through materials, ask the children whether air is one of the substances that magnetism passes through. How can they tell? Recall with the children that even though we cannot see air or magnetism, we have discovered that both are real things.

2. Set up a waterplay game that depends upon magnetism passing through water. Let the children make barge-shaped boats from pressed Styrofoam, and fasten a paper clip to it with a rubber band. Stack three blocks under each end of a shallow cake pan. Fill the pan with water and launch the Styrofoam boats on it. Children can guide their boats through the water with magnets held beneath the pan.

3. Combine buoyancy and the principle of attraction and repulsion of like magnetic poles in a waterplay activity. Help the children magnetize 2″ blunt needles, then place them on top of barge-shaped Styrofoam boats. Float the boats in a pan of water. Push the boats ahead by approaching the end of the needle with the like pole of a magnet; pull boats back with the unlike pole of the magnet. If a needle rolls off a boat, the children can go fishing for it in the water with a magnet.

Parent Involvement

Parents can provide the best field trip experience related to magnetism: a visit to the scrap metal yard where a giant electromagnet picks up huge loads of steel. They can also help children look for gadgets in the house that make use of magnets: pot holders, reminder pads, flashlights, and pin and paper clip holders. In addition, they can use small magnets to fasten children's art work to the refrigerator door.

References

Blough, Glenn, and Schwartz, Julius. *Elementary School Science and How To Teach It.* 5th ed. New York: Holt, Rinehart and Winston, 1974.

Freeman, Mae. *The Real Book of Magnets.* New York: Scholastic Book Services, 1967.

Holden, Raymond. *Magnetism.* New York: Golden Press, 1962.

Keen, Martin. *The How and Why Wonder Book of Magnets and Magnetism.* New York: Wonder Books, 1963.

Pine, Tillie, and Levine, Joseph. *Magnets and How to Use Them.* New York: Scholastic Book Services, 1963.

Podendorf, Illa. *The True Book of Science Experiments.* Chicago: Childrens Press, 1972.

Reuben, Gabriel, and Archer, Gloria. *What Is a Magnet?* Chicago: Benefit Press, 1959.

Wyler, Rose, and Ames, Gerald. *Prove It.* New York: Scholastic Book Services, 1967.

7

The Effects of Gravity

Children who have felt the tug of invisible magnetic attraction with their own hands can move from this awareness to simple understandings about the effects of gravity. These children are ready to put credence in the far stronger invisible pull that can hold people and houses and schools onto the ground: the force of the earth's gravity. The learning experiences in this chapter amplify one central concept:

GRAVITY PULLS ON EVERYTHING

Drawing children's attention to an ever-present effect that is rarely noticed or labeled calls for more preliminary description than we usually offer to action-loving children. The first suggested gravity experience is a story that provides basic information. The active experiences involve measuring and comparing gravity's pull on objects; trying a pendulum; and bringing things into balance.

Lead into the gravity story by crushing a piece of paper into a ball and holding it between your fingers. "What will happen to this ball of paper if I open my fingers?" Find out if the children's predictions are correct. "Do you think the ball might do the same thing another time, or might it fall up instead? Did you ever stumble and fall up? Here is a story about the reason for this."

Use a flannel board and felt figures to illustrate your story. It could be stated something like this:

Once a girl had a dream. Everything seemed very strange. The girl was floating in the air looking for her house. Se saw her friend floating close by with a ball in his arms. They wanted to play catch, but when the boy threw the ball, it drifted up out of reach. Then the girl saw her house bobbing up and down gently in the breeze. Her mom was very upset because somebody had spilled milk all over the ceiling. When the girl woke up, she was glad that her house was standing still!

Something important was missing in that dream. Houses and balls and children don't float around. Milk doesn't spill up! There is a reason why those things don't happen. There is a very powerful force pulling down on everything in the world: the force called earth's *gravity*. We can't touch gravity, or see it. We can just see what gravity does.

Can you think of something else invisible that pulls some kinds of things? Yes, it reminds us of the way magnets pull on iron and steel. But gravity is much, much stronger than magnetism! Gravity pulls from inside the earth. *It pulls on everything all of the time.* We are so used to it, that we don't even notice it happening.

(Show the picture of an astronaut in his space suit.) The astronauts who walked on the moon had a strange experience. They had to wear very heavy boots to stand on the moon, because the moon's gravity pull is too weak to hold people to the moon's surface.

You can find out how much earth's gravity is pulling on you at the science table.

Concept: Gravity Pulls on Everything

---

1. How Much Does Gravity Pull on Different Objects?

LEARNING OBJECTIVE: To experience changes in gravity's pull on one's body while holding sand bags in different positions.

MATERIALS:

Bathroom scale

Kitchen scale

4 small, sturdy bags

Sand, pebbles

Market bag with handles

Containers, scoops

Long mirror, if possible

GETTING READY:

Fill each small bag with 2 pounds of sand or stones.

SMALL GROUP ACTIVITY:

1. "When we weigh ourselves on a scale, we are finding out how much gravity pulls on us."
2. Find out how much gravity pulls on each child. Record the weights.
3. Weigh each child again, while he holds a sand bag in each hand. Compare with first weight record. Does gravity pull more on him now?
4. Put both sand bags in the market bag. Have children hold it in one hand so the weight is on one side. Weigh each child again.
5. "Look in the mirror. Are you standing up straight now, or leaning over? You lean away from the heavy side to keep your balance."

Let children weigh objects on both scales. Containers of sand make good materials to weigh. Provide objects of varying weight and size. Let children discover that size does not always determine weight.

Group Discussion: Recall the earlier discussion about gravity holding everything down. Encourage children to share ideas about things that they see being pulled down from the sky by gravity (leaves, seeds, snowflakes, raindrops).

Mention that some things go up and stay up for a long time (planes, birds, gliders, and so on). How do they get up in the air, away from the ground? How do they move through the air? Wind, motors, and jet engines can lift planes up and keep them up for a while. Can the children lift themselves all the way off the ground for a little while by using their muscles to push against gravity?

READ: "How Birds Fly," from *Great Big Air Book,* by Richard Scarry.

2. Can We Compare Gravity's Pull on Objects?
Making a Balance

LEARNING OBJECTIVE: To explore ways of achieving equilibrium using varied small objects as weights in balance cups.

MATERIALS:

Scrap lumber: 2′ piece of 1″ x 1″ or broomstick; 8″ x 8″ piece of shelving

Nails: 6d and 4d sizes

Yardstick

Pipe cleaners

Small paper cups

Small objects to weigh: washers, bottlecaps, etc.

GETTING READY:

Drill holes or saw small notches 3″ apart on yardstick markings.

Make a hole at 18″ mark with the 6d nail.

Make 2 holes on opposite sides of each paper cup near top.

SMALL GROUP ACTIVITY:

1. To make base: mark center of shelving square. Nail 2′ stick perpendicular to center of base. (Let children do the hammering.)
2. Nail yardstick loosely near top of the upright stick, driving a 4d nail through hole at the 18″ mark. Yardstick should swing easily.
3. Insert pipe cleaners into yardstick holes. Hook them into paper cups. (Put one cup on each side. Let children add more cups as they wish later.) If notches were made instead of drilled holes, make pipe cleaner handles for cups, hang in notches.
4. Let children fill cups with small items to balance.

Provide materials as different in weight as cotton balls and bottle caps. Do 5 cotton balls balance 5 bottle caps? Is the balance arm lower on the cap side? What does this mean? (Gravity pulls more on caps: we say they weigh more than the cotton balls.) A balance can be made from a paper towel tube by following directions in *Adventures With A Paper Tube,* by Harry Milgrom.

Try to keep the balances and containers of weighing materials accessible to the children for as long as they show interest in them. Put them away for a while, bring out periodically.

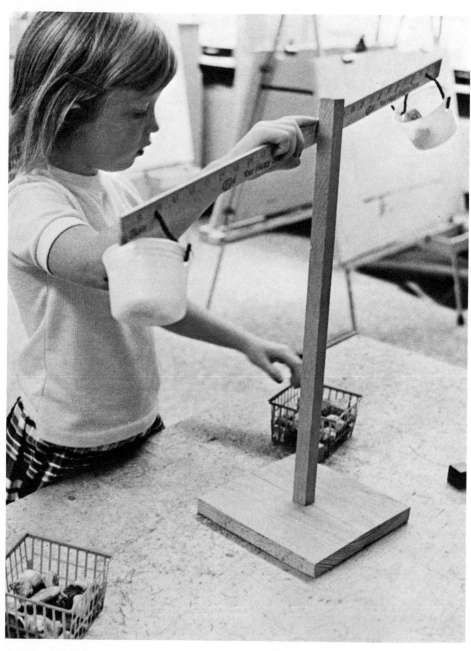

Group Discussion: Tie a small doll at the end of a foot of string. Hold the other end of the string, letting the doll dangle. "How could I make the doll go higher without lifting up the string? Good, I could swing the doll higher. Look, it is going high now. But it doesn't stay up high. Why? Let's watch what happens when I stop swinging the string. Is it moving up as high now? It's going slower and lower, and it has almost stopped swinging. Is something pulling it?

"Is this what happens to you when you're on the swing? What happens to you when you start to pull and push with your muscles? What happens when you stop working your muscles that way? Are you close to the top of the swing set, or close to the ground when the swing stops? Why?" Tape the doll and string pendulum to the edge of a table for children to try later.

READ: *Gravity At Work and Play*, by Sune Engelbrektson.

3. Can We Keep Objects in Balance?

LEARNING OBJECTIVE: To explore ways to achieve equilibrium by placing rocks on a ruler which is on a block resting point.

MATERIALS:

12" rulers

Half-circle blocks

Small rocks

Tinkertoys

Desirable: Acrobat balance toy from India, sold by mail order gift shops

SMALL GROUP ACTIVITY:

1. Gently place a ruler on a block, with the 6" mark resting on top of the curve. "Let's see if the ruler will tip or balance. Can you try this?"
2. "Can we balance two rocks on the ruler?" Show how to slide a heavier rock toward the center (resting point) to balance a lighter rock at the other end of the ruler.
3. Make a platform of 2 tinkertoy wheels and one long stick. Insert 2 sticks in a connector wheel, add small connectors to the stick ends. Rest connector wheel on the platform edge as shown.
4. Remove one, then both sticks from the connector wheel. What happens? Is the connector wheel stable without them? (The location and weight of the sticks changes the way gravity pulls on the connector wheel.)

FIGURE 11

```
┌─────────────────────────┐
│       REMEMBER          │
│                         │
│  Finding out takes time.│
│  Keep the learning pace │
│  relaxed. Listen to the │
│    children's ideas.    │
└─────────────────────────┘
```

Primary Reinforcements

Music

When children are investigating the effects of gravity, they enjoy singing three nursery rhymes as though gravity were not operating:

"Jack and Jill Went Up the Hill" might be sung:
. . . "Jack fell *up*, and broke his cup,
And Jill bent over with laughter."

"London Bridge" might be sung:
. . . "London Bridge is floating up,"

"Ring Around the Rosy" might be sung:
. . . "One, two, three and we fall up in the tree."

Here is a gravity song to sing:

Gravity Song

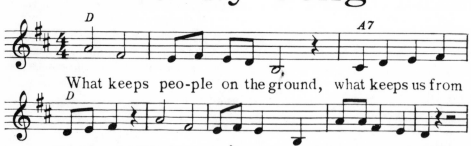

What keeps peo-ple on the ground, what keeps us from

float-ing up? What keeps ev'ry-thing down? Grav-i-ty, that's what!

Math Experiences

When they experiment with a pan balance and weights, children can strengthen their understanding of numerical equivalence. Sets of standard weights are available commercially. In some types the size and weight are related. To devise substitute weights fill screw-top plastic or metal containers with sand and gravel to one-, two-, and four-ounce weights as desired. Mark the corresponding numeral on each container.

Number balance equipment is made in several forms. One type uses weighted plastic numerals to make the mathematical equation balance as the weight balances. Keep a set of weights and boxes of materials to weigh next to a pan balance for children to use casually.

Stories and References for Children

Berger, Melvin. *Gravity*. New York: Coward-McCann, 1969. A careful explanation of the astronauts' experiences with weightlessness and with the moon's weak gravity pull.

Branley, Franklyn. *Gravity Is a Mystery*. New York: Thomas Y. Crowell, 1970.

Bright, Robert. *Georgie and the Magician*. New York: Doubleday & Company, 1966. Georgie is a gentle ghost who does some floating in a magician's show. One involved child-listener said, "Now I know ghosts aren't real things, cause gravity pulls on everything real."

Engelbrektson, Sune. *Gravity at Work and Play*. New York: Holt, Rinehart and Winston, 1963. This is a good first book about gravity for young children.

Freeman, Mae. *A Book of Real Science*. New York: Scholastic Book Services, 1970.

————. *Gravity and the Astronauts*. New York: Scholastic Book Services, 1971.

Goudey, Alice. *The Day We Saw the Sun Come Up*. New York: Charles Scribner's Sons, 1961. A beautiful book about one day's happy experiences. Earth's rotation is discussed.

Minarik, Else. *Little Bear*. New York: Harper & Row, 1961, chapter 3, "Little Bear Goes to the Moon."

Rey, H. A. *Curious George Gets a Medal*. New York: Houghton Mifflin, 1957. George takes a rocket ride into outer space.

Viorst, Judith. *I'll Fix Anthony*. New York: Harper & Row, 1969. The protagonist balances on his head, masters balancing on a two-wheel bike, and stretches out on water to float, while gravity pulls hunched-up Anthony to the bottom of the pool.

Zion, Gene, and Graham, Margaret. *All Falling Down*. New York: Harper, 1951. The story contains a confusing reference to night falling that must be corrected as it is read.

Swinging, sliding, blockbuilding, and falling down are part of many other children's stories as well. Casually refer to the effects of gravity's pull whenever possible.

Poems (See Appendix 1)

Gravity doesn't seem to operate in this poem:
"The Folks Who Live in Backward Town," by Mary Ann Hoberman. In *Poems Children Will Sit Still For*, de Regniers, Moore, and White.

This classic is among the poems about swinging:
"The Swing," by Robert Louis Stevenson, in *A Child's Garden of Verses*.

Art Activity

Use drinking straws, thread, and Styrofoam meat trays to make simple mobiles.

Children will need some help with this project, yet they can use their own ideas in a satisfying way.

Advance preparation for each mobile: sew a doubled-knotted thread up through the exact center of the straw length. Tie thread into a 6″ hanging loop. Sew an 8″ single thread down through the straw, ½″ from one end; sew a 6″ single-knotted thread down through the straw 1½″ from the other end.

Give each child a 4″ square and a 2″ square of Styrofoam to shape with scissors. Offer crayons for decorating the shapes. Older children can then punch a hole through the top of each shape, tie the 6″ thread through the large shape, the 8″ thread through the small shape. Younger children can join shapes and threads with pieces of tape.

Slip the hanging loop over a door knob or tape it temporarily to a table edge so that the mobile can hang freely. Help children adjust the balance by winding the short thread toward the center of the straw. Quickly tape the thread to the straw in its balanced position, as shown in figure 12. Tape completed mobiles to a ceiling beam or a door frame.

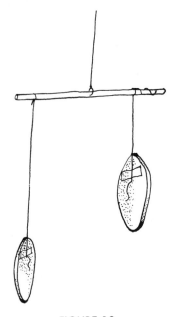

FIGURE 12

Dramatic Play

1. STORE. Put a pan balance or old kitchen scales, containers of materials like horse chestnuts, and artificial fruit and vegetables in the store play area.

2. BLOCK PLAY. Help blockbuilders think about why their structures collapse. Suggest making broad, sturdy bases for tall towers, so that gravity will pull more on the bottom of the tower than on the top. When appropriate, ask if gravity is pulling equally on both sides of the weight-supporting blocks, or whether an unbalanced load will tip over.

3. SPACE SHIP. Try to find a refrigerator shipping carton for the children to convert into a space ship. Help them improvise space helmets with small cartons and coils of telephone cable wire like the one worn by Little Bear on his imaginary trip to the moon. Before setting up the space ship play, supply play ideas by reading *Little Bear* by Else Minarik; *Curious George Gets A Medal* by A. A. Rey; or the last part of *A Book of Real Science* by Mae Freeman. If you can provide it, put out the astronaut puzzle made by the Judy Company.

Food Experience

Take the class to the nearest food store where purchases are weighed on a balance beam scale. Buying and sharing a half-pound of peanuts with the children is a very good investment in gravity learning.

Thinking Game

Use gravity pull as a topic to stimulate creative thinking. Ask, "What would happen if there were no gravity pull from earth?" Be sure to include the way playground fun would change if gravity did not return balls that have been tossed up, pull children down the slide, and so forth.

Field Trips

Knowing how much gravity pulls on objects is an important part of many businesses and services. Try to include a look at weighing devices during the field trips you plan to the post office, grocery store, feed store, airport, drugstore, medical offices, or the loading docks of factories. It can be great fun for a whole class of children to be weighed together on loading dock scales.

Creative Movement

Help your children recognize the way their bodies involuntarily adjust to changes in body position in order to maintain their balance when they dance or exercise. When they lean in one direction, their bodies automatically compensate for gravity's pull by extending an arm or leg in the opposite direction.

Pretend that the children are on a ship in a storm, rocking from side to side. They will stretch their legs into a wide-based stance—or tip over. Suggest moving like ice skaters, swinging their arms and bending their bodies as they glide and stride on the ice. Now they are tight rope walkers sliding one foot in front of the other on a swaying rope—arms extended. Next imagine that they are going to lift a heavy, heavy rock, working very hard with their muscles to force it up against gravity's pull, bit by bit. Now put the rock down carefully and push it ahead— slowly, slowly—then move like the astronauts on the moon where the gravity pull is weak.

In *Creative Movement for the Developing Child*, Clare Cherry suggests two poems as stimulus for balancing movements: "The Cat on the Fence" and "The High Wire Walker."

Secondary Reinforcements

Keeping Concepts Alive

Ian applied gravity concepts in a judgmental way when he picked himself up from a fall complaining, "That ol' grabbity pulled me down!" Many of the large muscle-play activities provide opportunities to point out how gravity pull makes some of our fun or work easier, such as balancing block towers; enjoying a slide, a teeter-totter, or swing; playing catch; or pouring water from a pitcher. Some activities are difficult to do because of gravity's pull. This is why children become tired when they put away blocks, climb the jungle gym, walk up the stairs, or trudge up a hill.

Relating New Concepts to Existing Concepts

1. GRAVITY-AIR RELATIONSHIP. Balancing two air-filled balloons is a vivid way to demonstrate that gravity pulls on air. To make a long balance arm, insert one drinking straw part-way into another straw. Insert a hanging loop in the center, as in making the mobile. Blow up two balloons to equal size, tie one to each end of the arm. Be sure that the balloons are the same color. Some children may believe that balloons of different colors are also different in the amount of air they contain.

Hang up the arrangement and let the arm come to rest. Add bits of masking tape to the end of the arm that is higher, until balance is achieved. It is hard to blow exactly the same amount of air into two balloons. Explain to the children that you are going to prick one balloon. "What will happen to that balloon? Some children become scared when the balloon pops, and forget to watch what happens to the balance. Put your hands over your ears if the noise might bother you." Pop the balloon. "Which side of the balance went down? Why did that happen? Gravity pulls on air, too!" (If the pricked balloon flies apart, gather the pieces and tape them onto the end of the balance stick so a comparison of empty and air-filled balloons may still be made.)

2. GRAVITY-WATER RELATIONSHIPS. Introduce the idea that gravity's pull plays a part in determining which objects sink and which float. Gravity pulls on water more than it pulls on corks, for instance. Recall that raindrops are pulled down to earth when they become too heavy to float as droplets of vapor in clouds.

Involving Parents

Parents often have opportunities to show their children things that go up and away from gravity's pull. Big motors help elevators and escalators lift people. Jet propulsion or propellers help lift airplanes off the ground. Heavy motors are needed to lift loads of materials at building construction sites which they could visit together.

References

Hawkins, Francis P. *The Logic of Action: Young Children At Work*. New York: Pantheon, 1974.

Milgrom, Harry. *Adventures With a Cardboard Tube*. New York: E. P. Dutton, 1972.

Parker, Bertha. *Gravity*. Evanston, Ill.: Row, Peterson, 1957.

Pine, Tillie, and Levine, J. *Gravity All Around*. New York: Whittlesey House, McGraw-Hill, 1963.

Podendorf, Illa. *The True Book of Science Experiments*. Chicago: Childrens Press, 1972.

8

Simple Machines

Throbbing motors and turning wheels are little-noted daily background noises for youngsters in the Western world. Children are proud to learn how to move and lift things with the help of simple machines. The knowledge invites interest in the complex machines they have previously taken for granted. The learning experiences in this chapter explore these concepts:

FRICTION MAKES HEAT; IT SLOWS AND WEARS AWAY OBJECTS
A LEVER HELPS LIFT OBJECTS
A RAMP SHARES THE WORK OF LIFTING
A SCREW IS A CURVED RAMP
SIMPLE MACHINES HELP MOVE THINGS ALONG
SOME WHEELS WORK TOGETHER, SOME WORK ALONE
SINGLE WHEELS CAN TURN OTHER WHEELS
SINGLE WHEELS LET US PULL DOWN TO LIFT THINGS UP

Experiencing the advantages and disadvantages of friction is a useful preliminary to the experiments that follow. The simple machines experiments illustrate the lever, ramp, screw, wheel and axle, and pulley.

Introducing Friction: "Rub the palms of your hands together as fast as you can like this. Keep going. Do you feel something happening to your hands? What we are doing makes heat. What we are doing has a name: friction."

Concept: Friction Makes Heat; It Slows and Wears Away Things

---

1. Does Friction Slow Sliding Objects?

LEARNING OBJECTIVE: To experience firsthand the slowing effect of friction on a slide.

MATERIALS:

Art gum erasers

Small pieces of waxed paper
Magnifier

Indoor slide or teeter-totter plank, propped against a table

Sheets of waxed paper

Rubber sink or tub mat

LARGE GROUP ACTIVITY:

1. Pass around pieces of waxed paper. "Try rubbing this on your arm. Does it slide fast? Try sliding the rubber eraser. Does it slide fast on your arm? Why not? We can say the rubber makes more friction."
2. Pass the magnifying glass. "Does an eraser look fuzzy? Does paper look smooth?"
3. Let children take turns on the slide, sitting first on waxed paper, then the rubber mat. "Smooth paper doesn't make much friction, so you move fast."

2. Does Friction Make Heat and Wear Away?

LEARNING OBJECTIVE: To experience firsthand the heat produced by friction and to actively wear away materials by producing friction.

MATERIALS:

Scrap lumber (6" pieces)

Coarse sandpaper, cut into 3" squares

Hammer

Common nails

Magnifying glass

GETTING READY:

Hammer a few nails half their length into a chunk of wood. (To use the hammer as a lever: catch nail in claw and roll hammer back on curve of claw. Pull down on handle to lift nail up, and out.)

SMALL GROUP ACTIVITY:

1. Give each child sandpaper and scrap lumber. "Feel these. Are they smooth or rough? Do they look smooth or bumpy with the magnifier? Rub them together hard and long. See what happens."
2. "Are your fingers feeling warm? Why? Rough things rubbing together make lots of friction. Are bits of wood wearing away? Look at your wood. Feel it. Is it getting smoother? Is the sandpaper getting smoother too? Does friction wear things away?"
3. "I'm going to pull a nail from this wood. Do you think that will make friction? Let's feel the nail quickly after it comes out. Is it warm or cool? Did the nail and wood rub together?"

3. Can We Cut Down Friction?

LEARNING OBJECTIVE: To notice how lubricating materials cut down friction.

MATERIALS:

Coarse sandpaper

Vaseline

Meat trays

Peanut butter

Soda crackers

Waxed paper

Table knives

GETTING READY:

Cut sandpaper into 2″ squares.

Put a spoonful of peanut butter on pieces of waxed paper for each child.

SMALL GROUP ACTIVITY:

1. Give children two pieces of sandpaper. "Rub these together fast. What happens? Do bits of sand rub off?"
2. "Look at the sandpaper. Is it bumpy and rough? Would it be smoother if something filled up the bumpy places? Try this vaseline on it. Will it help the pieces slide smoothly past each other?"
3. Give each child two crackers on a tray. Repeat steps 1 and 2. Offer peanut butter as lubricant. Eat the experiment.

Group Discussion: Show the children a small can of household oil. Ask what they know about it; why it is used at home. Develop the idea that oil makes a smooth sliding surface on objects that rub together. It cuts down friction that makes heat, wears bits away, makes things difficult to use, and makes things squeak.

4. Can Friction Be Useful?

LEARNING OBJECTIVE: To notice that friction is needed for writing, drawing, and gripping things.

A.

MATERIALS:

Chalk

Dark colored paper

Small pieces waxed paper

Pencils

SMALL GROUP ACTIVITY:

1. Give children paper and chalk. "What sound does the chalk make on the paper? Scraping? Scratching? Why?"
2. "Try dipping your chalk into the vaseline. Now does it rub and scrape? What happened to the chalk mark? Do you need friction to draw?"
3. Let them try to draw on waxed paper with pencils. Explain that the wax coating is like a lubricant.

B.

MATERIALS:

Screw-top plastic containers, such as small paste jars

SMALL GROUP ACTIVITY:

1. "Are your hands strong enough to unscrew this jar cover? You can do it well."

Two pans of water

Soap

Towels

2. "Try it again, but this time get your hands wet and soapy first. Why is it hard to do now? Do you need friction to hold the jar tightly?"
3. "Try the doorknob with wet hands. Can you turn it?"

Group Discussion: Ask the children to check each other's shoe soles. Are some smooth and slippery? Do some have rubber heels; do some have one-piece rubber bottoms? Are sneakers good for running and stopping, or do they skid? Are car tires smooth and slippery, or more like the soles of sneakers. Why? Talk about slippery road conditions; slippery bath tubs; and wet bathroom floors. Can friction make these places safer?

Concept: A Lever Helps Lift Objects

---

1. What Can a Lever Do?

LEARNING OBJECTIVE: To discover how to arrange a plank and resting point as a lever to lift and to be lifted.

Introduction: "One day I watched Amanda on the playground pushing *down* to lift David *up* in the air. Then David pushed *down* to lift Amanda *up*. What were they doing? (Using a seesaw.) Could Amanda lift me that way? Gravity pulls much more on me than on her. Let's see if we can find a way."

MATERIALS:

Six foot seesaw plank

Block, books

12" rulers, pencils

String

Hammer, common nails

Scrap lumber

Sturdy box large enough to hold two seated children

SMALL GROUP ACTIVITY:

1. Put a block below midpoint of the plank. Have a child stand on one end. Ask another to stand on the raised end to lift the other.
2. "Could one of you lift me up that way? Try. Now let's see what will happen if we move the resting point block closer to me. Now can you lift me? Yes! We changed the resting point and made a lever. It helped her lift me *up* when she pushed her weight *down*."
3. To show the importance of the resting point, place the box on one end of the plank. Put the block nearby. Ask two children to sit in the box. "Can someone use the plank to lift this load?" The load tips if the *plank* is *lifted up*. The load is lifted only when the plank is used as a lever: with the block placed under the plank near the load and the child *pushing down* on the plank at the end opposite the load.

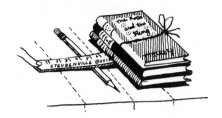

FIGURE 13

Children who are waiting for turns to lift the box with the plank lever could try out two other levers. Tie two or more books together with a string. Loop one end of the string so children can try to lift the bundle with one finger. Offer a ruler and a pencil for a resting point to make a lever. "It was hard to lift up the bundle pulling *up* with one finger. Try pushing *down* on the ruler lever to lift the books up."

Drive nails into the wood about half the nail length. "It can be very hard work to pull a nail out by pulling up. Try using the hammer as a lever, pushing down to lift the nail up."

Group Discussion: Look at the picture of a cave man using a branch and a small rock to move a huge rock in *The How and Why Wonder Book of Machines,* by Jerome Notkin. Open an empty cocoa can lid, with the handle of a spoon. Ask if the spoon was a lever. Show that the resting point was the edge of the can. Talk about oars on a rowboat serving as levers that are pulled *back* to push the boat *forward.* Sing "Row, Row, Row Your Boat."

Concept: A Ramp Shares the Work of Lifting

The inclined plane (ramp) is another simple machine that helps us lift things against gravity's pull.

1. Can A Ramp Help Us Lift?

LEARNING OBJECTIVE: To find out firsthand if a ramp helps one lift a heavy load.

MATERIALS:	SMALL GROUP ACTIVITY:
Old, sturdy suitcase	1. "Can you pick up this heavy case by the handle and lift it onto the table? Try."
10 pounds of objects, to fill suitcase	2. "Could this plank make it easier to get the case up on the table?" Lean plank from the floor to the table top. Place the suitcase near the bottom of the plank. "We call this a ramp."
Plank, at least 4' long	3. "A ramp holds some of the weight of the suitcase
Table	

GETTING READY:

Fill the suitcase with enough weight to make it hard for a child to lift by the handle.

as you slide it along. Now you can get the suitcase up there."

Group Experience: Make a miniature steep mountain of damp sand in a long cake pan, or in the sand table if you have one. Use a tiny matchbox car as a demonstrator. "Could a car go straight up the side of a steep mountain like this? Let's try it. Will it stay on the side of the sand if I let go? No. Gravity pulls it down fast! Could we curve a ramp road around this mountain to help the car go up?" Make a road like this, then let children try the car on the road. Will the car fall off the road if the children let go of it? (It may stand still in the damp sand, but on a real mountain road gravity could slowly pull a car down.)

Concept: A Screw is a Curved Ramp

Introduction: Draw a thick crayon line diagonally from one corner of a sheet of typing paper to the other. Cut along the line, leaving a crayon edged triangle. Bring the triangle, a pencil, a large screw, and a collection of nuts and bolts to a class discussion. "Does the line on this paper triangle look like a ramp? Let's see what we can do with it." Wind the triangle around the pencil so the line looks like a screw thread. Trace the spiral path from the bottom of the ramp up to the top. Compare it with a screw. Give children the bolts and nuts. "Can you make the nut go up the ramp that curves around the bolt? Try it."

1. Can Screws Lift Objects?

LEARNING OBJECTIVE: To investigate how threaded objects move up the corresponding threads of a screw.

MATERIALS:

(Use as many as possible)
Screw-type cookie press
Tissue
C-clamps
Playdough
Old lipstick tube
Screw-type nut cracker
Screw-top plastic jars
Plumbing pipes and joints (now available in plastic as toys)

SMALL GROUP ACTIVITY:

1. Remove design plate from the cookie press. Stuff a tissue in the press. Let children see what happens when the screw knob is turned. "What lifted up the tissue?"
2. Put a small ball of playdough on the end of the C-clamp turning screw. Hold clamp upright, turn the screw till the playdough rides up to be squashed by the top.
3. Show how two screws can be threaded together so they can't be pulled apart. (jars and pipes)
4. Let children enjoy working with the small materials you have assembled before presenting the most fun: the experience of being lifted by a screw on

Old piano stool or office swivel chair

GETTING READY:

The bottom half of a lipstick tube is usually two pieces. Separate them to reveal the spiral ramp that the lipstick moves along as it is twisted up.

a piano stool or office chair. Take time to examine the emerging screw as it turns.

===

Concept: Simple Machines Help Move Things Along

===

1. How Do Rollers Move Things?

LEARNING OBJECTIVE: To experience and compare the difference between dragging a box, pushing it over rollers, and pushing it with wheels under it.

MATERIALS:

Grocery cartons or Community Playthings nested hardwood crates*

Jumpropes

4 cut-off broomsticks, or cardboard cores from newsprint rolls, to use as rollers

Platform dolly or board and 4 caster wheels

GETTING READY:

If the school custodian doesn't have a platform dolly for scrub buckets, make your own by screwing 4 swivel casters into a 1" thick plank.

SMALL GROUP ACTIVITY:

1. Loop jumpropes around cartons. Let children take turns pulling each other in boxes, using jumprope handles in each hand. (Cardboard boxes fall apart soon, so have many.) "Is pulling easy or hard?"
2. Place rollers side by side on the floor. Put box on top. Repeat 1. "Do rollers help move the box? But they don't stay under the box! Put them back for the next child's turn."
3. "Which way made less friction?" Feel box bottoms after the dragging and after rolling.
4. "Let's try rolling wheels that will stay under the box now." Put box on the platform dolly. "Which is the easiest way to pull the box? Dragging, with rollers, or with wheels?"

* The nested hardwood crates have metal glides on the bottom to reduce friction. The largest crate has swivel casters.

Group Discussion: Recall the rollers experiment. "Was the carton moved very far by four rollers? Would rollers be a good way to move cars and trucks? What if someone had to keep putting rollers in front of the car to keep it moving? Rollers are used that way when whole houses are moved a short distance. They give good support to the house. Rollers are also used to unload big trucks at the grocery store. Rollers are part of checkout conveyor belts and escalators."

Concept: Some Wheels Turn Alone, Some Turn Together

---

1. How Do Single Wheels and Pairs of Wheels Work?

LEARNING OBJECTIVE: To notice the difference between things that move on single wheels and those that move on pairs of wheels joined by axles.

MATERIALS:

A light piece of furniture on 4 swivel wheels (office chair, typewriter stand, utility table, crate on casters, platform dolly)

Toy car with axles exposed

Small paper plates

Masking tape

Plastic drinking straws

Compass

GETTING READY:

Find the exact centers of paper plates with compass. Mark each center, push out a 1/4" hole with pencil tip. Have one for each child.

Cut 1" pieces of tape, stick lightly on a nearby table edge for children's use.

SMALL GROUP ACTIVITY:

1. Divide children into two facing rows, at least 5 feet apart.
2. "Let's take turns pushing the chair to children across the way. Watch what happens. Does it move easily? . . . Straight ahead?"
3. "Now let's push these cars across. Do they move straight ahead or from side to side?" Try the swivel again watching the wheels very closely. Turn the swivel and the cars upside down to see if they look the same. Supply the word *axle*, if a child doesn't offer it. Point out pairs of wheels that turn together on an axle.
4. Let children try to roll their plates across to another child. Offer straws and tape, suggesting that two children could join wheel plates to see if they will roll better as a pair with an axle.

Group Discussion: Talk about the advantages of single wheels and pairs of wheels. If there is an old upright piano or a classroom storage chest on casters, push it with the children. Tiny, single wheels can make it easier to push something very heavy for a short way.

"Do wagons, cars, busses, and trucks have a single wheel on each corner? Why not?" Show some pictures of wheeled objects cut from catalogs. "Do these things use single wheels or pairs of wheels on axles?" Children are surprised to learn that door knobs are pairs of wheels on an axle. Can you bring in an old one, or unscrew a school doorknob? Look together at a manual typewriter for rollers, wheels, and axles.

Concept: Single Wheels Can Turn Other Wheels

1. How Do Gears Work?

LEARNING OBJECTIVE: To observe how sets of gears mesh to operate mechanisms.

MATERIALS:

Egg beater (hand operated)

2 deep mixing bowls

Soup spoons

Water

Detergent

Gear toys, visible clock, visible music box works, old clock to open

Crayon

Newspapers, sponge

GETTING READY:

Put ½ cup water and 1 teaspoon detergent in each bowl.

Spread papers on the floor. (Suds are slippery—they cut down friction!)

SMALL GROUP ACTIVITY:

1. "Have you ever looked very closely at a beater? Do you see some wheels? How many? (Some wheels may look different.) Watch what happens when the big wheel is turned. Does it turn little wheels?" Introduce the term *gear:* a wheel with teeth that mesh with teeth of the wheels next to it.

2. "Let's take turns using the beater to find out how the gears work. Let's try to beat up bowls of soap suds with the beater, and with a spoon to see which works more easily."

3. Help children see that the big gear turns the little gears on the beater blades much faster.

Group Discussion: Try to borrow a one-speed bicycle to examine with the group. Turn it upside down and look at the gears. "Sometimes gears turn each other without touching each other. Instead they fit into a chain that moves them. Is one gear large and one small, like the egg beater? Let's turn the pedals and watch the chain make the small gear turn. Count how many times the back wheel turns while I turn the pedal one time." Count one turn when the air valve reaches the top.

Look at the tire tread. "Does a bicycle need friction to stop and keep from skidding? Does the chain look greasy? Why would it need grease? Does it need friction? What is inside the tires?"

Concept: Single Wheels Can Help Us Pull Down to Lift Up

1. Does a Pulley Make Lifting Easier?

LEARNING OBJECTIVE: To experience by comparison how a pulley makes a lifting task easier.

MATERIALS:

Small pulley

Firm cord, double the length of floor-to-pulley distance

Small school chair

Desirable: stopwatch

Screw hook

GETTING READY:

Install screw hook in a ceiling beam or door frame (ask custodian).

Pass the cord over the pulley wheel, hang pulley on screw hook.

SMALL GROUP ACTIVITY:

1. Show children the pulley. "Could this single wheel make it easier to lift a chair?"
2. "First let's see how long you can hold this chair with one hand. Lift it as high as you can. I'll time you." Record length of time each child can hold chair.
3. Tie cord firmly to chair back. "Now try pulling down on this cord to lift the chair. I'll time you to see how long you can hold it up." (Demonstrate careful lowering of chair, but stand by in case someone lets it down too fast.) "You are pulling down on the rope to lift the chair up. Does the pulley make the lifting job easier?"

Group Discussion: (Try to find pictures of the following things to show.) "Pulleys help people load big ships, trains, and barns. Pulleys are used on steam shovels, on sailboats, on flagpoles, on scaffoldings, in draw-drapery rods, and inside the casing of windows. A pulley arrangement moves people up in large buildings on elevators and escalators! Single wheels help people and machines pull *down* to *lift up* or *pull across.*" Richard Scarry's book, *What Do People Do All Day?* is a fine and funny source for pulley illustrations.

Primary Reinforcements

Music (See Appendix 1 for references)

1. Sing this song about friction to the tune of "Here We Go Round the Mulberry Bush":

Friction Song

This is the way we warm our hands, warm our hands, warm our hands.
  (Rubbing hands together)
This is the way we warm our hands, out in chilly weather.
Friction is what warms our hands, warms our hands, warms our hands.
Friction is what warms our hands, rubbing them together.

2. Beatrice Landeck's song, "Little Red Wagon" (8) is a lively reminder of the usefulness of wheels and axles. John added three verses to his favorite song:

"Both wheels are off and the back end's dragging. . ."
"Four wheels are off and we're not even moving. . ."
"Now we're going to the repair shop. . . ."

3. Sing this tricycle song with appropriate arm and leg movements to the tune of "One, Two, Three O'Leary":

Pump, pump, pump, the pedals,
Turn, turn, wheels-on-the axles,
Steer, steer, steer the handles,
When we ride our tricycles.
(Change to bicycles for older children.)

Math Activities

1. FORMING SETS. Using plastic cars (sold by the bagful at variety stores) and macaroni wheels as members of sets links simple machine study with math activities.

2. CAR CLASSIFICATION GAME. Let children park plastic cars in the correct parking area according to color. Use red, yellow, and blue construction paper as the parking garages where the cars of each corresponding color are parked. Add a second dimension to the classification so that red cars with tops are parked on one side of the red garage, red cars without tops are parked on the other side of the red garage, and so on.

3. WHEEL QUANTITY CLASSIFICATION GAME. Cut out and mount catalog pictures of wheeled objects. Ask children to sort them into groups according to the number of wheels each object has. (A record player turntable could be used as a one-wheel object example.)

Stories and References for Children

Ardizzone, Edward. *Little Tim and the Brave Sea Captain*. New York: Scholastic Book Services, 1968. The use of pulleys can be pointed out in lifeboat launching and in the rope rescue of Tim and the Captain.

Burton, Virginia Lee. *Katy and the Big Snow*. Orlando, Fla.: Sandpiper Press, 1974.

Freeman, Don. *Corduroy*. Seafarer ed. New York: Viking Press, 1970. Corduroy rides an escalator, which operates on rollers.

Hoban, Russell. *What Does It Do and How Does It Work?* New York: Harper & Brothers, 1959. Large illustrations of the working parts of heavy machines, such as a power shovel, almost put the reader into the driver's seat.

Holland, Ruth. *A Bad Day*. New York: David McKay Company, Inc., 1964. Lack of friction causes a jar of applesauce to smash.

Koren, Edward. *Behind the Wheel*. New York: Holt, Rinehart & Winston, 1972. Illustrations of transport and construction equipment viewed from the driver's seat.

McCloskey, Robert. *Make Way for Ducklings*. Seafarer ed. New York: Viking Press, 1969. The Mallards make a mistaken assumption about the paddlewheel swanboats in the Boston Public Garden.

Rey, H. A. *Curious George Rides a Bike*. New York: Scholastic Services, 1973. A hammer is used as a lever to open a crate. Gears, chain, and pedals on George's bike, and pulleys on a circus wagon cage are shown in this adventure.

Rockwell, Anne and Harlow. *Machines*. New York: Macmillan Co., 1972. Beautiful water colors illustrate simple machines. The text is direct, brief, and very appropriate for young children.

Scarry, Richard. *What Do People Do All Day?* New York: Random House, 1968. A profusion of funny illustrations show wheels, gears, pulleys, rollers, and screws in use.

Seymour, Dorothy. *The Crate Train*. New York: Wonder Books, 1963. Read this book to stimulate train play.

Watts, Mabel. *Timothy Tinker, The Wonderful Oilcan*. Racine, Wis.: Western Publishing, 1968. Timothy overcomes some friction problems with a few drops of oil. (Skip the ideas of oiling a watch, and oil "melting" into a wheel. It spreads.)

Wright, Ethel. *Saturday Walk*. New York: William R. Scott, 1960. Construction equipment is seen on father and son walks.

Fingerplays

The familiar fingerplay, "The Wheels of the Bus," calls for arm rolling and active bouncing.

> The wheels on the bus go round and round,
>   Round and round and round and round.
> The wheels on the bus go round and round,
>   As it goes down the street.
> The people on the bus go bounce, bounce, bounce,
>   Bounce, bounce, bounce, bounce, bounce, bounce, bounce.
> The people on the bus go bounce, bounce, bounce,
>   And fall right off their seats!

> —Author unknown

Art Activities

1. COLLAGE. These collage materials are strongly suggestive of simple machines: macaroni wheels; pieces of thick string; bottle caps; popsicle sticks; and round, triangular, and rectangular construction paper shapes. (The macaroni wheels may become essential parts of pulleys and cars, or they may be quietly eaten by a child whose inspiration is not as strong as his curiosity about new tastes.)

2. CUTTING AND PASTING. Young children enjoy making their own books or contributing pages to a group book for classroom use. For individual books: staple a few sheets of folded paper together. For group books: use cardboard punched with holes at the top. Fasten with leather thongs or notebook rings.

Provide scissors, paste, and pages cut from catalogs illustrating things with simple machine parts: clocks, egg beaters, wheelbarrows, wheeled toys, mechanical toys, tools, carts, pepper mills, and so forth. If the supply of pictures is sufficient, they could be part of a math experience, making separate pages to show one-wheeled objects, two-wheeled objects, and so on.

3. FRICTION AS AN ART MEDIUM. Sometimes when children are drawing with pencils and crayons, or making chalk rubbings, remind them that friction is involved in making colors stay on the paper.

4. A FRICTION PROJECT. This satisfying work requires at least two days. Let the children sand 3″ x 5″ pieces of scrap lumber to satin smoothness. Next, draw a design on paper with magic markers to cut out and glue to the sanded wood. The teacher can coat the plaque and picture with clear varnish and allow at least a day of drying time. Insert a small screw eye in the top edge of the plaque for hanging. This makes an appreciated gift for parents.

Dramatic Play

1. PACKING CARTON VEHICLES. Children usually need little more than grocery cartons, paper plate wheels, and paper fasteners to create play cars and trains. A real steering wheel from an auto salvage yard, an inner tube and tire pump, and some sets of discarded keys add fun to the play. Books like *The Crate Train*, by Dorothy Seymour, and *Behind the Wheel*, by Edward Koren, can supply play ideas.

Community Playthings sells a fine demountable, two-seat car for children to assemble and use. Initial adult guidance on connecting wheels and axles will be needed. Completing the car requires teamwork and problem-solving ability.

2. ELEVATOR. A tall refrigerator packing carton can become an elevator with a door cut in one side and numerals marked above it to indicate floors. It can be part of block or housekeeping play as desired.

3. PULLEY FUN. Make an elevator for a skyscraper. Ask children to build a three-sided block tower directly below a pulley. Fasten a milk carton elevator to one end of the pulley cord. Cut a door in one side of the carton and fill it with toy passengers.

Attach two small pulleys to opposite sides of the block play area, a few feet above the floor. Tie the handle of a small basket to the pulley cord and knot the cord into a continuous, taut loop running between the two pulleys. It can be an aerial tramway for toy passengers or a conveyor belt for block construction workers.

4. OTHER INDOOR FUN. A toy conveyor belt ramp is sold commercially. It can be an airplane baggage loader or a piece of play farm equipment. The two rollers that move the belt are operated with a small crank.

Add a toy sand or water wheel to sandbox or water play arrangements. They are sold seasonally as beach toys.

Provide pieces of perforated hardboard and hardware odds and ends to attach to it: cupboard door knobs and hinges; nuts; bolts; and washers. Short screwdrivers are easiest for children to control.

Many commercial toys with visible working parts extend the simple machine concepts in play. Examples include construction sets such as Tinker Toys and gear sets, toy clocks, music boxes, and locks with visible working parts.

A broken hand-wound alarm clock is a fine source of firsthand information about gears and springs. Provide small screwdrivers, such as those sold as sewing machine accessories, and let the children take apart the clock. Springs can be sharp, so adult supervision is recommended for the dismantling.

Supply the workbench with bottle caps, metal ends from food container tubes, spools, and empty typewriter ribbon reels to inspire the construction of wheel-, gear-, and dial-encrusted inventions.

Food Experiences

Children feel very important when they turn a crank that contributes to good eating. Several simple machines can be used to prepare food in the classroom:
1. Make molded cookies with a cookie press.
2. Use a hand cranked grinder to make graham cracker crumbs for unbaked cookies, to make toast crumbs for the birds.
3. Use a rolling pin roller to make cut-out cookies.
4. Use the gear-driven egg beater to mix instant pudding.

Thinking Games

1. WHAT HELPS US WORK? "What is helping me to do this work? I am (pantomime) twisting and twisting to lift something up . . . pulling down to lift something up." Let children reach into a bag for pictures of simple machine applications. They can pantomime the action and offer clues for other children to guess.

2. WHAT IF? Collect pictures to illustrate a family picnic outing: getting food ready, climbing into the car, and gathering fishpoles and playthings. Ask, "What if there weren't any friction anywhere one day? What would be different for this family on a picnic? Yes, the mother would have trouble opening the peanut butter jar to make the sandwiches, the children would skid and fall down trying to walk to the car, the baseball bat would slip out of the boy's hands when he hit the ball, the fishpoles might slide out of their hands."

Field Trips

1. Field trips to see simple machines in action can be as simple as a walk to the school kitchen. A well-timed visit might allow the children to see a food order being unloaded from a delivery truck on a hand truck. Hand trucks have one pair of wheels on an axle, and they use the lever principle to lift loads. The kitchen may have a swivel-wheeled utility cart and a large can opener that has a sharp wheel to cut metal, gears to turn the can, a crank that turns an axle, and a screw to clamp the opener to a table.

2. The school office may have a manual typewriter that is full of wheels, gears, axles, and a visible roller. Can the typewriter be turned upside down carefully for inspection? There may be a ditto machine with a huge roller and crank.

Are there chairs with swivel wheels, swivel seats, screw-type back adjustments? Look closely.

3. A repairman working in the building could show children his array of tools and equipment that apply simple machine principles.

4. The nearest driveway could be the scene of an impressive sight, if the teacher can demonstrate the screw or lever principle by jacking up her car. (Be sure to observe the safety precaution of blocking the wheels on the ground with a brick.)

Be sure to check for safety hazards when planning the following field trips. The locations are not intended for general public use. Children should be well supervised.

5. A visit to an auto repair shop can verify the usefulness of simple machine principles. Mechanics in small garages may use scooting platforms on caster wheels to get under cars. A mechanic might demonstrate the tire changer, using a crowbar as a lever to pry off the tire.

6. Many wheels, rollers, conveyor belts, and pulleys are used in the work areas of the post office. Each one also has a flagpole with a pulley to raise the flag.

7. Supermarket backstage operations include hanging meat from overhead rolling tracks, using sets of rollers enclosed in metal frames to slide cases of food from trucks to storerooms, and moving groceries on checkout counter conveyor belts.

8. It is easy to find ramps, wheels, rollers, axles, and pulleys in use in the milling area of a feedstore. A warehouseman might demonstrate how a hand truck helps him move huge loads.

9. An older retail store in your community might still use a hand operated dumbwaiter to bring stock upstairs from a basement storage room. In some types of dumbwaiters the pulleys and ropes are visible. See if there is an enclosed freight elevator near your school where the whole class could take a ride together. It's fun to do.

There are so many opportunities to see simple machine principles in action that it would be easy to overdo the effort. Don't risk wearing down children's interest by trying too many field trips.

Creative Movement

MECHANICAL TOYS. Children enjoy acting out the stiff, jerking movements of wind-up toys. Offer to wind up one child-toy at a time, so that other children can guess what kind of toy they are watching, or wind up all the toys at once so they can all move to music. In addition, children can try to move like the Tin Woodsman both when he was too rusty to move, and after friction was cut down by oil so that he could move well.

Secondary Reinforcements

Keeping Concepts Alive

There are countless opportunities to bring simple machine principles to light during everyday school activities. When we want things to move or spin or slide easily, we can mention the need to cut down friction with a few drops of oil. There are times when too little friction poses safety hazards for young children: shoeless children moving fast on slippery floors, or unwary children crossing streets on rainy or icy days.

For a vivid application of the lever and a pair of wheels, let children help trundle heavy sandbags to the sandbox with a hand truck. Encourage them to try moving the sandbags without the hand truck so that they will realize how much the hand truck helps them.

Simple machine concepts are part of workbench use. Examples include the friction of sanding and sawing; the lever action of pulling out nails with the hammer; and the interlocking screw threads that hold wood tightly in a vice or clamp.

Whenever possible, let children watch the repair and maintenance of classroom and playground equipment. Better still, enlist the help of a shy child, or one who needs a chance to get attention and approval. One child who broke toys and mistreated other children to attract attention was able to give up these undesirable behaviors when he became our chief mechanic. He took such pride in manning the oilcan and tightening tricycle bolts that he became a good steward of school property and a friend to other children.

Relating New Concepts to Existing Concepts

Simple machines help overcome the effect of gravity's pull. This can be brought out by speaking about the weight of the objects being lifted or moved in terms of gravity's pull. The effect of magnetism could be used to discover what a strong axle or wheel frame is composed of, or to learn what kind of hinge rusts and needs oiling when it works hard and squeaks from too much friction.

Simple machine principles are used to move boats on water. Easy examples are the levers called oars, and the paddle wheels that power the swanboats seen in Robert McCloskey's book, *Make Way For Ducklings*.

Parent Involvement

Ask parents if they would be willing to lend equipment or demonstrate skills that involve simple machines. Todd's mother loaned us a butter churn that her grandmother had used. Jenny's mother made bread with us, using her hand-cranked kneading bucket. Both children gained new status as a result of their parents' contributions.

Suggest that parents help in a simple machine hunt at home. Some of the common things they might find are drapery pulleys, can opener wheels, or overhead garage door wheels on tracks.

Also, tell parents about places they could visit with their children to see simple machines. A visit to a shoe repair shop permits the best boosted-up-high-enough view of the long axle that turns grinding wheels and polishers. A really good look at the impressive gears inside a bank vault door also calls for a long visit with a patient parent.

References

Lewellen, John. *The True Book of Toys at Work*. Chicago: Childrens Press, 1953.

Notkin, Jerome. *The How and Why Wonder Book of Machines*. New York: Wonder Books, 1960.

Pine, Tillie S., and Levine, Joseph. *Friction All Around*. New York: Whittlesey House, McGraw-Hill, 1960.

————. *Simple Machines and How We Use Them*. New York: Whittlesey House, McGraw-Hill, 1965.

Schneider, Herman and Nina. *Now Try This*. New York: William H. Scott, 1957.

Sharp, Elizabeth. *Simple Machines and How They Work*. New York: Random House, 1959.

VanAmerongen, C. *The Way Things Work: An Illustrated Encyclopedia of Technology*. New York: Simon and Schuster, 1967. This book gives the teacher the same revelations of "So that's how it works!" that the children will gain from their study of simple machines.

9

Sound

The discovery that sound occurs when something vibrates can help children overcome fears about scary noises. Vibrations cause sound whether they originate in the distant clouds or in our own throats. The concepts explored in this chapter are:

SOUNDS ARE MADE WHEN SOMETHING VIBRATES
SOUND TRAVELS THROUGH MANY THINGS
DIFFERENT SIZES OF VIBRATING OBJECTS MAKE DIFFERENT
SOUNDS

The experiences begin with a group activity to clarify the term *vibration,* and to establish the idea that vibrations cause sounds. This is followed by experiencing vibrations; experimenting with mediums through which sound travels; and relating the pitch of sound to the size of vibrating objects.

Introduction: Help children understand what a vibration is by producing one. Say something like this: "Can you lift your arm and let your hand dangle from your wrist? Now, shake your hand as fast as you can. What do you call what is happening to your hand? Shaking? Wiggling? Jiggling? Wobbling? Those are good words. *Vibration* is another word that means moving back and forth very fast. Does your hand look different when it is vibrating? Some vibrating things move back and forth so fast that they look blurry. Another thing happens when something vibrates. You can find out if you listen very quietly. Hold your hand near your ear, then vibrate your fingers and hand very fast. What happens? Does someone hear a soft, whirring sound?

"Now put your fingers very lightly on the front of your throat, near the bottom. Very, very softly sing a sound like *eeeeee*. Do you feel something with your fingertips? Try it again. Did something inside your throat vibrate? Yes, you made a sound in there. Whenever we hear a sound, it is being made by something vibrating. Try touching your lips while you say *hummmmmm*. What's happening?"

Concept: Sounds Are Made When Something Vibrates

1. Can We See Things Vibrate?

LEARNING OBJECTIVE: To learn the meaning of the term **vibration** by creating and watching a vibration.

MATERIALS:

Binding strip from vinyl folder cover, or flexible ruler

Coffee can with plastic lid, or sturdy drum

Sand, rice, or Styrofoam packing chips

Quart milk carton

Rubber bands

GETTING READY:

Cut window opening in one side of milk carton.

Stretch rubber band around length of milk carton.

SMALL GROUP ACTIVITY:

"Watch and listen to this."
1. Extend folder strip from edge of table or chair, like a diving board. Bend free end down, then release. "What did you see? . . . hear?"
2. Show the milk carton. "What will happen if I pluck the rubber band?" Watch, listen.
3. "We could see the plastic strip and the rubber band vibrate easily. Can you see the can lid vibrate easily? No? Let's put something light on the lid that will show us how the lid is vibrating." Put sand, rice, or chips on lid. Tap the lid. What happens? Let the children experiment.

2. Can We Feel Things Vibrate?

LEARNING OBJECTIVE: To learn the meaning of the term **vibration** by creating and feeling a vibration.

MATERIALS:

One or more of these:
Wind-up alarm clock, kitchen timer, toy music box

Any motor-run school equipment, aquarium air pump

SMALL GROUP ACTIVITY:

1. Pass unwound clock, timer, and music box among children. "Do you feel these things vibrating now? Are they making sounds?"
2. Wind the equipment, pass again. "Now what do you feel? . . . hear?"
3. "Try making some music with vibrating air and

motor, record player, water cooler

Combs

Waxed paper (tissue paper disintegrates when damp)

GETTING READY:

Cut pieces of waxed paper to fold over teeth of combs.

paper. Hold the paper at the bottom of the comb lightly between your lips. Now try to hum and blow a tune at the same time. The vibrations feel funny, but the sound is nice."

4. Tour the room and halls to feel vibrating electric motors.

Read a story about how to pucker the lips tightly to blow out another kind of vibration: *Whistle for Willie*, by Ezra Jack Keats.

Concept: Sound Travels Through Many Things

1. Does Air Carry Sound?

LEARNING OBJECTIVE: To become aware that sound vibrations can make air vibrate to carry sound.

MATERIALS:

12″ pieces of plastic garden hose

Plastic golf club cover tubes (very inexpensive at sports stores)

SMALL GROUP ACTIVITY:

1. "Is there anything inside the pieces of hose? Yes, air. Put one end next to your mouth, the other next to your ear. Whisper your name into the hose. Could you hear yourself? What could be vibrating inside the tube?"
2. "You can *feel* what is vibrating if you put your hand at the end of the hose. Try saying words like *toot* and *tut*. Can you feel something pushing on your hand each time you say a word?" (Air carried vibrations from their throats through the tubes.)
3. Let seated children enjoy speaking to each other through the long golf-club tubes.

READ: *Goggles*, by Ezra Jack Keats.

Group Discussion: "Peek into the ear of the child sitting next to you. Do you see anything inside the ear that is vibrating? Could something invisible be in there?"

Recall how the sand or foam chips bounced around when someone tapped the coffee can lid. One vibrating thing made the things next to it vibrate. "Air vibrates when something next to it vibrates. That is the way sound is carried by air. It is the way sounds usually come to our ears. The air inside our ears also vibrates so we hear the sounds." Let children experiment with this idea by covering and uncovering their ears with their hands as they listen to some music. Could the air inside their ears vibrate very well when their hands were covering them?

Safety note: "Our ears have an outside part that we can see and an inside part that we can't see. The inside part is so delicate that vibrating air can vibrate it. That is how we hear. We must be very careful with our ears to keep that delicate part working well. Can you think of some good safety rules for our ears?"

2. Does Water Carry Sound?

LEARNING OBJECTIVE: To become aware that sound vibrations can make water vibrate to carry sound.

MATERIALS:

Two similar containers: such as plastic buckets

Pair of blunt scissors

Sponge, plastic sheet, or newspaper for spills

Golf club tube cut into 12" lengths

GETTING READY:

Half-fill one container with water.

SMALL GROUP ACTIVITY:

1. "Take turns pressing one ear to the side of the bucket to listen to the sound I'll make." Open and shut scissors to make a steady clicking noise, holding them inside the empty bucket.
2. "I'll make the same sound in the water in this bucket. Listen the same way here. Do you hear the clicks? Are they louder or softer in the water? Put the golf tube in the water, then put your ear at the other end to listen. Is the sound louder coming through the air, or through water?" Let the children make the scissor clicks for each other.

Note: If children in your class have gone fishing, they will understand now why people try to be very quiet when they are fishing.

3. Do Solid Things Carry Sound?

LEARNING OBJECTIVE: To become aware that sound vibrations can make solid objects vibrate to carry sound.

MATERIALS:

Table

Bottle caps, sticks, small rock, anything that will make a noise on the table

Desirable: clock, aquarium pump motor, musical toy works

SMALL GROUP ACTIVITY:

1. "We're going to make sounds for each other. Some may be very soft, so we'll have to listen closely." Tap one fingertip on table top. "Can you see what I am doing? Does it make a loud sound? Now cover one ear with your hand and press the other ear on the table top while I do the same thing again."
2. "Which way was the sound louder, through the air, or through the wooden table? Now put

your ears to the table and close your eyes. Each one of you can take a turn tapping on the table with these things. We'll try to guess what made the sound."

Finding out takes time. Keep the learning pace relaxed. Listen to the children's ideas.

3. Later compare sounds made by the clock, motor, or music works when held in the hand, placed on the table while heads are up, and on the table while ears are pressed to the table. Which sounds loudest?

4. Will String Carry Sound?

LEARNING OBJECTIVE: To become aware that sound vibrations can make taut string vibrate to carry sound.

MATERIALS:

Light string

Metal spoons

Bar of soap

Empty frozen juice cans, 2 for each telephone

1½" nails

Hammer

GETTING READY:

Cut string into 2½' lengths for spoon chimes.

Make a hole in center of each can bottom.

Cut string into 5' lengths for tin can telephones. (String can be longer for use at home. Short lengths are best when many children will be using phones in the same room—avoids tangles.)

SMALL GROUP ACTIVITY:

1. Dangle short string over a finger. "Do you think loose string will vibrate to make a sound if I pluck it? Will it make sound if it is held tightly by both hands? Try it both ways with your string." (Loose string vibrates too slowly for audible sound.)
2. "Let's add heavy vibrating metal to the string ends and listen to find out if tight string will carry sound." Tie a spoon to each end of strings. Fold string in half; press folded end to ear. Lean over so that spoons dangle freely. Swing string to make spoons strike each other. Listen to the sounds traveling up the string.
3. Make tin can telephones with children. To stiffen string ends, pull across soap bar. Put a string through the holes in two cans from the outside. Pull string into the can, tie around a nail. Wedge the nail inside the can. "Keep the string straight and tight. You talk into one can, your friend hears through the other can."

Group Discussion: Give each child a rubber band to pluck when it is limp and when it is stretched. What did the tin-spoon chimes and tin-can telephone makers find out about how string vibrates to carry sound? How many things vibrated to carry the sound of their voices? (Air in cans, the cans, and the string.)

READ: *Timmy and the Tin Can Telephone,* by Branley and Vaughn.

5. Do All Materials Carry Sound Well?

LEARNING OBJECTIVE: To become aware that materials that are not firm and solid do not carry sound vibrations well.

"We found out that a loose string and a loose rubber band don't carry sounds well. They don't vibrate fast enough to make a sound we can hear. Everyone can take a turn to find out if we can hear sound better through something firm and solid, or through something fluffy."

MATERIALS:

Kitchen timer or a loud wind-up alarm clock

Fluffy cushion

Masking tape

Crayon and paper

Low table

GETTING READY:

Place a dividing strip of tape across the center of the table.

Tape a piece of paper to each section of the table top.

Tape cushion to one side of the divider. Put ticking clock or timer under the table on floor.

ACTIVITY:

1. "Put one ear flat on the table top, cover your other ear with your hand. Listen carefully."
2. "Then put your ear lightly on the cushion, still covering your other ear. Listen carefully."
3. "Decide which way you could hear the ticking best. Make an X on the paper taped to the side of the table where the ticking sounds loudest. When everyone has had a chance to listen and decide, we'll count the X's."

Concept: Different Sizes of Vibrating Objects Make Different Sounds

---

1. Do Different Vibrating String Lengths Sound Alike?

LEARNING OBJECTIVE: To hear pitch differences when different string lengths vibrate.

MATERIALS:

Three sizes of plastic boxes, such as 3″, 4″, 5″

Three sizes of small rubber bands

Empty covered boxes like a 2 pound cheese box or small shoe boxes

Rubber bands large enough to

SMALL GROUP ACTIVITY:

1. Pluck rubber bands on the plastic boxes. "Do these all sound alike? Which one sounds highest? Lowest? Try it."
2. "Now try this." Stretch long rubber bands around lengths of covered boxes. Slip block under band near left end of the box. Pluck the length of rubber band to the right of the block. Listen. Now slide block slowly, still plucking, to the right of the block. "Is pitch changing? Is it higher or

stretch around the length of covered boxes

Small blocks

Desirable: autoharp or guitar

GETTING READY:

Stretch small rubber band over each opened plastic box. Smallest band on smallest box, etc. (The effect won't be the same if same size rubber band is used on all three boxes. Try it to find out why.)

lower? Does the whole rubber band length vibrate, or just the side being plucked? Is the part that vibrates getting shorter and higher?" Let children experiment, sliding the block and plucking. Can you play the scale this way? Play a tune?

Group Discussion: The autoharp shows the relationship between string length and pitch very clearly. (A real harp, an upright piano with the front panel removed, or a grand piano with the top raised will show the same thing.) If a guitar is used for this purpose, be sure to make clear which part of the string is vibrating, so that the relationship between vibrating string length and pitch can be understood.

2. Do Different Vibrating Air Column Lengths Sound Alike?

LEARNING OBJECTIVE: To hear pitch differences when different air column lengths vibrate.

MATERIALS:

Carton of 8 empty 16 oz. bottles

Pitcher of water

Funnel

Masking tape

Sponge

Bicycle tire pump or bellows step pump

GETTING READY:

Experiment at home with levels of water needed to produce tones of the octave. Internal shape of bottles vary, but these levels may be about right: (1) empty; (2) $1\frac{3}{4}''$ water; (3) $2\frac{1}{2}''$ water; (4) $4''$

SMALL GROUP ACTIVITY:

1. "What is inside these bottles? What will happen if the air inside the bottles vibrates? When air moves across the top of the bottle, it makes the air inside vibrate.* Listen." Have a child use the pump while you direct a stream of air from the hose *straight across* the bottle top.

2. "We put some water in these bottles. Is there space for as much air in this bottle as in this one? Let's see what happens when we make different amounts of air space vibrate."

3. Arrange bottles in order, 1 through 8. While a child pumps air, direct air from the hose across tops of bottles to play the scale. Try to play "Yankee Doodle." Let children play your bottle organ. (Put bottles in two cartons to prevent breaking, or keep bottles on the floor.)

water; (5) 4½″ water; (6)
5¼″ water; (7) 5½″ water;
(8) 6″ water.

Place band of tape around
each bottle, with upper edge
of tape at measurement level.

Let children pour water to
marked levels of bottles if
possible.

* If air moves too fast across the bottle, shrill tones one octave higher are produced
(harmonics).

   Note: This would be a good time to invite a flute player to visit. Ask the player to
show children how air is blown across the mouthpiece, and how the air column is lengthened
and shortened by pressing keys to cover holes on the flute.

3. Do Different Sizes of Vibrating Metal Sound Alike?

LEARNING OBJECTIVE: To hear pitch differences when different sizes of metal objects vibrate.

MATERIALS:

Assemble as many of these items as you can:

Set of four steel measuring cups

Set of four steel measuring spoons

Nesting steel bowls

Metal bells of different sizes (any kind)

Finger cymbals, child-size cymbals

Heavy aluminum pan lids of different sizes

New unsharpened pencils, pieces of dowel, or sticks

String

GETTING READY:

Tie loops of string through handle holes of measuring cups and spoons.

SMALL GROUP ACTIVITY:

1. Introduce each type of object separately to avoid confusion. "Do you think these measuring cups will sound alike when they vibrate? Mary, please tap each one with the pencil to find out. Which sounds highest?"
2. Point out the difference in sound when the spoons are held by the string, and when they are cupped in your hand.
3. Suggest that children try out the sounds of one kind of object at a time; that they try to stop the vibrations with their hands.

Group Discussion: Recall with the children which sizes of metal objects made the highest sounds, which the lowest. If you have a child's xylophone, ask for predictions about the metal plate that will make the highest note. Try it. Play a tune to sing along with.

Primary Reinforcements

Music

Many of the familiar children's songs are easy extensions of the learnings about vibrations and pitch as they describe bell sounds and animal sounds. The concepts can be applied when rhythm instruments are used. "Charles, try holding your triangle by the string loop instead of with your hand. See if it vibrates more now." Prolong the life of the school drums by suggesting that they vibrate better when lightly tapped rather than when thumped very hard.

Children can really make pleasant music with a classroom made box harp. Excellent directions for making this no-cost instrument are given in *Music and Instruments for Children to Make,* by Hawkinson and Faulhaber (see page 119). Young children can help with taping the box shut, but most of the remaining steps require the strength of an adult.

This song is about the cause of sounds:

Sounds

Sounds are made by vi - bra - ting things like
met - al or wa - ter or air or strings.

Math Experience

ORDERING BY PITCH AND SIZE. The mathematical relationship between the size and the pitch of vibrating objects is fun to explore. Sets of bells and sets of detached metal chimes that can be placed on a molded framework to form a xylophone are available commercially. The bells and chimes can be arranged by children in one-step tone order visually according to size, largest to smallest; or auditorily according to tone, lowest to highest.

Older children can have fun converting the bottle organ (page 111) into bottle chimes when they tap the bottles lightly with a pencil. They discover that the tone order is reversed. The bottle with little air space and a large amount of water produces a high tone when the air vibrates, and a low tone when the water vibrates. Young children may be confused by the reversal. It would be wiser not to present this activity to them in two different ways.

Ideas for playing tunes on the water chimes are given in *Wake Up and Sing*, by Beatrice Landeck [(7), Appendix 1]. However, Landeck's suggestion of using drinking glasses seems less safe for young children than using heavy bottles.

Stories and References for Children

Alexander, Anne. *Noise In The Night*. Chicago: Rand McNally, 1960. Sherri identifies a mysterious vibration that makes a friendly noise in the night.

Alexenberg, Melvin. *Sound Science*. Englewood Cliffs, N.J.: Prentice-Hall, 1968. Sound experiments illustrated in bright colors with imaginary creatures wandering about.

Borten, Helen. *Do You Hear What I Hear?* New York: Abelard-Schuman, 1960. A sensitive description of sounds.

Branley, Franklyn, and Vaugh, Eleanor. *Timmy and the Tin Can Telephone*. New York:

Thomas Y. Crowell, 1959. Two children devise an early morning communication system between their houses that won't disturb their families.

Hoban, Russell. *A Baby Sister for Frances*. New York: Harper & Row, 1964. Frances competes for parental attention by making and using a rattle from a gravel-filled coffee can, "rattley bang!"

Keats, Ezra Jack. *Whistle for Willie*. Seafarer ed. New York: Viking Press, 1969. Peter has the thrill of discovering how to whistle!

_____. *Goggles*. New York: Collier-Macmillan, 1971. Peter sends his voice through an empty drain pipe to confuse the big boys who are trying to catch him.

Scarry, Richard. *Great Big Air Book*. New York: Random House, 1972. The story, "Orchestra Practice," deals with sound waves traveling through the air. Amusing and informative.

Schwartz, Julius. *Now I Know*. New York: Whittlesey House, McGraw-Hill, 1955. Sensitive commentaries about the causes of sounds that often worry young children.

Showers, Paul. *The Listening Walk*. New York: Thomas Y. Crowell, 1961.

Steiner, Charlotte. *Listen to My Seashell*. New York: Alfred A. Knopf, 1959. A book of sounds for young preschool children that can be used as a stimulus for discussion. "What vibrates when we hear the harp?" and so forth.

White, Laurence B., Jr. *Investigating Science With Rubber Bands*. Reading, Mass.: Addison-Wesley, 1969. Describes such things as making a rubber band banjo, and changing pitch and volume.

Zolotow, Charlotte. *The Storm Book*. New York: Harper & Row, 1963.

Poems (References found in Appendix 1)

Many poems for children recreate sounds. The following three extend the learning activities about sound:

From *Poems To Grow On*, by Jean McKee Thompson:
"Kitchen Tunes" by Ida Pardue
"The Storm" by Dorothy Aldis
From *Poem Children Will Sit Still For:*
"Wind Song" by Lilian Moore

Fingerplays

This fingerplay relates size to pitch and volume:

The Clocks

(slowly, loudly)
    When I'm a big tall clock,   (stand & stretch tall)
    I go TICK TOCK, TICK TOCK, TICK.   (swing arms like a pendulum)
(faster, softer)
    When I'm a middle-size clock   (stoop over)
    I go tick tock, tick tock, tick.   (swing arms faster)

(even faster, softer)
When I'm a *very small* clock   (crouch low)
I go tick-tick-tick-tick-tick   (move hands fast)
So fast that I fall over!

—Author unknown

Recall the tin-can telephone fun with this fingerplay:

Tin-Can Telephone

I called my friend on a tin-can phone.   (make cylinders with hands)
Two tin cans were joined by a string.   (extend little fingers to touch each
                                                           other)
I put it to my mouth,   (one cylinder up to mouth)
I put it to my ear,   (move cylinder to ear)
I could hear my friend
Say everything!

Art Activities

Children enjoy making musical instruments they can use.

1. TAMBOURINES. Let children make crayon designs on two paper plates. Punch holes at regular intervals around the edges of the pair of plates. Children can lace the plates together part way, fill the tambourine with bottle caps, then complete the lacing. Plastic margarine tubs can also be used, but they are difficult to decorate.

2. DRUMS. Use salt or oatmeal boxes, or cans with air-tight plastic lids. Glue construction paper to the side of the drum, slipping rubber bands around the paper to hold it firmly while the glue dries. Children can decorate with crayons.

3. HOOTING HORNS. Let children glue and wind lengths of yarn around paper towel tubes. (The pressure children use when crayoning will squash most tubes.) An adult can punch an air-vent hole near one end. Help children fasten a single piece of waxed paper over one end of the tube with a tight rubber band. A reedy sound is made by hooting tunes into the open end of the tube.

4. JINGLE STICKS. For each stick, make a hole through the center of six bottle caps using a hammer and thick nail. Let children sand eight-inch lengths of dowel, 1¼″ in diameter. Secure the dowel in a clamp or vise. Let children loosely attach three pairs of bottle caps (open edges together) near one end of the dowel with roofing nails.

Dramatic Play

1. A pair of tin-can telephones can add interest to the block corner airplane, ship, or spaceship play. They can also be fun to use in a pretend office, home, or hospital.

2. Medical play can include the experience of actually hearing each other's heart beats. Use a real or an improvised stethoscope to "gather" the sound so it can be heard more clearly. Insert the tube end of a soft plastic funnel into a short length of narrow-gauge plastic tubing. Place the funnel on a child's chest. Hold the tubing end close to (not in) the ear to hear the beats.

Thinking Games

1. MATCH MY SOUND. Gather pairs of matching items that will produce sounds, such as: metal spring "crickets"; two squares of sandpaper to rub together; small brass bells; jingle bells; two bottle caps to tap together; blunt scissors to click; small pieces of corrugated paper to scrape with a fingertip; pocket combs and waxed paper to blow on; two finger cymbals. Put one of each item in a teacher's bag. Distribute the matching sound makers as evenly as possible into lunch-size paper bags. Fold down the tops and present a bag of secret sounds to each child at the table. While children keep their eyes tightly shut, the teacher reaches into her bag and makes a sound with one of the items. The children then search through their bags to see who can find things that produce a matching sound. Allow plenty of time for this game. The children may want to trade bags and begin again when you finish.

2. SOUND MATCHING TRAY. Use a divided cutlery tray and color film cans or small opaque plastic bottles to adapt a Montessori sensory training exercise. Loosely fill two matching containers with materials that make distinctive sounds when shaken, such as gravel, sand, pennies, rice, or puffed cereal. Mark matching pairs with matching numerals or letters on the container bottom as a self-correcting aid to success. Put one set of containers on one side of the tray, have children find the matching sound containers and place them next to their mates on the other side of the tray.

Field Trips

Look around your school area for a place that will produce an echo. An empty gymnasium or a high, windowless wall that borders an empty lot might be good places. Tell children that when they shout their names toward the walls, the vibrations touch the walls and bounce back to them. Try it.

As you walk together for any special purpose, suggest walking very quietly so that you can listen for sounds to identify. An old church or auditorium with visible organ pipes, within walking distance of the school, is a good destination for this study.

Creative Movement

Children can show their perception of high or low sounds by moving to the tones of an instrument played by an adult. When the notes are low the children move in a low position close to the floor; when they are high the children move in a stretched up position. They can also rise from a crouch to tiptoes in response to a slowly ascending scale, and return to the crouch as the descending scale is played.

Secondary Reinforcements

Keeping Concepts Alive

Occasionally two of the loudest and most frightening sounds occur while children are in school: thunder and sonic booms. Children who are afraid of thunder could be reminded of the air experiment with the balloon that swelled when the cold air inside of it was warmed. When lightning moves through the air, that air suddenly gets warm and it swells so fast that it vibrates. Thunder is the way we hear the vibration from that fast swelling air far up in the clouds.

The unexpectedness of sonic booms add to the scariness of that particular sound. Adults can agree with frightened children that surprise noises startle us. That acknowledgment and the example of our calm response are helpful to children. You could explain that when a jet goes very, very fast, it sometimes bumps into the air ahead that is already vibrating with its own sound! Sound travels fast, but sometimes a jet can travel faster than sound. People on the ground below hear that bump like a big explosion of air.

Relating to New Concepts to Existing Concepts

Some of the suggested experiences relate to the children's existing concepts about the presence of air in empty-looking places and moving air pushing things. Friction is also involved in the production of some sounds, such as rubbing sandpaper together and unlubricated metal parts rubbing together to produce squeaks from the vibrations.

A nice way to relate sounds to animal life is to play the Tom Glazer record, *Now We Know (Songs to Learn By)*, to hear, "What Makes the Bee Buzz."

Parent Involvement

Any parent who is able to bring in and play a musical instrument can enrich the children's awareness of sound making. Parents could be encouraged to lend things like a bell collection or wind chimes for the children to enjoy. Suggest points of soundmaking interest in the locality which they might visit with their children, such as hand operated church bells, a pipe organ, or a special musical event.

References

Blough, Glenn, and Schwartz, Julius. *Elementary School Science and How to Teach It.* 5th ed. New York: Holt, Rinehart and Winston, 1974.

Bonsall, George. *The How and Why Wonder Book of Weather.* New York: Wonder Books, 1960. Includes an explanation of the cause of thunder.

Hawkinson, John, and Faulhaber, M. *Music and Instruments for Children to Make.* Chicago: Whitman, 1969. Excellent instructions for making a box harp that will withstand the wear and tear of child use. It will produce good clear tones.

Keen, Martin. *The How and Why Wonder Book of Sound.* New York: Wonder Books, 1962. Contains an explanation of sonic booms.

Pine, Tillie, and Levine, Joseph. *Sounds All Around.* New York: McGraw-Hill, 1959.

Podendorf, Illa. *Sounds All About.* Chicago: Childrens Press, 1970.

Wyler, Rose, and Ames, Gerald. *Prove It.* New York: Scholastic Book Services, 1963.

10

Light

From the day of birth, infants are able to perceive light. Later the playpen explorer may try to catch a sunbeam; the toddler may try to pounce on his shadow. Growing young children are fascinated by the sparkle of reflected light and the beauty of the spectrum. The experiences that capture some children's closest attention, however, are those that help to allay their worries about darkness—the absence of light. The light concepts suggested for investigation in this chapter are:

NOTHING CAN BE SEEN WITHOUT LIGHT
LIGHT APPEARS TO TRAVEL IN A STRAIGHT LINE
SHADOWS ARE MADE WHEN LIGHT BEAMS ARE BLOCKED
NIGHT IS EARTH'S SHADOW
EVERYTHING WE SEE REFLECTS SOME LIGHT
LIGHT IS A MIXTURE OF MANY COLORS
BENDING LIGHT BEAMS MAKE THINGS LOOK DIFFERENTLY

Children can experiment by examining a box full of darkness; using a flashlight beam to note the straight line path of light; creating shadows; and looking through filters. Other experiences explain night and day, reflection, and refraction.

Introduction: For a comfortable lead into experiences with light, read one of these stories about the mastery of nighttime anxiety: *Bedtime for Frances,* by Russell Hoban, or *Switch on the Night,* by Ray Bradbury, the science-fiction writer.

Concept: Nothing Can Be Seen without Light

1. What Can We See in a Dark Box?

LEARNING OBJECTIVE: To become aware that nothing can be seen without light.

MATERIALS:

Pen flashlight

Extra batteries

Shoebox with cover

Small picture

Old heavy blanket

Low table

GETTING READY:

Cut a dime-size peephole in one end of the shoe box.

Cut a flap in top of box.

Paste picture to inside of box at end opposite the peephole.

Cover table with the blanket

SMALL GROUP ACTIVITY:

1. "Let's stretch out on the floor and put just our heads into the dark place under the table."
2. "Here is a dark box. It has a hole in one end to look into. Do you see anything in there?" Pass the box to everyone.
3. "Now I am going to change something, then you can look into the box again." Turn on the flashlight, push it under the flap on top of the box. "Can you see something in the box now? It was there before, but you couldn't see it. Let's try to find out why."
3. Remove flashlight, pass the box again. "The picture is still in there. Can you see it? Why not? Right, there is no light. *We always need light to see anything. Nothing can be seen without light.*"

so it drapes to floor on all
sides, making a dark place.

Be prepared to repeat this experience. Children are impressed with their ability to make
the dark go away and come back at will. Listen to: "Why Can't I See In The Dark?" sung
by Tom Glazer in *Now We Know (Songs to Learn By)*. (See Appendix 1)

Concept: Light Appears to Travel in a Straight Line

1. Does a Flashlight Beam Curve around Things?

LEARNING OBJECTIVE: To notice that light appears to pass along in straight lines.

MATERIALS:

Pen flashlight

Extra batteries

3 sheets of 8" x 11" paper

Blanket and low table

Blocks

Masking tape

GETTING READY:

To prepare 3 screens: stack
2 blocks. Tape flashlight to
top block. Turn it on. Fold
paper as shown. Stand it in
front of the light. Cut a small
hole where beam hits center
of paper. Cut holes in same
location in other screens.

SMALL GROUP ACTIVITY:

1. "Let's find out how a beam of light travels. Lie
   down along the sides of the table. Put your heads
   under the blanket. I'll be at this end, no one will
   be at the other end."
2. Turn on the flashlight. "Is the light shining on the
   blanket at the end of the table? Is it coming
   through each hole in the screens?"
3. "Tom, will you put your hand in front of one hole,
   please? Is the light still shining on the blanket?
   Why not? Did Tom's hand block the light? Did it
   curve around the paper to shine in the next
   holes?"
4. "Take turns blocking the light beam as Tom did.
   Does the light curve around things? No. Light
   travels in a straight path." Let children use the
   flashlight to check and recheck the path of light.

FIGURE 14

Line up screens a few inches
apart so that the light beam
can pass through all the holes.
Cover table with blanket.

Concept: Shadows are Made when Light Beams are Blocked

1. Does Light Shine through some Things and not Others?

LEARNING OBJECTIVE: To perceive light differently as it shines through different materials and
to become aware of shadows as results of blocked light.

PART 1

MATERIALS:

Small flashlight

Blanket and low table

Waxed paper

Cardboard

Large shoebox

Clear glass jar

Water

Colored tissue paper

Clear vinyl folder

GETTING READY:

Cut a large opening in shoebox bottom.

Cut simple 3" cardboard doll
figure.

Fill jar with water.

Cover table with blanket.

SMALL GROUP ACTIVITY:

1. "Let's find out what light will shine through. You
   stretch out along that side of the table, I'll be
   across from you."
2. Put the box on its side, opening facing children.
   Shine light through the opening. "Does light shine
   through air?"
3. Put water jar in the opening. "Does light shine
   through water?"
4. "Do you think light will shine through waxed paper
   in the same way?" Cover opening with waxed
   paper. "Does the light shine in one spot, or spread
   out?" Try colored tissue paper and clear vinyl at
   opening.
5. "Do you think light will shine through this cardboard doll?" Remove box, place doll so that it
   makes a shadow on the blanket.
6. Help children notice that light shines on only one
   side of the doll. "Why is there a dark place behind the doll? It blocked the light and left a
   shadow."

PART 2

Move outdoors on a sunny day. Trace the outline of children's shadows with chalk
on a paved area. As you trace, ask other children "Is sunlight shining right through Amy
or does she block the light? I'm tracing the darkness that Amy's body makes where the
sunlight can't shine through her."

Concept: Night is Earth's Shadow

1. Why Do We Have Day and Night?

LEARNING OBJECTIVE: To begin to understand night's darkness as the shadow of the turning earth.

Group Experience. Needed: globe or ball; projector or flashlight; chalk; and a darkened room.

"We had fun blocking the sunlight to make shadows. Did you know that the whole earth does the same thing? That is the way day and night happen. Let's pretend that this light is the shining sun. This globe is a model of our huge earth. I'll put a chalk mark here on the globe to show where our part of the world is. Watch the mark as I turn the globe the way the earth always slowly, slowly turns. Is the mark in the light now? Does the light curve around the globe to keep shining on our part of the world? No, the light shines in a straight line. Our part of the world is in a shadow now—the shadow of the other side of the earth."

Continue to turn the globe, so that children can see the marked part of the globe alternately in the light and in the shadow. "What do we call the time when our part of the world is in the earth's shadow? When it is in the sunlight?" Let the children turn the globe.

READ: *The Day We Saw The Sun Come Up,* by Alice Gouday. The children in this beautiful story do the same experiment to grasp the meaning of day and night.
LISTEN TO: "Where Does the Sun Go At Night?" sung by Tom Glazer on: *Now We Know (Songs To Learn By).* (See Appendix 1.)

Concept: Everything We See Reflects Some Light

Introduction: Put a lighted purse-size flashlight into your cupped hands. Open your hands to let the children see where the light is coming from. "Is the flashlight making this light?" Hold a pocket mirror in your hands. "Is the mirror making a light?" Now shine the flashlight beam onto the mirror. Tilt the mirror so that the light is reflected onto the walls or ceiling. "Which thing made the light that is bouncing up there, the flashlight or the mirror?" Turn the flashlight off and on several times so children can verify that the spot of light is *reflected* by the mirror to the ceiling only when the flashlight makes the light.

1. Do Some Things Reflect Light Better Than Others?

LEARNING OBJECTIVE: To become aware that various materials reflect different amounts of light.

MATERIALS:

Strong sunlight, or spotlight study lamp

Large sheet of stiff white paper or cardboard

Aluminum foil pans

Shiny baking sheets

SMALL GROUP ACTIVITY:

1. Prop white paper on a chair seat at a right angle to the light source.
2. "Can you stand facing the light, holding a pan so it reflects light to the sheet of paper on the chair? See the reflection glow? Try to reflect light on the paper with these other things. See which

Colored construction paper: yellow, red, black

Dark carpet sample, velveteen, or bath towel

Add more things to try, if possible. Small pocket mirrors are fun, but may be hazardous. Tape edges of unframed mirrors if you decide to use them.

ones reflect light well, which ones do not." Start with things that reflect well. Children may be discouraged as they try things if they don't get results right away.

READ: *The Rain Puddle,* by Adelaide Holl. What confused the animals?

Concept: Light is a Mixture of Many Colors

1. Can Some Things Bend Light to Show its Colors?

LEARNING OBJECTIVE: To observe the effect of light passing through a prism, or prism-like materials, and spreading into spectrum colors.

MATERIALS:

Magazine

Strong sunlight or a projector

Small piece of thick plate glass or plastic, edges taped*

Prisms, or chandelier drops

Small, clear plastic boxes

Water

Soap bubble materials

Desirable: an aquarium

* Do *not* use a magnifying glass.

SMALL GROUP ACTIVITY:

1. "There is a secret in light beams. This magazine can help us find it." Hold magazine: cut edges toward children, bound edge toward you. "When pages are pressed together, does the edge look like one thick line? I'll bend it back toward me. Now can you see that line spread out to show many edges of paper? Try it."
2. Hold plate glass in front of light source. "When light comes through this glass it looks clear. Let's see how it looks when it is spread by glass that is bent."
3. Hold prism edge in front of light beam, rotate till a spectrum can be seen in the room. "Now you see the secret! Light really has seven colors in it (spectrum), but we only see them when it shines through something clear that is bent or curved." Let the children try it.
4. If possible, place an aquarium near sunny windows. Fill with water. Help children stand where they can see the spectrum through the aquarium corners.
5. Let children experiment with water in small plastic

boxes outdoors on a sunny day. Can they see the spectrum through the corners?

6. Try to make soap bubbles near a sunny window to see colors.

FIGURE 15

Group Discussion: Talk about how raindrops sometimes act like prisms to form a rainbow in the sky. Listen to "Seven Colors Make A Rainbow" sung by Tom Glazer in: *Now We Know (Songs To Learn By)*.

Concept: Bending Light Beams Make Things Look Differently

1. How Do Things Look through a Curved Drop of Water?

LEARNING OBJECTIVE: To notice that things change in appearance when seen through transparent, curved materials.

MATERIALS:

Small bottles

Water

Medicine droppers

Waxed paper

Newspapers

Magnifying glasses of all sorts

Sponges or paper towels

Small objects to examine

SMALL GROUP ACTIVITY:

1. "What happens when you put *just one drop* of water on your piece of waxed paper? Look at the newspaper through the drop of water. What do you see? Is the water drop curved?"
2. "Now add more water to the drop. Is it still curved, or is it a flat spot of water? Do words beneath still look bigger? Why not? What has changed?"
3. "Absorb the water with a sponge and try again."
4. Show children the curved profile of a magnifying lense. "Hold up the curved water bottle. Look at your finger through the bottle and water. Does it look differently?" (Light bends when it goes through

GETTING READY:

Fill bottles with water for each child.

Cut waxed paper and printed sections of newspaper into 3″ squares. Give each child a square of newspaper with waxed paper covering it.

curved glass or a curved drop of water. Things seen through them look differently.) "We looked through curves that made things look bigger."

Group Discussion: Try to find a simple microscope to show the children. "What could this mirror be used for? It reflects light up into the microscope." Read Milicent Selsam's book, Greg's Microscope. Try to make salt crystals to examine under the microscope the way Greg did. If a child in your class wears glasses, ask him how the glasses help him.

Primary Reinforcements

Music (References found in Appendix 1)

Sing this song after children have used prisms:

Prism Song
(To the tune of "Good Morning Merry Sunshine") (4)

Good morning merry sunshine,
Your light comes straight to me.
When glass or water bend your line,
Your colors I can see.

Stories and References for Children

Alexenberg, Melvin. *Light and Sight*. Englewood Cliffs, N.J.: Prentice-Hall, 1969. An activities book about reflection, refraction, color, and magnification.

Bradbury, Ray. *Switch on the Night*. New York: Pantheon Books, 1955. A child learns to control his fear of darkness.

Bulla, Clyde R. *What Makes a Shadow*. New York: Scholastic Book Services, 1962.

deRegniers, Beatrice. *The Shadow Book*. New York: Harcourt Brace, 1960. A good story for children like our Dawn who was "skeert of shaddas, cause Grandmaw said they would git me if I didn't git to bed."

Duvoisin, Roger. *The House of Four Seasons*. New York: Lothrop, Lee, and Shepard, 1958. This story about color includes a spinning color wheel demonstration of the way the spectrum colors blend into white light.

Goudey, Alice. *The Day We Saw the Sun Come Up*. New York: Charles Scribner's Sons, 1961. A beautifully written and illustrated story that informs children about night and day.

Hoban, Russell. *Bedtime for Frances*. New York: Harper & Row, 1960. Monstery shapes become familiar chairs and robes when father turns on the light in Frances' bed-room.

Holl, Adelaide. *The Rain Puddle*. New York: Lothrop, Lee and Shepard, 1965. Evapora-tion of water and reflections confuse some farm animals.

Kinney, Jean. *What Does The Sun Do?* New York: Young Scott Books, 1967. Shadows, reflections, and the spectrum are part of this story of a boy's interest in the sun.

Lionni, Leo. *Little Blue and Little Yellow*. New York: Ivan Oblensky, 1959. A simple color story.

Schwartz, Julius. *Now I Know*. New York: Whittlesey House, McGraw-Hill, 1955. Re-flections on night windows are explained,

————. *Magnify and Find Out Why*. New York: Scholastic Book Services, 1972. This paperback is sold with a small magnifying glass included. It includes more facts about objects magnified than about magnifiers.

Selsam, Milicent. *Greg's Microscope*. New York: Harper & Row, 1963.

Simon, Seymour. *Let's Try-It-Out: Light and Dark*. New York: McGraw-Hill, 1970. Simple light experiments for young children in a pleasant story form, beautifully illustrated.

Tison, Annette, and Taylor, Talus. *The Adventures of the Three Colors*. New York: World Publishing, 1971. Clever designs printed on colored transparent overlays create new patterns in secondary colors with the pages below them.

Storytelling With Lights

1. Tell Leo Lionni's story, *Little Blue and Little Yellow,* using a small study lamp and blue and yellow plastic colored paddles to blend and separate the color families in the story. Let the children experiment with the light and colored paddles afterward. Have a sheet of white paper under the lamp. A set of colored plastic construction squares can also be used this way.

2. Use a small high-intensity lamp and three dimensional objects to animate and tell a simple shadow story. Do this on the floor of a darkened room, with the children sitting in a circle around the story setting.

Small dolls can be children playing shadow tag outdoors. A cardboard tree or a wall of blocks can form a shady place for the dolls to rest after the game. A cardboard cloud could pass between the dolls and the lamp to perplex the story children. They can't find their shadows for the tag game, and think they've lost them. Walk the dolls over to the children watching the story to ask them for help finding the shadows.

Poems (References found in Appendix 1)

There are many poems for children dealing with light.

From *Poems to Grow On,* by Jean McKee Thompson:
About shadows: "Shadow Dance," by Ivy O. Eastwick
"Kick A Little Stone," by Dorothy Aldis

About reflections: "Mirrors," by Mary McB. Green

About the spectrum: "I Wonder," by Virginia Gibbons

From *Poems Children Will Sit Still For*, compiled by Beatrice deRegniers:
Reflection: "A Coffeepot Face," by Aileen Fisher
Shadows: "8 A.M. Shadows," by Patricia Hubbell

"My Shadow," by Robert Louis Stevenson, from *A Child's Garden of Verses*, may need a bit of translating for children who know babysitters, but not nursemaids. It should be part of their poetry experience.

Art Activities

1. A REFLECTING COLLAGE. Let children make collages with pieces of foil gift wrap, aluminum foil, sequins, glitter, and gummed stars.

2. REFLECTOR HANGING. Let the children cut pairs of simple shapes from foil paper or aluminum foil. Help them place three or four shapes face down in a line. Put a few drops of white glue in the center of each shape. Place a 15″ length of string on the glue spots, then let the children cover each shape with its mate. Tie a gold plastic thread spool to the bottom of the string. Tape to the ceiling or to a doorframe.

3. "STAINED GLASS" MEDALLIONS. Cut apart separate rings of plastic "six-pack" holders from frozen juice or drink cans. Pierce a hole at the top of each ring with a heavy threaded needle. Tie a thread loop. Let children dot glue around the ring and press colored tissue paper and cellophane over it, then trim away excess paper. Hang the medallions in the windows. Does light come through?

4. WAXED PAPER TRANSLUCENTS. Let children cut shapes from colored tissue paper and arrange them as they wish between two sheets of waxed paper. Children seal the papers together by placing them on a newspaper-covered food warming tray, and rubbing firmly across the waxed paper with a pizza roller.

5. COLOR BLENDING. After reading *Little Blue and Little Yellow*, by Leo Lionni, children may be interested in blending paint colors. Younger children can try two primary colors at a time. Older children can try to create all the colors of the rainbow with three primary colors.

6. SUBMARINE. Provide a milk carton periscope to help convert a block construction boat into a submarine.

Dramatic Play

1. SHIP PLAY. The crew of a building-block ship will enjoy using a periscope. Let them see how mirrors reflect light to create this interesting effect. Instructions for making an open periscope are found in *The How and Why Wonder Book of Light and Color*, by Harold Highland. Directions for making the sturdy enclosed milk-carton periscope are given in *The How and Why Wonder Book of Beginning Science*, by Notkin and Gulkin. Other mirror fun is described in *Light and Sight*, by Melvin Alexenberg.

2. SHADOW FUN. Draw the shades during active playtime on a rainy day, and set up a projector at one end of the room. Turn on dancing music and let the children enjoy creating shadows as they dance in a designated area. Outdoors on a sunny day play shadow tag with the children.

Creative Movement

BE MY MIRROR. Suggest to the children that they pretend to be your reflection in a mirror. They silently move as you move. You may be surprised at the number of movements you and the children can invent while you are seated, using your head, neck, shoulders, arms, hands, and fingers. This is a good activity to calm a restless group.

Thinking Games

WHAT IF. "What if none of the lights could be turned on in your house one night?" How could things be identified in the dark? Pass a feeling bag containing several objects that can be identified with closed eyes, by feeling or smelling.

Secondary Reinforcements

Keeping Concepts Alive

1. Point out reflections when you notice them in the classroom: in door knobs, in a child's shiny brass button, in the spoons at lunchtime, or in the rain puddles on the playground.

2. Hang a prism in a classroom window that gets direct sunlight. Experiment with balance and location to produce a good spectrum.

3. Use the opportunities that arise to comment on the need for light to see well: when raising the shades after rest time, when looking closely at a scraped knee, and so on.

4. Store magnifying glasses in a place where children will have access to them when they want to examine something. If you have a classroom microscope, let the children know that you will get it out for them when they want to examine a specimen. Talk about reflecting more light onto the specimen with the adjustable mirror.

5. Keep track of the length of the shadow made by a special tree or building near the school playground. Use a chalkmark on a paved surface, or stones on a grassy area, to compare its length when you are outdoors in the morning, at noon, and in the afternoon.

Relating New Concepts to Existing Concepts

Relate the bending of light beams to the surface tension experiences. Recall that the pull on the outside of the water drop makes it curved. Light coming through this curve of water bends and changes the way in which we see through it. Surface tension keeps soap bubbles curved, and lets us see the rainbow colors of spread-out light beams.

Parent Involvement

Perhaps some of these things are available in your area for parents and children to visit: a telescope, a lighthouse, stained glass church windows, and electric eye counting devices at public building entrances.

References

Blough, Glenn, and Schwartz, Julius. *Elementary School Science and How To Teach It.* 5th ed. New York: Holt, Rinehart and Winston, 1974.

Craig, Jean. *Questions and Answers About Weather.* New York: Scholastic Book Services, 1969. A fine weather reference book geared to young children's comprehension level. It describes the darkness before a storm and how rainbows are formed.

Healey, Frederick. *Light and Color.* New York: Golden Press, 1966. The nicely illustrated information about light and color includes a lucid example of how a prism breaks up light into the spectrum.

Highland, Harold J. *The How and Why Wonder Book of Light and Color.* New York: Wonder Books, 1963. Basic experiments for older children that provide background information and adaptable experiences for younger children to enjoy.

Keen, Martin. *The How and Why Wonder Book of the Microscope.* New York: Wonder Books, 1961. Describes the lens and magnification principles.

Notkin, Jerome. *The How and Why Wonder Book of Beginning Science.* New York: Wonder Books, 1960.

11

Static and Current Electricity

Young children often encounter static electricity during dry times of the year. A sneakered child scuffles across a nylon rug and receives a small shock upon touching the doorknob. Sweaters crackle as they are pulled on, hair flies into a halo when it is brushed. Why? The answer can help conquer fears about that giant electrical charge—lightning. These concepts underly the experiences in this chapter:

FRICTION BUILDS STATIC ELECTRICITY ON SOME THINGS
STATIC ELECTRICITY MAKES A SPARK WHEN IT JUMPS
CURRENT ELECTRICITY TRAVELS IN A LOOP
CURRENT ELECTRICITY DOES NOT MOVE THROUGH SOME
    THINGS

An initial group activity is suggested to label the effects of static electricity. Other experiences with static electricity follow this. A demonstration and discussion introduce the idea that current electricity is pushed through wires by batteries or generators. It concludes with a safety discussion. Children can try to complete a simple circuit, add a knife switch to the circuit, and experiment to find materials that conduct electricity.

Note: The experiences with static electricity will not be successful in a humid atmosphere. It is best to save these experiences for dry weather.

Part 1: Static Electricity

Introduction: Show the children a two-inch square of plastic wrap, held between your thumb and forefinger. "What do you think will happen when I let go of this plastic?" Find out.

"Let's see if friction might make a difference in what happens to the plastic." Rub the plastic on a piece of wool or nylon fabric. Pick it up again and let go. "Look at this. I have let go, but the plastic hasn't let go this time. Friction did change something on the plastic: something so tiny that it is invisible. That thing is part of everything; even part of us. It is a kind of electricity that usually stays still. It is called static electricity." The number of ideas children already have about static electricity may be surprising. Listen to their comments.

Give the children their own pieces of plastic to try. A sample of nylon carpeting, or garments that the children are wearing can be good sources of synthetic fiber to rub against the plastic.

"Static electricity is part of everything, but we don't notice it until friction charges it and it moves a bit. You can have fun using friction to make some little things jump with the static charge."

Concept: Friction Builds Static Electricity on some Things

---

1. Can We Build Up Static Electricity to Make Things Move?

LEARNING OBJECTIVE: To observe the effects of static electricity charges on noncharged materials.

MATERIALS:

Clear, flat plastic boxes

Tissue paper

Combs (plastic or nylon)

Small pieces of cotton thread

Scraps of wool, fur, silk, or nylon

SMALL GROUP ACTIVITY:

1. Ask children to tear up tissue paper into rice-size bits. Put some in the boxes.
2. "Let's rub a box top with a bit of fabric very fast. The friction can make static electricity move. It's called building a charge. Watch the bits of paper. They move when the static charge moves."
3. Suggest turning boxes over after tissue bits jump

FIGURE 16

and cling to the top. Try to build a charge on the bottom.

4. "Now try to build a charge on the comb with the fabric. Hold it near the thread. What happens? Did the thread jump when the static charge jumped?"

5. "Hold the charged comb near your hair. Does some hair move with the moving electricity?"

2. Can Static Electricity Make Things Stick Together or Push Away?

LEARNING OBJECTIVE: To observe the clinging effect of unlike-charged materials and the repelling effect of like-charged materials.

MATERIALS:

Styrofoam meat trays

Small, long balloons

Wool, silk, or fur

String

GETTING READY:

Mark children's initials on balloons with felt-tip pens.

Tie a foot of string to each of two balloons.

SMALL GROUP ACTIVITY:

1. "Will this tray stick to a wall by itself? Find out." It won't.

2. "Let's see if static electricity will help." Rub fabric very fast on tray underside to build up a static charge. "Now will it stick to the wall?"

3. Carefully build a charge on balloons. Will they stick to the walls?

4. Now build a charge on string-tied balloons. Holding by string, bring charged sides of balloons together. (Bits of fiber stick to charged sides of balloons.) Do they cling together, or push each other apart?

Did this remind someone of the way like ends of magnets push away, and unlike ends cling? There are negative and positive electrical charges. Like charges push apart, unlike charges cling.

Concept: Static Electricity Makes a Spark When it Jumps

1. Can We Make a Tiny Lightning Flash?

LEARNING OBJECTIVE: To begin to understand the nature of lightning.

Introduction: "Let's see if we can make a tiny lightning flash in our dark place. We'll pretend that balloons are storm clouds full of water. Water drops rub together in a storm cloud to build up a big charge of static electricity."

MATERIALS:

Small, long balloons

SMALL GROUP ACTIVITY:

1. Show children how to stroke the balloons on the

Small wool or nylon rug, or carpet sample

Heavy blanket, table

GETTING READY:

Drape table with the blanket to make a very dark place.

Place rug on the floor under the table.

Blow up balloons.

rug to build the static charge. Count 20 strokes with them.

2. "Now pretend my finger is another cloud or the earth. I'll bring the charged balloon close to it. Watch! Listen! Did you see the spark jump to my finger? Now you try it."

Group Discussion: "You can make a tiny lightning flash at home in a room that is almost dark. Scuffle your feet on a wool or nylon rug, then touch something metal. You can feel, hear, and see a small charge of static electricity jump from yourself to the metal.

"A small static spark like this is not dangerous, but lightning from storm clouds is very powerful. That is why we take shelter in a building or a car during an electrical storm."

Part 2: Current Electricity

Group Discussion: Use an air pump, a flashlight battery, and the simple circuit materials to introduce the topic of current electricity. Show the children the air pump. "Do you

remember how we used the pump to push air into the bags (innertube, air mattress)? Does the pump make the air? No, it pushes along the air that comes into it through this air hole."

Show the battery and dry cell. "These things also push along something we can't see." Some children will recognize them as batteries that make flashlights shine and electrical toys work. "Batteries don't *make* electricity. They push the electricity that is already in something to make it flow along. When it moves we call it electric current. It flows through wires in a special way. Small batteries like these can push only a small amount of electricity through the wires, so it is safe enough for children to touch. *The electricity that is pumped by giant generators into wires for houses and schools is so powerful that it is too dangerous for people to touch.* If the powerful electricity does not move through the wires the right way, it can burn things, or very badly hurt people who touch it."

Children can find out how to make a safe amount of electricity flow through the wires to make a tiny light shine.

Concept: Current Electricity Travels in a Loop

---

1. Can We Complete a Simple Circuit?

LEARNING OBJECTIVE: To find out with safe materials that electric current only moves in a complete loop.

"Current electricity can move only in a loop pathway. You can find out what this means by trying to light a small bulb."

MATERIALS:

For two children at a time:

#6 dry cell (1½ volts)

Insulated copper wire

1½ volt light bulb

1½ volt socket

2 tiny screwdrivers

GETTING READY:

Cut wire 12" long.

Cut and peel off ½" of insulation from each end of wires.

Bend exposed wire into hooks, by folding around a pencil tip.

SMALL GROUP ACTIVITY:

1. Have materials for one circuit out. Show the children how to loosen a dry cell terminal cap, hook end of wire beneath it, and tighten the cap.

2. Loosen (don't remove) a socket screw, hook other end of the wire around it and tighten it.

3. "The light didn't go on yet. Did we make a complete loop for electricity to move on? It has to flow from the dry cell, through the light socket, back to the dry cell. Can one of you complete the loop to make the light go on?"

4. Later ask if children can find ways to turn the light off.

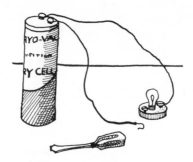

FIGURE 17

With a finger, trace the path of the completed circuit. Start at one terminal, follow the wire to the socket. Remove the bulb to show the metal pathway in the socket. Follow the second wire back to the dry cell. Have the children trace the path.

Explain that if a wire or piece of metal touches both terminals on top of the dry cell, the current will travel in just that small loop, and it would use up all the power too fast. The dry cell could not be used to make the lights shine after that. No metal or wire should ever touch both terminals. Try to keep the equipment available for children to return to many times.

2. How Does a Switch Stop Moving Electricity?

LEARNING OBJECTIVE: To find ways with safe materials to complete and break an electric circuit.

MATERIALS:

#6 dry cell

Insulated copper wire

1½ volt light bulb

1½ volt socket

2 tiny screwdrivers

Knife switch

Desirable:

Flashlight

Wall switch and cover

GETTING READY:

Cut a 6" piece of wire, trim away insulation, and bend ends into hooks.

SMALL GROUP ACTIVITY:

1. Let children complete a simple circuit.
2. "How are lights turned on at home? Right! With a switch." Show how the knife switch opens to make a gap in its metal pathway and closes to complete it.
3. "Can you find a way to add the switch and a new wire to the completed circuit?"
4. "Is there a complete loop for electricity to move through with the handle down? What happens to the light when the handle is up?"

Let the children open and examine the parts of the flashlight. The metal case takes the place of wires to make a pathway. Compare the wall switch parts with those of the knife switch. Could it work in the same way to complete and break the circuit?

Group Discussion: The Instructor Primary Science Concept Charts on Electricity provide leads for discussing how the circuits were made and how the switch works. Show the children an extension cord. How many wires does it have side by side? Look at the two prongs on one end, two holes on the other end. Why are two wires needed? Would electricity flow if the extension cord were plugged into itself? What is missing? Children must never play with electrical outlets. Why?

Concept: Current Electricity Does Not Move through Some Things

1. Which Materials Let Current Electricity Pass Through, Which Do Not?

LEARNING OBJECTIVE: To discover with safe materials which materials conduct electricity.

MATERIALS:

#6 dry cell

1½ volt socket and bulb

Electrical wire

SMALL GROUP ACTIVITY:

1. Let children set up a switch circuit, winding exposed ends of two wires around the two nails instead of connecting to a switch.
2. Is electricity moving to make the light shine? Why not?

Roofing nails, or large head tacks

Small blocks of wood

Test materials: string, rubber bands, sticks, long nails, keys, plastic spoon, 1″ tile squares, stones, leather, glass, paper clips, paper

Desirable:

Glass or ceramic insulator

Trays or box lids

GETTING READY:

Hammer 2 nails an inch apart into blocks of wood.

Label the trays: yes, no.

3. "Will the circle pathway be complete if a key lies across the two nail heads? Try it. Put the key on the yes tray, see if electricity moves through it."

4. Let children try placing other materials across the space between the two nail heads to discover which things let electricity pass, which do not. Use terms: conductor, insulator.

5. Change one wire, using a new wire with the insulation still covering the end. Does electricity pass through, even though the circuit looks complete? Why not?

Group Discussion: "It is important to know about two other things that electricity can flow through: people and water. We must never touch a light switch when we have wet hands, or when we are standing on a wet floor, or in the bathtub. If a wire were loose inside the switch, powerful electricity would pass from the wire through the wet person. That is also why lifeguards tell swimmers to come out of the water when an electrical storm starts."

Primary Reinforcements

Music (References found in Appendix 1)

Try singing about static electricity:

The Static Song
[To the tune of "I'm A Little Teapot" (4)]

When we scuff a rug with feet so quick,
We touch some metal and get a prick.
If we do the same thing in the dark,
When static jumps, we see a spark.

Stories and References for Children

Bradbury, Ray. *Switch on the Night*. New York: Pantheon Books, 1955. Children can point out the lights that are electric, those that are not.

Branley, Franklyn, and Vaughan, Eleanor. *Rusty Rings A Bell*. New York: Thomas Y. Crowell, 1957.

Scarry, Richard. *What Do People Do All Day?* New York: Random House, 1968. Electricians are installing an electric circuit in a new house. Safety features can be seen. The continuous pathway of wires running behind walls is well illustrated.

Schneider, Herman and Nina. *How Big is Big? From Stars to Atoms.* New York: William R. Scott, 1946.

Schwartz, Julius. *Now I Know.* New York: Whittlesey House, McGraw-Hill, 1955. Lightning is described in terms of the static that a child can build up scuffing his shoes on a rug.

————. *Magnify and Find Out Why.* New York: Scholastic Book Services, 1972. Suggests using a magnifying glass to see how coils of wire inside a light bulb heat up to make light when electric current passes through.

Zolotow, Charlotte. *The Storm Book.* Illustrations by Margaret Bloy Graham. New York: Harper & Row, 1952. The illustrations draw attention to the beauty of a summer storm. The text is more poetic than accurate in describing thunder and lightning. Suitable alterations should be made in reading this book aloud to children, so they will not confuse static and current electricity.

Three stories for children are illustrated with pictures of homes without electricity. The last one listed shows the homes of four generations of one family. Children are interested in noting the differences in kitchens and in lighting.

Sawyer, Ruth. *Journey Cake, Ho.* Seafarer ed. New York: Viking Press, 1970.

Ward, Lynd. *The Biggest Bear.* New York: Scholastic Book Services, 1975.

Zolotow, Charlotte. *The Sky Was Blue.* New York: Harper & Row, 1963.

Poems (References found in Appendix 1)

From *Poems To Grow On,* by Jean M. Thompson, read Dorothy Aldis's poem, "The Storm." Point out that lightning and thunder are part of the same event. We see the spark before we hear the vibration.

Fingerplay

Adapt a familiar fingerplay to include the children's new awareness of the biggest static spark of all:

This little girl	(Hold up right forefinger)
crawls into her bed.	(Place it on open left palm)
She pulls the covers	(Fold left fingers over palm)
over her head.	
She turns off the light	(Move left thumb down)
to sleep through the night.	
Till a loud thunder crash	
and a bright lightning flash,	
Make her jump out of bed	(Release right forefinger)
to watch static, instead .	

Art Activities

1. COLLAGE. Let children cut out and paste catalog pictures of electric appliances to make a "We Use Electricity" collage.

2. WIRE ART. Heavy telephone cables consist of bundles of copper wires coated with insulation of varied, attractive colors. Telephone repairmen can give you discarded lengths of cable. Twelve inch lengths of wire are easy for children

to work with. Pull out wires from the bundle as needed. Discuss the nature of the material as you give it to the children. Let them use it for:

A. Lacing or weaving: through pieces of wire screen or burlap.

B. Sculpture: as sculpture bases, either staple a loop of wire to scrap lumber, or let the children poke their wires into chunks of Styrofoam. (It is fairly easy to saw large pieces of molded foam packing material into usable sizes.) Show the children a few techniques, such as winding wire around a crayon to make a spiral, or threading other materials—paper or foam chips—onto the wires.

Dramatic Play

1. A flashlight can now be added to medical play, camping play, or service station play.

2. Let the children help you convert a cardboard carton into a table top "control panel" for their imaginative play. Use the knife switch and light on the outside of the box, attaching them to wires poked through the box to connect with the dry cell inside. Draw dials and gauges on the outside of the box, add a paper plate wheel.

3. Wire a shoebox doll house by cutting doors and windows in the sides of a shoebox. Put two wires through small holes in the box top, connect them to the dry cell and the light bulb socket to make a ceiling light. Children enjoy making furniture for the house from egg carton sections, and dolls from clothespins and pipecleaners.

Food Experience

A toaster provides a safe vantage point from which to observe and use electricity in a food experience for young children. The children can help to prepare buttered toast for a snack or for lunch, while they see what happens when electricity passes through a special kind of wire. The glowing wires are held in place with insulators. Can the children see them? Check the safety of using the toaster in your room beforehand.

Thinking Games

Play a "What If?" game to think about the many ways we depend upon electric power. "What if we couldn't use any electricity tomorrow? How would we start the day? Would an electric alarm clock wake us up? . . ." Follow through the day as the children know it. What can they do to use electricity conservatively?

Field Trips

Two simple field trips can extend young children's information about using electric power, at their level of understanding.

1. Ask a hardware store manager if he would show children electrical fittings such as switches, receptacles, and light sockets. He could point out where two

wires must be connected to let the current pass through and where light bulbs must touch sockets to complete a circuit.

2. Walk to the utility pole nearest your school. Look for the insulators that keep the wires from touching the pole. If possible, follow the lines back to your building, checking to see if insulators are used where the wires might otherwise touch the building. If you should ever pass a telephone or electrical repair crew at work while walking with your children, stop to watch. Perhaps a repairman would be willing to show the children the equipment he wears on his belt, especially the rubber or plastic insulation on tool handles.

Secondary Reinforcements

Keeping Concepts Alive

Whenever you notice the effects of static electricity mention them to the children. "Did some of your hair seem to stand up when you were brushing it this morning? Mine did." The children will probably tell you why it happened. When you are ready to turn on a record player or a projector for use in school, ask what is needed to complete the circuit to make the electricity flow into the equipment. Talk about stormy weather when it occurs. "Were you awake during the storm last night? What did you see in the sky? Did you watch it a while? Did you remember how we made our tiny lightning sparks at school?"

Relating New Concepts to Existing Concepts

When the children are experimenting with static electricity charges, making unlike materials cling and like materials push away from each other, recall that the same ends of two magnets also pushed each other away, and the unlike ends pulled together. Magnetism is somewhat like electricity in this respect.

Parent Involvement

Parents can help their children look for things at home that use electricity. Suggest that they let their children watch the unloading of a clothes dryer. Do nylon synthetic garments cling to other things in the load? (They will unless a fabric softener was used.) Can the children hear crackling sounds when the clinging things are separated? If the area is not brightly lighted, perhaps tiny sparks can be seen when the static electricity jumps.

Parents can also let children watch when they change a lightbulb. They can discuss safe and conservative use of electricity.

References

Bonsall, George. *How and Why Wonder Book of Weather.* New York: Wonder Books, 1960.

Branley, Franklyn M. *Flash, Crash, Rumble and Roll.* New York: Thomas Y. Crowell, 1964.

Notkin, Jerome, and Gulkin, Sidney. *The How and Why Wonder Book of Electricity.* New York: Wonder Books, 1960.

Pine, Tillie, and Levine, Joseph. *Friction All Around.* New York: Whittlesey House, McGraw-Hill, 1960.

Podendorf, Illa. *True Book of Magnets and Electricity.* Chicago: Childrens Press, 1972.

Shepherd, Walter. *Electricity.* New York: Golden Press, 1966.

CHARTS

Magnetism-Electricity. The Instructor Primary Science Concept Charts. Danville, New York: F. A. Owen Publishing, 1964. These charts will be meaningful to children who have tried to complete a circuit and experimented with the conducting properties of many materials.

12

Rocks and Minerals

". . . Oooooh! This one has shiny speckles!" "Look! This one is all little rocks joined up into one." "These three are a family." "Mine has a stripe all around and around." Children relish sifting through piles of rocks to find favorites. They are awed to hear that our earth is a giant ball of rock and that rocks can be millions of years old. Learning about the importance of rocks seems to promote feelings of security in youngsters, just as the Rock of Gibraltar symbolizes trust and stability to adults. Experiences in this chapter lead to the following concepts:

THERE ARE MANY KINDS OF ROCKS
ROCKS SLOWLY CHANGE BY WEARING AWAY
CRUMBLED ROCKS AND DEAD PLANTS MAKE SOIL
OLD PLANTS AND ANIMALS LEFT PRINTS IN ROCKS
MINERALS FORM CRYSTALS

An unstructured experience in washing and finding variety in ordinary highway gravel is suggested as a beginning activity. This is followed by classifying and hardness testing. Basic information is given about rock formation. Grinding soft rocks; breaking rocks open to compare the fresh surfaces with the worn exteriors; pulverizing rock to compare it with complete soil; and forming crystals complete the suggested experiences.

Introduction: Tuck a small rock into your hand, then comment quietly, "I have something quite small but very, very old in my hand. It is so old that it might have been here long before any people lived on earth, or even before the dinosaurs were alive. "Can you guess what it could be?" Slowly open your hand to reveal the humble, but now significant, rock.

Concept: There are Many Kinds of Rocks

Note: Children seem to be drawn to a material that is available in quantity for them to explore freely. A heaping dishpan of common rocks will have more durable appeal than a box of neatly labeled special rocks.

1. How Do Rocks Look Dry and Wet?

LEARNING OBJECTIVE: To notice and describe the appearance of a variety of rocks.

MATERIALS:

Bucketful of #67 washed gravel (builder's supply store)*

Dishpans, water

Few drops of detergent

Old newspapers under pans

Trays for clean rocks

Cleanup sponge

Smocks for children

GETTING READY:

Fill dishpans to ¼ depth with water.

SMALL GROUP ACTIVITY:

1. Invite the children to enjoy looking at and washing the rocks. "Do wet rocks look the same as they did when dry?" Listen to children's comments.
2. Leave the gravel out for children's independent use during unstructured times, if possible.

2. Can We Find Rocks That are Alike in Some Ways?

LEARNING OBJECTIVE: To group rocks into simple classes.

MATERIALS:

Bucketful of #67 washed gravel*

Sorting containers: egg cartons, margarine tubs, divided plastic snack trays, old muffin tins

SMALL GROUP ACTIVITY:

1. Suggest putting rocks that are alike in some way together in containers.
2. Classifying decisions are easy for many children to make: by color, size, shape, texture, pattern.
   If your group can't get started on their own, offer easy ideas: "Put the flat rocks here, put rocks that aren't flat there."

* 67 washed gravel consists of varied rocks (from old riverbeds) that range from almond to egg size. For school use, some building suppliers might give you a bucketful without charge. It is usually sold by the ton.

3. Which Rocks are Hard, Which are Softer?

LEARNING OBJECTIVE: To use hardness tests as the basis for grouping rocks.

MATERIALS:

#67 washed gravel

Blackboard chalk (pressed gypsum)

Pumice (inexpensive, from the drugstore)

Pennies with firm edges

Three trays or boxes

GETTING READY:

Make two labels: *soft* and *hard.*

Place trays next to each other. Put *soft* and *hard* labels in first and third boxes, leave middle box unlabeled.

SMALL GROUP ACTIVITY:

1. "Some rocks are soft enough for a fingernail to scratch them. Rocks just a bit harder can't be scratched that way, but a penny edge will scratch them."

2. Let children experiment with scratch tests. Suggest sorting rocks by degree of hardness:

   Put rocks scratched by your fingernail into tray marked *soft,* on the end.

   Put rocks scratched by penny into middle tray, between *hard* and *soft.*

   Put rocks that can't be scratched by a penny into the end tray marked *hard.*

If children find it hard to form three classes of rocks, simplify the experience to form two classifications of hardness: hard rocks, not scratched by a penny; and softer rocks, scratched by a penny. Make a separate activity to find soft rocks, scratched by a fingernail, and harder rocks, not scratched by a fingernail. Perhaps a teacher is wearing the hardest rock of all on her finger—a diamond (crystallized pure carbon).

Rock Formation

As children engage in the suggested experiences, they can be fed bits of simple information about the mineral content of rocks, and about the way rocks were (and are) formed.

Mineral Content

When children question the specks and streaks of color they see as they sort rocks, tell them that most rocks are mixtures of many kinds of material. The materials are called minerals. There are about 2,000 different minerals, but only about twenty minerals are abundant. Different mixtures of minerals make different kinds of rocks. (You might want to recall baking experiences with them. Talk about how sometimes the same materials are put together in different ways to make different things to eat. Cornbread and cookies are almost alike in ingredients.) Sometimes the mineral mixtures are easy to see as specks, sparkles, and stripes. Rocks may contain many different combinations of minerals.

Three Types of Rock Formation

1. IGNEOUS. Some rocks were once mixtures that melted deep inside the earth. When they cooled, they formed rocks.

2. SEDIMENTARY. Some rocks were formed in layers or parts, like a sandwich. Layers of sand, clay, and gravel were pressed together very hard at the bottom of old lakes, rivers, and oceans. Sometimes animal shells were mixed into the rock. It takes thousands of years of very hard pressure to form rocks this way. Some of our rocks have stripes of color or line marks in them. Some feel sandy. Some have tiny rocks stuck together. They were all made under pressure.

3. METAMORPHIC. Sometimes rocks that were already formed by pressure, or by the cooling of melted mixtures, were changed again by more heat and pressure. Thus changing the rocks into still different types.

Try to find out something about the rocks in your area, both the visible outcroppings and the rocks beneath the soil. Were rocks heaved up into mountains and hills in your areas millions of years ago? Did ancient rivers wear away rocks and carve out valleys? Mention this to the children when it seems a suitable time.

===
Concept: Rocks Slowly Change by Wearing Away
===
---

1. Can We Wear away Bits of Rock?

LEARNING OBJECTIVE: To acquire a beginning understanding of the ways rocks change.

Go outdoors for this experience. It's noisy and fun.

MATERIALS:

Pieces of soft, crumbly-looking rock (shale, soft sandstone)

Tin cans with lids: coffee cans, large tobacco cans, cocoa tins

SMALL GROUP ACTIVITY:

1. Put several soft rocks in each can. Ask children to feel the rocks. Cover the cans tightly. Let children hold them tightly and shake them as long and as hard as they can. Open cans. "Has anything changed? Is there dusty stuff at the bottom?"

2. If this must be an indoor activity, try briskly rubbing two crumbly rocks together over a piece of white paper.

Children really like being able to change something through their own vigorous efforts.

Group Discussion: Talk about the results of the rock shaking activity in terms of wearing away pieces of rock. Look together at the edges of the smoothest pebble you can find, and the edges of a freshly broken rock. (One you have broken open with a hammer.) Encourage children who have visited natural beaches to recall whether they found smooth pebbles or jagged rocks on the sand. Talk of how pieces of rock break from large rocks; how waves tumble the rocks against each other and smooth them;

how sand bits are rubbed off. If there are nearby rock formations with which children are familiar, speak of how they were slowly changed and worn by winds or running streams of water.

2. Can We Draw with Rocks?

LEARNING OBJECTIVE: To apply the idea that bits of rock wear away.

(Small or whole group, as circumstances permit.)

If there is a safe sidewalk area where this activity can be performed, give children assorted soft rocks to use for outdoor sidewalk art. Mention that cavemen made pictures on rock walls with soft rocks of different colors.

Later show the children two other rocks we use for writing: pencil "lead" (graphite) and blackboard chalk (pressed gypsum). They make marks because they are so soft that worn-away bits are left on the paper as the drawing or writing we see.

Does your schoolroom have an old-fashioned real slate blackboard to draw on? (Slate is a metamorphic rock.) Perhaps you can buy an inexpensive one in the dime store. Slabs of slate can sometimes be found in salvage stores, after wrecking crews have taken off old slate roofs. (They are fine to use under flowerpots on the windowsill, after the writing experience is over.)

3. Do Rocks Look Differently on the Inside?

LEARNING OBJECTIVE: To discover firsthand that weathering changes the outside appearance of rocks.

MATERIALS:

Rocks

Old heavy cloth

Hammer

Safe sidewalk area

SMALL GROUP ACTIVITY (Do on a sidewalk):

1. Cover a rock with the cloth. Strike it hard with the hammer. (Children experienced with hammers can do this successfully. A two-handed grip may help.) Very hard round rocks may not split well. Other rocks will split with one hammer blow.
2. Enjoy examining the inside; compare it with the outside appearance.

Note: This is a very exciting activity, that may lead to rock fever! What will be found inside a rock: the glint of mica flakes, a streak of mineral, a sleek surface? The worn outside surface of the rock was once the same color and texture as the inside—before wind, rain, or temperature changes weathered the outside.

Concept: Crumbled Rocks and Dead Plants Make Soil

1. What Happens When We Pound Soft Rocks?

LEARNING OBJECTIVE: To develop a beginning awareness of soil formation.

MATERIALS:

Pieces of crumbly rock (shale, soft sandstone, etc.)

Heavy paper bags

Hammers

Newspapers

Sieve

Empty can

SMALL GROUP ACTIVITY:

1. Put one bag inside another. Put a few rocks in the bags, place on sidewalk. Let children take turns pounding rocks, checking results often.
2. Spread newspaper on the ground. Fit sieve over the can. Shake contents of bags into sieve, catching spills on newspaper.
3. Keep pulverizing until bags are tattered, and children are tired.
4. Examine the powdered rock in the can, save for the next experience.

2. What Does Soil Look Like?

LEARNING OBJECTIVE: To develop an awareness of soil composition.

MATERIALS:

Trowel

SMALL GROUP ACTIVITY:

1. Let children scoop up a trowelful of soil in a

Container

Newspapers

Top soil

Sieve, sticks

Magnifying glasses

Container of pulverized rock
from previous experience

2 paper cups

Water

2. Spread the soil on newspapers, examine with
   magnifying glass. Compare with rock pulverized
   by children.
3. Put soil through sieve. Good topsoil contains bits
   of leaves, twigs, roots, and worms. Some of this
   matter will be left in the sieve.
4. Put some sifted soil and powdered rock in separate
   cups. Stir a bit of water into each. Compare.

Note: Clay is like the moist powdered rock. It must have lots of old vegetable and
animal matter, and perhaps sand, added to it to make good soil for growing things.

Concept: Old Plants and Animals Left Prints in Rocks

Surprisingly young children show interest in dinosaurs, thanks to television cartoons.
However some have the confused idea that dinosaurs and cave men existed on earth
at the same time. This notion can be clarified by reading *My Visit to the Dinosaurs,* by
Aliki. Recall splitting rocks open to find unexpected color, sparkle, and texture inside.
Add that prints of animals, shells, and plants that lived on earth millions of years before
people did can be found pressed between layers of rocks. These rocks are called *fossils.*
(Perhaps there are some fossils in the bucket of highway gravel that the children have been
using.)

Children can have fun making prints of their hands, shells, or leaves, using the kind
of powdered stone that became clay. They can make prints similar to fossils, though they
won't be as old or as hard as fossils.

1. Can We Make a "Fossil" Print?

LEARNING OBJECTIVE: To become aware of one way that fossils are formed.

Let children roll out moist clay slabs about $1/4''$ thick with small rolling pins. Show
them how to press a leaf, shell, or their hand firmly into the clay. It may take several
tries to get a clear print. "Erase" unsatisfactory leaf prints by rubbing clay with water
and lightly re-rolling. Cut the slab into a plaque shape with an empty coffee can as a
cutter. Poke a hole through the top of the slab for a hanging loop of string. Scratch
child's initials in the clay. Allow several drying days. Teacher may shellac the dried
clay to preserve it, if desired.

Concept: Minerals Form Crystals

Do this after children understand evaporation.

   Introduction: Look together at some mineral crystals: a diamond or other precious stone jewelry; the rocks you cracked open to reveal glittering bits of mica or quartz crystals; or some large or small salt crystals. Say that when minerals are dissolved in liquid which evaporates, or when they melt and cool slowly, they form into *crystals*. Each type of mineral forms into its own special crystal pattern. "We can try to dissolve a mineral in liquid that will evaporate to leave pretty, powdery crystals."

1. Will Crystals Form on Coal?

LEARNING OBJECTIVE: To observe the formation of crystals.

MATERIALS:

Coal, broken into small chunks (charcoal briquettes may be used)

Glass pie pan, or low ceramic bowl

Old tablespoon

Pint jar for mixing

4 tablespoons *plain* salt

4 tablespoons water

2 tablespoons *clear* household ammonia*

4 tablespoons laundry bluing

Food coloring in squeeze bottles

GETTING READY:

Spread newspapers on work area.

Have smocks for children.

* Keep ammonia bottle tightly capped until needed. Open well away from face. *Keep out of the reach of children.*

SMALL GROUP ACTIVITY:

1. Heap chunks of coal (a rock, by the way) in pie pan.
2. Let children take turns measuring salt and water.
3. *Warn children* to stand away from table when ammonia is opened, and to hold their noses. *Adult measures ammonia* and bluing (it stains). Mix all ingredients in jar until salt is dissolved.
4. Slowly pour mixture over coal pieces to saturate. Let children sprinkle drops of food coloring in separate areas on the coal.
5. Place dish where it can be observed, but not disturbed.

Crystals may begin to form on the coal within a few hours, and may continue to form for several days. The dissolved minerals move to the surface of the coal as the liquid evaporates and the mineral residue forms crystals. Liquid will continue to move to the surface of the newly formed crystals to form crystals on top of crystals. Some children may think they are growing as a plant grows. Point out that minerals can change, but only living things grow.

2. Will Crystals Form from Salty Water?

LEARNING OBJECTIVE: To observe the formation of crystals.

(Here is a surprise for children: we eat bits of one kind of rock every day!)

MATERIALS: SMALL GROUP ACTIVITY:

2 tablespoons rock salt (halite)   1. Pour hot water into the pint jar. Let children
                                              measure rock salt into water, stirring, until dis-
1 cup hot water   solved.

Glass pint jar   2. Tie string around the pencil. Place it across the
                                              jar top so the string dangles in the salt solution.
String
                                          3. Place jar on a sunny windowsill. Check the next
Pencil   day for beginning crystal formation. Look at the
                                              underside of the pencil. Watch for several days.

READ: *Greg's Microscope*, by Milicent Selsam. If you have access to a simple microscope
(40X will do) follow Greg's method for forming salt crystal. Through the microscope tiny
crystals can be seen as perfect, sparkling cubes.

Primary Reinforcements

Music (References found in Appendix 1)

1. A familiar folk song can be easily adapted to help children remember that
mountains are rock formations:

"The Bear Went Over the Mountain":
Substitute ". . . But all that he could see, was the rocky
        part of the mountain."

                    for

". . . But all that he could see, was the other part of the
mountain."

You could mention that some mountains are covered with soil and growing
things, and other mountains are bare rock on top.

2. Listen to: "What's Inside Our Earth?" sung by Tom Glazer on the recording, *Now We Know (Songs To Learn By)*.

Math Experiences

1. COUNTING. The Grab Bag Game may be played with stones: place a
container of stones in the center of a circle of children. Let them take turns reach-
ing in to scoop out as many stones as they can hold in two hands, then count the
results. Keep score with an abacus, a numbered spinner, or make dice from 4"

squares of cardboard to determine how many rocks players win.

2. BURIED TREASURE. If a sandbox is available, bury a specific number of stones (or stones and shells, if you wish to include classifying) for children to hunt. A large sandbox may be "staked out" with string as separate territories for several children to use amiably.

3. COUNTING CANS. Mark numerals from 1 to 10 or more on the sides of low tin cans. Line up the cans in order on a table or shelf. Place a coffee can full of gravel beside them for independent counting of appropriate quantities of stones to put in numbered cans.

4. ORDERING. Search through the bucket of gravel to find stones of conspicuously different sizes. Place them in a paper bag. Pass the bag among the children so they can shut their eyes to choose a stone. Allow time for much fingering and feeling in choice making. Ask for the smallest stone of all. Next ask children to compare their stones with the smallest one to find the stone just a bit larger to put next to it. Build up to the largest stone. Older children who have had experience measuring with rulers could use them for this activity. Suggest ordering rocks according to texture, from smoothest to roughest; and to color, from lightest to darkest.

5. WEIGHING. Keep two coffee cans full of stones near the classroom balance for casual use by the children.

Stories and References for Children

Aliki. *My Visit to the Dinosaurs*. New York: Thomas Y. Crowell, 1972. A child's reaction to a natural history museum visit. Facts about fossil formation.

Baylor, Byrd. *Everybody Needs A Rock*. New York: Charles Scribner's Sons, 1974. A young child's view of rock hunting.

Bradfield, Roger. *Hello, Rock*. Racine, Wis.: Western Publishing, 1965. A small boy's appreciation for his rock that becomes a special gift.

Cole, Joanna. *Dinosaur Story*. New York: Scholastic Book Services, 1974. Read selectively to young children.

Hoban, Russell. *Baby Sister for Frances*. New York: Harper & Row, 1964. Frances keeps her collection of gravel in a can and uses it as a noisemaker.

————. *Nothing To Do*. New York: Scholastic Book Services, 1969. Father gives Walter a stone, polished smooth by the river, calling it a magic something-to-do stone.

Kinney, Jean. *What Does The Sun Do?* New York: Young Scott Books, 1967. A child takes shelter from the rain in a rock-ledge cave in this desert locale story.

Koch, Dorothy. *Up The Big Mountain*. New York: Holiday House, 1964. Two children collect rocks as souvenirs of their mountain climb.

Lobel, Arnold. *Frog and Toad Together*. New York: Harper & Row, 1972. In the story, "Dragons and Giants," Frog and Toad climb a mountain; run from an avalanche of rocks; and take shelter beside a rock.

McGovern, Ann. *Stone Soup*. New York: Scholastic Book Services, 1971. A stone and some fast talk win food and shelter for hungry travelers in this retold folk tale.

Meek, Pauline P. *The Hiding Place*. Racine, Wis.: Western Publishing, 1971. A young child needs a new hiding hole for his treasured rock and marbles when he moves to a new apartment. Stone steps and buildings can be seen in the illustrations of city life.

Podendorf, Illa. *The True Book of Pebbles and Shells.* Chicago: Childrens Press, 1972. Simple statements about the three ways rocks are formed and how rocks change into smooth pebbles.

————. *The True Book of Rocks and Minerals.* Chicago: Childrens Press, 1972.

Schwartz, Julius. *Magnify and Find Out Why.* New York: Scholastic Book Services, 1972. Sand, soil, and salt are some of the materials discussed and seen through the magnifying lense.

Selsam, Milicent. *Greg's Microscope.* New York: Harper & Row, 1963.

White, Anne Terry. *Rocks All Around Us.* New York: Scholastic Book Services, 1959. Portions of this book for older children can be read aloud to young ones.

Wyler, Rose, and Ames, Gerald. *Secrets in Stones.* New York: Four Winds Press, Scholastic Magazines, 1970. This child-oriented book starts with what a child can see and find, then explains how rocks or formations came into being. A good reference book for younger children; a readable guide book for older children.

When rock formations are used in illustrations of other children's stories, point them out. *The Biggest Bear,* by Lynd Ward, and *One Morning In Maine* and *Blueberries For Sal,* both by Robert McCloskey, have nicely illustrated rocky settings. (See Appendix 1.)

Poems (References found in Appendix 1)

Read three profound lines (from "Rocks," by Florence Parry Heide, in *Poems Children Sit Still For)* to children who have been wearing away sand from sandstones.

Read this poem with a box of your favorite rocks at hand:

My Rocks

Here in this box
I keep my rocks.
They came from under the ground.
Some are striped, some are plain,
Some are tiny as a grain.
My favorite is round!

Art Activities

1. ROCK SCULPTURE. Let children create additive sculpture by joining rocks of assorted sizes, using white glue. The resulting sculpture forms may be painted with tempera. Sculptures that have been coated with shellac (adult work) can be used as paperweights. Older children enjoy trying to create fantasy by gluing dyed aquarium stones, seeds, and tiny shells to their sculptures.

2. ROCK OR SAND COLLAGE. Small stones, painted if desired, can be

glued in patterns onto heavy cardboard. Color sand by shaking it in a tightly covered jar with dry tempera paint. Punch nail holes in the lids to make sand shakers. Let the children paint swirls of diluted white glue on construction paper, using cotton swabs, then sprinkle colored sand over the glue patterns. Surplus sand can be tipped onto a small tray and reused.

3. CHALK DRAWINGS. When children use chalk as an art medium, recall that the chalk material was once a rock.

4. PLAYDOUGH. Let children help mix playdough using: 1 cup salt, 2 cups flour, 2 tablespoons salad oil, about ½ cup water, and dry tempera paint as desired. Talk about the gritty feeling that the salt produces when the dough is newly mixed; the smooth texture that results after thorough blending and kneading with flour and water.

5. ROCKS AS RAW MATERIALS FOR CRAFTS. A box of small rocks is a good design resource for children's projects. Maria was inspired by two black, curved rocks to create a hand puppet from an upended paper cup and much scotch tape. The rocks became ears, two round rocks became eyes, and a red-crayoned slash was the mouth of the puppet that entertained Maria and her friends.

Dramatic Play

Introduce rocks as a play material in the indoor or outdoor sandbox. Rocks can be formed in lines to make the floor plan of a house. They can also be piled up to make furniture, and sticks or clothespins can become the people who live in the house. Lines of rocks can also outline highways for toy cars to travel through sand-table dunes and deserts. In addition, children find relaxed enjoyment using sifters to separate the rocks from the sand at cleanup time.

Food Experiences

Children are surprised to find that we eat small amounts of one kind of rock every day—salt! Show them some rock salt if available. Mention that all the salt that is mined under the ground was once part of ancient oceans.

Another link between food and rocks is the use of rocks to grind seeds into meal and grain. Perhaps you can find a bag of stone-ground flour or cornmeal in a fancy foods shop. A student teacher let fascinated children grind dried corn between two rocks as part of a study of American Indians.

Field Trips

Walk around the school neighborhood to look for rocks in their natural setting; rocks that have been cut for use in buildings; and products made from rocks and minerals. Look closely at the natural rock for signs of weathering, such as cracks or surfaces worn smooth by years of exposure to heat, cold, wind, and rain. Young children personalize familiar rocks according to the events they associate with them: our picnic rock; our sitting-on rock; our storytime rock; the where-we-found-the-turtle rock. Use the special rock names when you can.

Look for old stone steps or stone curbings that have been worn down into sloping shapes by thousands of feet treading upon them. Look for monuments; stone walls; stone windowsills in old brick buildings; and flagstone or crushed limestone paths.

Man-made materials containing rocks and minerals are everywhere: concrete or blacktop playground surfacings contain coarse or fine gravel bonded together with concrete or asphalt, both of which derive from rocks. Cement blocks, bricks, tiles, terazzo flooring, porcelain sinks, glass, iron railings, steel slides, and fences around school playgrounds are made with rock or mineral raw materials. No school is without structures of this sort to visit. Talking about these strong, solid parts of their environment seems to contribute to children's feelings of security.

Creative Movement

Take a rock walk. Children enjoy moving in a circle, interpreting movement suggestions, and following the rhythm of the teacher's drumbeats or clapping. Adult participation in the activity encourages the involvement of children. Suggest ways to move in a story form such as this: "Let's go for a rock walk. Let's pretend to be barefooted. We'll start on this gravel path. Oh! It's *hard* to put our feet down on the broken rocks. We'll have to move quickly and lightly to the end of the path. Step . . . step . . . step . . . step. There, that's better. We've come to a sandy place. Let's scuffle our feet in the sand. Scuffle . . . scuffle . . . push up little piles of sand with each step. Oh look, we've come to a wet place where we have to walk on moss-covered rocks. They are so slippery to walk on, let's move very carefully with each step . . . step . . . step. Look at that huge rock. Let's try to climb it, bending way over to hold on with our hands . . . climb . . . climb . . . slowly, slowly. Now we're at the top. Let's run down the other side to the beach ahead. Run, run, run to the sandy beach. But this sand is *hot* from the sunshine. We can't move slowly here: Let's move quickly down to the edge of the water to cool our poor feet. Now let's sit down to rest."

Secondary Reinforcements

Keeping Concepts Alive

Since rocks and minerals are so commonplace, the topic would become tedious if reference were made to them at every opportunity. Do mention rocks when something a bit different prompts a comment, "Is Lynn wearing a very special rock in her bracelet today? Tell us about it." Bring interesting rocks to share with the children whenever you come across one. Talk about its texture, color, or whatever appeals to you. The children will respond similarly with their favorites when they know of your appreciation of rocks.

Relating New Concepts to Existing Concepts

The inclusion of rocks as a material for experimentation is suggested for the topics of water, electricity, and the effects of gravity. It could be pointed out in discussing the effects of magnetism that the original source of magnetic material is a rock called lodestone (magnetite).

The tie between soil formation and growing things is an easy relationship to mention. Wet sand is sometimes used as a growing medium for rooting stems such as begonias or pineapple tops. The powdered rock made when children pounded soft rocks could be used in a seed germinating experience, comparing results with seeds growing in more complete soil.

An ecosystem can be experienced if the school playground has both deciduous shade trees and a sunny place for a small garden. Perhaps the local agricultural extension agent could talk to the children about making compost to enrich the soil, or adding a mineral (like powdered limestone) or sand to improve the soil that the plants will grow in. After a crop of radishes or lettuce is raised and harvested, children could put discarded leaves on the compost pile to contribute to the following year's soil enrichment process.

Parent Involvement

Invite parents to share special rocks or fossils with the class. Masking tape name labels are helpful for insuring the safe return of borrowed rocks. Suggest that they point out to their children areas of rock exposed to highway construction, or special rocks that are landmarks in the area. Win the hearts of mothers by forewarning them to check the pockets of their children's jackets and jeans before laundering them, once the children's interest in rocks has been whetted.

References

Cooper, Elizabeth K. *Science in Your Own Backyard.* New York: Harcourt, Brace, 1960. Soil, rocks, and fossils are discussed in this excellent book.

Evans, Eva Knox. *The Adventure Book of Rocks.* New York: Capitol Publishing, 1955.

Fenton, Carroll, and Fenton, Mildred. *Riches From the Earth.* New York: John Day, 1970. Clear descriptions of rocks and our dependence on them.

Shaffer, Paul. *The Golden Stamp Book of Rocks and Minerals.* Racine, Wis.: Western Publishing, 1968. Abbreviated informative descriptions of rocks and minerals.

Shuttlesworth, Dorothy. *The Story of Rocks.* Garden City, N.Y.: Doubleday & Co., 1966. Clear explanations of rock formation.

Sutton, Felix. *The How and Why Wonder Book of Our Earth.* New York: Wonder Books, 1960.

White, Anne Terry. *Rocks All Around Us.* New York: Scholastic Book Services, 1959. Places special emphasis upon the importance of rocks and minerals in our lives.

Wyler, Rose. *Exploring Earth Science.* Racine, Wis.: Western Publishing, 1973. Sections of this book on rocks, sand, and soil could be read to young children. Suggestions for experiments and collections.

Zim, Herbert, and Shaffer, Paul. *Rocks and Minerals.* New York: Golden Press, 1957. Comprehensive pocket guide for serious rock collectors.

13

Plant Life

They feed us, clothe us, shelter us, purify the air we breathe, and fill our visual world with beauty: the living things called plants. Children may be captivated by towering giant plants, or the tiniest weed blossoms underfoot. When we share their delight, we renew our own appreciation of nature's exquisite order. These plant life concepts will be explored:

THERE ARE MANY KINDS OF PLANTS: EACH HAS ITS OWN FORM
MOST PLANTS MAKE SEEDS FOR NEW PLANTS
SEEDS GROW INTO PLANTS WITH ROOTS, STEMS, LEAVES, AND FLOWERS
MOST PLANTS NEED WATER, LIGHT, MINERALS, WARMTH AND AIR
SOME PLANTS GROW FROM ROOTS AND STEMS
SOME PLANTS DO NOT HAVE SEEDS OR ROOTS
MANY FOODS WE EAT COME FROM SEEDS AND PLANTS

The first suggested experience will be limited by climate to areas where deciduous trees grow. The next group of activities calls for gathering natural materials. This may require the ingenuity of teachers in urban schools. (These teachers will find inspiration for the task by reading Ruth Howell's book, *A Crack in the Pavement.*) The concluding experiences with seeds and plant growing should be possible anywhere. Suggestions for seedling care and for transplanting are included.

Concept: There are Many Kinds of Plants: Each Has Its Own Form

1. Do the Parts of Different Plants Look Different?

LEARNING OBJECTIVE: To observe and describe similarities and differences in the leaves, bark, and flowers of different plant sources.

(Do this after a walk to collect nature materials.)

MATERIALS:

Large collecting bag full of found items such as:

Leaves (2 or 3 of each kind)

Tall grasses (include seeds or blossoms)

Flowers

Twigs

Bark

Seed pods, nuts

Mosses, lichen

Paper lunch bags

GETTING READY:

Sort the found materials.

Fill a teacher's bag with one of each kind of item.

Distribute an assortment of materials into small bags for the children.

Place a closed bag at each place at the science table.

SMALL GROUP ACTIVITY:

1. Take one object from your bag. "Look into your bags to see if you can find a leaf that just matches this one."

2. As children find similar items to compare, encourage them to notice details: "Is it just like mine? Are the tips of your leaf rounded like this one? It almost matches. Who found one with rounded tips?" (Children may have lots of information about plants already. Listen.)

3. Point out that all leaves from the same kind of tree have the same general shape. (Size and fall coloration may vary.) For example: "All sweet gum tree leaves have five points if they have finished growing. That's one way to know it is a sweet gum tree."

Note: Children may want to enjoy this activity several times. If you save the materials for a few days, check their condition before setting up the activity. Some leaves may crumble after being indoors a while; materials that were damp when collected may mildew unless they are spread out to dry.

2. How Do some Plants Rest for Winter?

LEARNING OBJECTIVE: To observe and describe seasonal changes in trees and shrubs.

MATERIALS:

Shopping bag

SMALL GROUP ACTIVITY:

1. When deciduous trees start to change color, take

Old, thick catalog

Newspaper

Waxed paper

Electric Iron

GETTING READY:

(Try to do this a week in advance. Save waxed leaves for another year.)

Get a good specimen leaf from each tree you plan to visit with the class.

Press leaves several days between newspaper, inserted into the catalog. Weight with the iron or bricks.

Fold waxed paper over each dried leaf. Press warm iron on paper to coat leaves with wax.

Tape to a low bulletin board. Label.

a tree trip. Have children circle a tree, holding hands. "What can you see above you? Below?" Repeat with an evergreen tree. (Old needles on the ground have been replaced by new ones, but not all at once.) Visit shrubs if trees are not within walking distance.

2. Supply these ideas, as needed:

    Leaves make food for trees to grow;

    Green stuff (chlorophyll) in leaves turns sunlight, water, minerals, and air into food;

    This work is finished for leaves on some trees when summer ends.

3. Gather leaves from the ground.

4. Let children put like kinds of leaves together when you get back. Ask them to try to match their finds with the mounted specimens. Encourage them to bring leaves from home to try to match them.

5. Save the surplus leaves for art activities or for compost.

Group Discussion: Recall the fun of collecting leaves. Ask what happens to the leaves from deciduous trees and shrubs that rest for winter. Introduce the idea that when chlorophyll goes out of these leaves, other colors that are also in the leaves show instead of only the green chlorophyll. (You might be able to find mottled leaves that fell before all the chlorophyll left.) Talk about how the leaves can still be valuable after they fall. If possible, start a compost bag or heap. See page 188.

Concept: Most Plants Make Seeds for New Plants

1. Are there Seeds in Fruit?

LEARNING OBJECTIVE: To become aware that most plants form seeds which may grow into new plants of the same type.

MATERIALS:

Any available seed pods: flower, tree, shrub, tall grass seed head.

SMALL GROUP ACTIVITY:

1. Show a seed pod. Open it. (Pods still attached to stalks are best.) Let children tell what they know about it. "Each kind of plant has a job to do: to

As many of these as can be brought in: apple, tomato, pomegranate, peach, ear of corn in husk, orange, squash, nuts in shells, cucumber, melon, squash, green beans, apricot, cucumber

Clean meat trays

Paring knife *(for adult use)*

Smocks

Newspapers

Nutcracker if needed

GETTING READY:

Wash fruits and vegetables.

Cover table with papers.

Hand washing for all participants.

Put out plants with seed pods at first, to minimize confusion.

make seeds for new plants just like it. Each plant forms seeds when its flowers stop blooming. Some seeds are protected by covers we like to eat. Let's try to find seeds inside these fruit and vegetable covers."

2. Take plenty of time to decide if seeds will be inside each fruit. Look at stems and blossom ends. Cut open, share tastes and sniffs with everyone.

3. Save melon and squash seeds. Later let children wash them, and dry them on trays. Save for bird feeding trays. If corn is fresh, pull back husks, hang to dry. Let children shell dried corn for the birds and for a spring sprouting project. Also, a whole dried husk can be tacked to a tree for the birds.

FIGURE 18

READ: *The Apricot ABC*, by Miska Miles. This is a lovely poem about the cycle from fruit, to tree sprout, to fruit. Try to read it without referring to the alphabet letters hidden in the charming illustrations. The story line can fade in importance when children concentrate on hunting for the letters.

2. How are Seeds Scattered?

LEARNING OBJECTIVE: To examine how different kinds of seeds are formed, thus enabling them to scatter.

An Indoor/Outdoor Activity

MATERIALS:

Locally available seeds from: garden plants; weeds (teasle, milkweed, burdock); grasses (wheat, oats); and trees (Ailanthus, locust, oak, pine (cones),* chestnut)

Magnifying glasses

Old fuzzy mittens and socks

Trays

SMALL GROUP ACTIVITY:

1. Arrange materials on trays. Encourage children to shake seeds from pods, brush hairy seeds against the mitten, beat grass seed spikes against trays to release grains, and take a close look at burrs and hairy seeds with the magnifying glass to see tiny hooks on the tips.

2. Take an envelope of winged seeds and a few heavier nuts to the playground. Let children launch them from a high place. Compare what happens to each kind of seed.

GETTING READY:

Gather ripe seed stalks in advance. Store in open containers or hang in tied bunches to dry. Preserve husks and pods intact. Find weeds in vacant lots or in roadside ditches.

* Seeds lie beneath separate cone scales. Old cones on trees may no longer contain seeds. Tightly closed new cones will dry and open in a warm oven with the heat turned off. Seeds can then be found.

Group Discussion: Talk about how different seeds came out of their coverings in different ways. "Can the wind scatter seeds? Which ones? Can animals carry seeds to new places in their fur? Can people carry them on mittens and socks? Have you ever seen plants growing in places where people couldn't plant them; in sidewalk cracks or rock crevices? How could seeds get there?"

READ: *Travelers All: The Story of How Seeds Travel,* by Irma E. Webber.
LISTEN TO: Tom Glazer, "How Do the Seeds of Plants Travel?" on *Now We Know (Songs to Learn By).*

Concept: Seeds Grow into Plants with Roots, Stems, Leaves, and Flowers

---

1. What is Inside a Seed?

LEARNING OBJECTIVE: To examine and notice the parts of seeds.

MATERIALS:

Dried lentils, lima, or navy beans

Peanuts in shells

Desirable if available: maple tree seeds, avocado, fresh green beans or peas

GETTING READY:

Soak seeds overnight in enough water to cover.

Keep a few seeds dry for comparison.

SMALL GROUP ACTIVITY:

1. Ask for children's ideas about what is in a seed.
2. Find out with them: carefully slip off a seed coat separating the seed into the two parts (cotyledon) that feed the seedling. Look together for the tiny new plant at the base of the seed (embryo).
3. Let the children enjoy doing this independently, sampling the edible seeds if they wish.
4. If a very ripe avocado is available, slice the fleshy part in half. Twist slightly to pull apart. Examine seed with children. Peel the seed coat at the base. A ripe fruit seed may already be split, revealing a root tip. Do *not* split it open.

Group Activity: Encourage the children who examined seed contents to share the secret inside of the seeds with the others. Discuss what a seed needs to start sprouting into a plant with roots, stem, and leaves. "Let's see what will happen to this big seed if we keep the bottom half in water for a few weeks." Slice ¼" at the base to hasten emergence of the root. Insert three round toothpicks midway through the seed. Suspend the seed in a tumbler of water. Place the jar in a warm spot away from direct or bright sunlight. Check for growth signs. Change the water if it begins to smell disagreeable; replenish evaporated water. Move it to a sunny, warm location after the root appears. Gently plant in a 5" pot after first leaves appear. Leave the top quarter of the seed exposed above the soil. Water and spray with water frequently.

2. How Do Seeds Start to Grow?

LEARNING OBJECTIVE: To observe initial seed sprouting.

MATERIALS:

Matching disposable plastic tumblers

Transparent tape

Cotton balls

Dried legumes: navy or lima beans, lentils (fresh stock)*

Water

Plastic prescription vial

Desirable: mung beans (natural foods store)

SMALL GROUP ACTIVITY:

1. Make a sprouting dome: wet 4 or 5 cotton balls, press out excess water, and flatten. Line the bottom and sides of one tumbler with cotton.
2. Let children see and feel the beans. Recall the secret inside the seeds as they help place four beans between the cotton and the tumbler side. (Try to use more than one kind of legume to see which sprouts first, which gets tallest, which grows for the longest time.)
3. Upend the matching tumbler on the rim of the prepared tumbler. Tape the rims to make a domed enclosure.
4. Place it away from direct sunlight where temperature will be even.

FIGURE 19

5. Put one of each kind of seed in the vial for later comparison. Start a calendar record of starting date, first root, first stem, and first leaf appearance. Crayon-mark daily growth level on the tumbler.

* Two common causes of germination failure are old seeds and an overheated, dry room. Don't expect good results with seeds of unknown vintage, nor with uncovered sprouting containers. Don't reject a gift of undated seeds from a child, but try to sprout a few at home before using them with the class. (Soak seeds with hard seed covers, such as morning glories, before sprouting them.)

Note: It's a good idea to start two germinating domes. Keep one available for children to pick up for a close look. If sprouts don't survive the inspection, the other dome will be available. It's hard to only look when leaves are showing beneath a rakish seed cover cap.

3. Which Direction Do Roots and Stems Grow?

LEARNING OBJECTIVE: To become aware of the tendency of roots to grow downward toward water and of stems to grow upward toward light.

MATERIALS:

Same as for the seed sprouting experience

SMALL GROUP ACTIVITY:

1. "Notice which direction the seedling roots and stems take. Is it the same for each seedling?"
2. Gently turn one seedling so the stem points down, the root reaches up. Mark an X on the glass beneath it.
3. Check each day for changes in root and stem growth direction. Look at the cotton behind the seeds. Roots may poke down into it toward water.

Group Discussion: Ask children if trees grow with their branches and leaves in the soil and their roots in the air. Do flowers blossom underground, or do plants send roots into the ground and other parts into the light? Why is this so? Help the children recall that leaves need light and air to perform their food-making job. Roots have the job of getting water and minerals from the soil so that the plant can live and grow. The upended seedling root and stem twisted and turned to grow in the directions where each could get what it needed.

Concept: Most Plants Need Water, Light, Minerals, Warmth, and Air

---

1. Can We Raise Plants from Seeds?

LEARNING OBJECTIVE: To become aware of and to provide the elements needed to promote seed germination and plant growth.

MATERIALS:

Zinnia or marigold seeds, package-dated for current year

Small package commercial potting soil (sterilized)

Teaspoons

Egg shells (as large as possible), one for each child, plus spares

Frozen pie pans with plastic dome cover intact*

Water

Sand or fine gravel

Punch-type can opener

Toothpicks

Medicine droppers

GETTING READY:

Collect egg shells in advance.

Cover table with newspapers.

Put an inch of sand in each pie pan.

Make tiny paper name tags and staple to, or lace with, a toothpick.

SMALL GROUP ACTIVITY:

Let the children:
1. Fill egg shells almost to the top with soil (cup a shell in one hand while filling).
2. Push shell gently into the sandfilled pie pan. Pans can hold about 12 shells.
3. Use droppers to dampen soil well. Place one seed on soil, then cover with spoonful of soil, press firmly, water again, and insert name tags in shells. Plant extra shells to replace possible failures.
4. After all shells are in place, tape plastic domes to pie pans. Place in a spot away from drafts, radiators, and direct sunlight.
5. Start a calendar record of seedling growth stages.

* If frozen pie containers are not available, use two egg cartons, one inside the other. Slide cartons into plastic bags, fasten with rubber bands during germination.

Seedling Care: After leaves appear, provide moderate light, such as a north exposure. Cover during nights and weekends to retain moisture. Allow children to water their own plants with the dropper. It's hard to overwater this way, but, if it happens, blot up standing water with absorbent material. Check each shell before covering pans at night in case someone forgot to water a plant.

Transplanting: For several days after the second pair of leaves appear, give seedlings a few hours of direct sunlight, preferably outdoors in a sheltered spot. Pack the shells in small milk cartons stuffed with crumpled paper for children to carry home. Tell parents that the eggshells can be planted directly into the ground if the soil is warm. Crushing the shells as they are placed helps roots become established.

If many children in the class are apartment dwellers, you may want to choose dwarf plant varieties to grow. Transplant the seedlings before sending them home. Use any container large enough to hold about three cups of soil. Punch a drainage hole in the bottom of cartons or cans, add a layer of small rocks, fill 2/3 full with soil. Crush the shell, plant firmly, cover with more soil, and water it.

About soil: To control one possible source of failure, commercially prepared potting soil is recommended for germinating seeds. For other classroom use, let children enjoy mixing their own potting soil: 1/3 ordinary soil, 1/3 sand, 1/3 peat moss. Talk about how soil is made of crumbled rocks, dead plants, and insect matter.

Group Discussion: Compare the calendar records of the germination dome and the plant raising experiences. "Were seeds treated alike in both experiences? Which seedlings stopped growing and withered? Which ones kept growing?" Moist seeds can grow only until their built-in food supply is used up. Plants rooted in soil can use minerals and moisture from the soil to help the leaves make their food for growth. Would the seeds grow in a freezer? Find out.

Additional Experiences: Keep some soil at hand all year to be ready for planting opportunities. Plant seeds used in the earliest investigations of seeds. Fresh peas or beans can be planted directly into the soil. Corn must be dry enough to be pried off the cob without breaking open. Plant some jack-o-lantern seeds after Halloween. Try growing plants from grapefruit seeds. Late season, tree-ripened grapefruit seeds seem to respond most promptly. Soak them in a small amount of water until the seeds sink to the bottom of the container (about three days) before planting. Try fresh date pits. A general rule for planting is that seeds should be planted at a depth twice the width of the seeds.

2. How Do Plants Take Up Water?

LEARNING OBJECTIVE: To observe how moisture is taken into the stem of a plant.

MATERIALS:

Two stalks of celery, with leaves

Two jars

Food coloring, blue or red (enough to make a dark color)

Water

SMALL GROUP ACTIVITY:

1. "How does water get into the leaves of a plant?"
2. "Let's see if we can figure out how water moves up these stalks of celery." Let children stir food coloring into one jar of water.
3. Check within an hour for signs of color in leaf tips. Separate a dyed strand from the stalk so the dye can be seen in whole length. Slice a cross section from the bottom of the stalk to examine.
4. "What do you think would happen to a stalk of celery if it had no water for a while? Let's find out." Leave the other stalk in the empty jar overnight. Check its condition the next day.
5. "Do you think water will change this stalk? Let's try it." Add water to the jar. Check it the next day. Has it revived? Clarify that celery plants have roots in the ground when they are growing. Roots take up water from the soil and the water travels up through the stalk strands.

Concept: Some Plants Grow from Roots and Stems

1. Can Plants Grow from Potatoes? Carrots?

LEARNING OBJECTIVE: To observe a different means of developing a new plant: by sprouting roots or stems.

MATERIALS:

White potato, or a sweet potato (do not try a kiln dried potato, local ones may be un- treated)

Onion

Carrot (fresh, an aged one with root hairs showing won't do much)

Ketchup bottle cap

Disposable plastic tumbler

Saucer

Glass jars

Water

Round toothpicks

SMALL GROUP ACTIVITY:

1. "Some plants can be grown from parts of the stem or root. A potato plant will start this way. Let's see if we can start one growing in water."
2. Stand, or suspend from toothpicks, potato in a jar of water. (About 1/3 of the tapered end of a sweet potato needs to be in water.) Add to or change water as needed during the growing pe- riod. What happens?
3. "Where does the potato vine get its food?" (Roots and tubers provide stored food for new growth.)
4. Keep a calendar record of growth. A successful sweet potato vine will flourish for months before its food supply is depleted. It may be planted in the ground when the old potato starts to cave in.
5. Cut the carrot top twice the bottlecap depth. "Perhaps this carrot top could feed a small new plant. Let's keep it wet and see what happens." Put it in the bottle cap, add water. Place on a saucer, invert the tumbler over the carrot top. Place in a light area, avoiding direct sunlight. Add needed water as long as the ferny plant continues to grow.

FIGURE 20

Group Activity: Try to plant some daffodil bulbs outdoors in fall. Later, if you should find a sprouting onion in your kitchen, slice it open vertically so the children can see the new plant tucked inside its food supply bulb. Talk about the bulbs outdoors waiting for the spring sunshine to warm the earth and the rain to start them growing. Try to start a few paper narcissus bulbs in the room. Follow packaged directions for growing conditions.

Concept: Some Plants Do Not Have Seeds or Roots

1. What Is a Mold?

LEARNING OBJECTIVE: To observe the ways simple plant forms grow and develop.

Group Discussion: Bring a piece of bread, two screw-top jars, and a drop-top bottle (like a soy-sauce bottle) of water to a group gathering. Recall with the children that most plants make new plants from seeds or root and stem parts. Say that a few kinds of plants grow from tiny dust-speck bits called *spores.* Millions of spores blow about in the air, but they are too small to see. When spores land on a warm, moist food source, they grow into plants that we can see.

"Perhaps we can grow a plant like that on a bit of bread." Put half of the bread in each jar. Cover one jar. Let the children sprinkle water on the other piece of bread. Leave this jar uncovered for an hour. Then cover it and store it in a warm, dark place for a few days. Compare the two pieces of bread. Do they look the same? Leave the moldy bread in the jar to develop a luxuriant fur coat, perhaps the black spore clumps will be visible as specks on the mold.

If you want to develop this concept further, experiment with the growth requirements of yeast. Examine mushroom gills, watch for algae and lichen growing on rocks, sample Roquefort or bleu cheese, watch for brown or green algae growth in an aquarium, bring in mosses and ferns to plant in a terrarium. The green spore-producing plants can make their own food. The colorless spore plants must use dead plants or other sources for food.

Concept: Many Foods We Eat Come from Seeds and Plants

1. Which Seeds are Good to Eat?

LEARNING OBJECTIVE: To find out firsthand that many seeds are used for food.

MATERIALS:

For Sprouting:
Mung beans, soy beans, alfalfa, wheat, or other legumes and grains (buy at a natural food store)

SMALL GROUP ACTIVITY:

Sprouting: Wash ½ cup mung beans. Soak overnight in water to cover. Drain water, compare soaked beans with dry beans. Put in opaque bowl. Cover beans with wet paper towels. Cover bowl with a plate. Keep at room temperature. Rinse, drain, and

Ceramic or steel bowl

Paper towels

Water

For Grinding:

Blender

Cracked wheat

Peanuts

Peppercorns

Peppermill

For Cracking:

Peanuts in shells

Whole sunflower seeds

For Toasting:

Hulled sunflower seeds

Hulled pumpkin seeds

Squash seeds

For Cooking:

Rice

Oatmeal

For Popping:

Popcorn, salt, margarine

Transparent dome popper

For Smelling:

Whole seed spices like: nutmeg, corriander, anise, poppyseed, or peppercorns

change damp towels daily. Sprouts about 1″ long should be ready to eat on the third day. They taste like fresh, raw peas. Store leftovers in refrigerator, in closed plastic bag. Excellent vitamin C source. Experiment at home to see how long it takes to sprout other grains and legumes.

Grinding: (To show how grain becomes flour.) Follow blending instructions to grind wheat. Use blender book recipe to make peanut butter.

Toasting: Toast hulled sunflower and pumpkin seeds in an electric skillet at low heat with a few spoons of margarine. Stir till lightly browned. Sprinkle with salt. Delicious and nutritious.

Cooking: Follow package directions. Compare dry and cooked foods, then eat.

Popping: Mention the bit of moisture in dry kernels that changes to steam, exploding the kernels, when heated. Plan carefully to use electrical equipment safely in the classroom.

Group Activity: Open a coconut, one of the biggest seeds that grows. Puncture soft spots at the end of it and drain the juice into a measuring cup, then let children sample spoonsful of juice. Crack the shell with a hammer, and scrape out small pieces of coconut for children to taste. If a blender is available, grate some of the coconut according to manufacturer's instructions to make this confection:

Seed Candy

Use the blender to grate: 1 cup of coconut

1 cup hulled sunflower seeds

Mix with: 2 tablespoons peanut butter

2 tablespoons honey, confectioners sugar, or maple syrup (both of the latter come from plants)

Form into a log, slice thinly, and enjoy.

Go on with other foods from plants as long as your enthusiasm lasts. Try, or talk about, root, stem, blossom, or leaf parts of plants that we eat.

Safety note: Do not suggest that children pick wild mushrooms. Do not give these things to children: castor beans, berries from pokeweed, nightshade, bittersweet, yew, holly, privet, or mistletoe. Do not allow experimental eating of buckeyes, daffodil bulbs, iris or lily tubers, or poinsettia leaves. Further information about poisonous plants can be found in *A Guide to the Medical Plants of the United States* by A. and C. Krockmal, New York: Quadrangle Press, The New York Times Book Company, 1973.

Primary Reinforcements

Music (References found in Appendix 1)

There are many children's songs about plants. Try these:

1. Adapt "The Paw-paw Patch" (8) to include other fruits and vegetables of interest to your children. For example, "Way down yonder in the carrot patch."

2. Sing the old English cumulative song (4) about a tree, its parts, and its occupants: "The Tree in the Woods."

3. Vary "Oats, Peas, Beans, and Barley Grow" (4) to sing about vegetables that might be more familiar to some children: "Corn, peas, beans and lettuce grow. . . ."

PLANTS AS MUSIC MAKERS. Dried gourd maracas are well known plant instruments. Drums or resonant rhythm instruments can be made from hollow logs and coconut shells. Don't forget willow whistles, dandelion or grass stem whistles, wooden flutes, and recorders.

Math Experiences

1. KEEPING RECORDS. Take a shopping bag on nature walks to hold things found along the way. Use these things in the classroom for sorting, classifying, and counting experiences. Record the results on a bulletin board or an experience chart:

We Found: 12 leaves, 10 acorns, 8 bits of bark, 1 piece of moss.

For younger children use numerals and samples of the material, for beginning readers, use numerals and words.

2. ACCUMULATE COLLECTIONS. Chestnuts, acorns, pinecones, sweetgum balls, and buttonwood "buttons" can be collected. Use them as materials to sort, match, count, and weigh. Use them as markers in bingo games. Group them on meat trays to make sets to match numeral cutouts, or numerals marked on cardboard squares. Seriate sticks by comparing lengths.

Commercial materials for number experiences include magnet-board apples, and felt tree and fruit cut-outs for flannel boards. Puzzles to arrange in time sequence include the subjects of seed germination and maple-sugar making.

3. ATTENDANCE COUNT. Cut leaf-shaped felt name tags for each child. Each morning place the leaves at the bottom of a flannel board. Let each child find his own name and move it to the top of the board as he or she comes in. Count the leaf tags out loud with the children to take attendance at group time.

Stories and References for Children

Bancroft, Henrietta. *Down Come the Leaves.* New York: Thomas Y. Crowell, 1961. Illustrated by Nonny Hogrogian. Holds together well as a story, while presenting clear botanical information. Beautifully illustrated.

Benton, William and Elizabeth. *How Does My Garden Grow?* Racine, Wis.: Western Publishing, 1969. A simple story about what plants need to grow. Cheerfully illustrated.

Blough, Glenn O. *The Tree on the Road to Turntown.* New York: McGraw-Hill, 1953. Portions can be read aloud to younger children.

Brown, Margaret Wise. *The Little Fir Tree.* New York: Thomas Y. Crowell, 1954. A tender Christmas story that describes a good conservation practice; includes seed scattering information as well.

Bulla, Clyde. *A Tree is a Plant.* New York: Thomas Y. Crowell, 1973. Describes the life cycle of the biggest plants that grow.

Downer, Mary Louise. *The Flower*. New York: William R. Scott, 1955. A nice story of plant life from a single seed through the cycle to an envelope of seeds for next year's garden.

Howell, Ruth. *A Crack in the Pavement*. New York: Atheneum, 1970. Every city-bound teacher should know this book. Nature's ability to triumph over asphalt and concrete permeates the text and photographs of school children examining plants and animal life in their urban environment.

Huntington, Harriet. *Let's Go To The Woods*. Garden City, New York: Doubleday & Company, 1968. Includes excellent photographs and descriptions of spore-reproduced plants, insects, and galls.

Jordan, Helene J. *How A Seed Grows*. New York: Thomas Y. Crowell, 1960. Simple concepts about a bean seed growing experience.

Koehler, Cynthia. *The Wonder Book of Trees*. New York: Grossett and Dunlap, 1974. A good reference book for children describing the functioning of tree parts.

Krasilovsky, Phyllis. *The Shy Little Girl*. Boston: Houghton Mifflin, 1970. A shy girl finds a best friend through shared fun with dandelion chains.

Krauss, Ruth. *The Carrot Seed*. New York: Scholastic Book Services, 1971. A simple story of a child's faith in a seed.

Lobel, Arnold. *Frog and Toad Together*. New York: Harper & Row, 1972. Toad has some funny ideas about coaxing seeds to grow.

Miles, Miska. *The Apricot ABC*. Boston: Little, Brown, 1969. Beautifully illustrated story of insects' responses to a fallen apricot that eventually becomes a bearing tree.

Podendorf, Illa. *The True Book of Plant Experiments*. Chicago: Childrens Press, 1972. Experiments with seeds, spores, and plants. Parts can be read to children to enrich experiences.

———. *The True Book of Weeds and Wild Flowers*. Chicago: Childrens Press, 1972. Nice illustrations of weeds and wildflowers in bloom.

Rinkoff, Barbara. *Guess What Trees Do*. New York: Lothrop, Lee and Shepard, 1974. Discusses uses of wood and wood byproducts, and the ecological role of trees.

Schwartz, Julius. *Magnify and Find Out Why*. New York: Scholastic Book Services, 1972. A close-up look at roots, seeds, and the seeds we use for spices.

Selsam, Milicent E. *Seeds and More Seeds*. New York: Harper & Brothers, 1959. Benny learns firsthand about seeds, beginning with his inquiry about whether a seed, a stone, or a marble will grow. He learns how seeds are formed and how they scatter.

Silverstein, Shel. *The Giving Tree*. New York: Harper & Row, 1964. A boy grows up with a tree that gives him shade, apples, shelter, and finally a resting stump.

Urdry, Janice May. *A Tree is Nice*. New York: Harper & Brothers, 1956. A child's view of tree appreciation.

Watson, Aldren. *My Garden Grows*. New York: Viking Press, 1963. Growing a vegetable garden is described in good story form, illustrating growth from seeds to mature vegetables.

Webber, Irma. *Up Above and Down Below*. New York: William R. Scott, 1953. A simple, concise presentation of plant and animal dependence upon sunlight, air, water, and soil.

Zion, Gene. *Harry By The Sea*. New York: Harper & Row, 1965. A funny story about seaweed that turns Harry into a temporary sea monster.

Poems (References found in Appendix 1)

The collection, *Poems To Grow On*, compiled by Jean McKee Thompson, has four poems about seeds appropriate to read during the seed investigations:

> "The Little Plant," by Kate Louise Brown
> "The Seed" and "Carrot Seeds," by Aileen Fisher
> "Seeds," by Walter de la Mare

Fingerplays

This traditional fingerplay fits well with the concept that living things reproduce in their own special form.

The Apple Tree

Way up high in the apple tree,	(Stretch arms up)
Two red apples, I did see.	(Make circles with hands)
I shook that tree as *hard* as I could.	(Shake "trunk")
MMMMM, those apples tasted good!	(Pat tummy)

—Author unknown

Substitute "orange carrots, green pears, two bananas," and so on, for "two red apples, I did see." The children will enjoy catching and correcting your mistake. Ask them why it must be apples growing on the apple tree. "Really? Don't carrots grow on apple trees? Then, where do they grow? Do they grow in the ground from apple seeds?"

Enjoy this fingerplay after collecting or raking leaves:

Leaves

The leaves are falling from the trees	(Arms rising and falling)
Yellow, brown and red.	
They patter softly like the rain,	(Tap fingers on floor)
One landed on my head!	(Hands on head)

—Author unknown

My Garden

This is my garden.	(Hold one hand palm upward)
I'll rake it with care.	("Rake" with curled fingers of other hand)
Here are the seeds	

I'll plant in there.	(Pantomine planting, seed by seed)
The sun will shine.	(Circle above head with arms)
The rain will fall.	(Fingers flutter down)
The seeds will sprout	(Spread fingers of one hand. Push up other fingers between them.)
And grow up tall.	(Bring hands and forearms together. Move up, spreading palms outward as arms move up.)

—Author unknown

Art Activities

1. COLLAGE. Dried grasses, leaves, pressed flowers, flat seeds, and small twigs make lovely collage materials. Tape may be needed when younger children include twigs and long grasses in their work. Vary the background colors to bring out the hues of the dried materials. Flat macaroni wheels, spaghetti, lentils, and similar foods can be used in plant life collages, after investigating plants that we eat.

2. PRINTING. Carve simple shapes from pieces of carrot or potato, or use halves of green pepper or citrus fruit as printing blocks. Make a simple stamping pad for the activity by folding paper towels into a plastic meat tray, and pouring liquid tempera on them.

3. RUBBINGS. Tape a single fresh leaf, or a pattern of small leaves, to the table in front of each child. Cover with a sheet of heavy paper. Let children rub a crayon over the paper to bring out the relief design of the leaf veins.

4. TRANSLUCENTS. Fresh leaves, flower petals, and grasses can be sealed between two sheets of waxed paper to make translucent window hangings. Do not use an electric iron in the classroom to seal the paper. For safety, and for maximum child participation, use a newspaper-covered electric food warming tray as a heat source. Give children a pizza roller or a child-size rolling pin to apply light strokes of pressure to the waxed paper.

5. EASEL PAINTING. Cut newsprint sheets into very large blossom shapes or leaf shapes for the children to paint at the easel. A border of painted flowers makes a charming room decoration for a special occasion.

6. CUT-PAPER MURAL. Offer strips of green paper for stems and leaves and assorted sizes of circles in blossom colors. Indicate ways to changes the texture and shape of the rounds such as notching; slashing for fringes; scoring with a ruler edge and pinching into cup shapes; cutting into spirals; and curling edges around a pencil. Put out scissors and white glue or paste. Assemble the completed fantasy flowers into a beautiful mural for your classroom door.

7. LEAF MOBILE. Let children cut out free-hand leaf shapes (or whatever satisfies them as appearing leaf-like). In spring use green paper; in fall use orange, brown, and red. Use five inch squares of paper. Suggest making the job easier by folding the paper in half. Let them punch a hole in each leaf and thread it with a small bit of yarn. Help them tie or tape their leaves to an interestingly shaped

branch. Hang the branch from a ceiling beam, or staple it to a bulletin board with some of the twigs extending into the room.

Let the children paint the branch with thick, real soapsuds in winter; hang soap-painted pinecones and fold-and-cut snowflakes. Scrape off the soap snow and save the branch. Hang paper hearts on it in February; blown, dyed egg shells in March; paper birds, butterflies, and green leaves in April.

Dramatic Play

1. FARMING. Playgrounds that offer a bit of shady ground for digging are natural settings for spontaneous farm play. Provide children with sturdy small rakes, hoes, shovels, buckets, and a wheelbarrow. They will find rocks or cones to plant and leaves, grasses, or pine needles to harvest without further suggestion. Children will need to know the boundaries of the permissible digging area. Listen to their planting ideas.

2. SANDTABLE INDOOR GARDENS. A collection of twigs, pinecones of several sizes, dried grasses and pods, or perhaps wild flowers, can be arranged by the children to create small landscapes in the sandtable. (Dampened sand will hold still better than dry sand.) Rubber toy animals and people can be added.

3. BLOSSOM FUN. If you can find an abundance of wild flowers for children to gather, use the blossoms to make beautiful, though short-lived, decorations. Show children how to make a split midway in a dandelion stem in which to insert another dandelion stem, and so on. The resulting rope can be looped into necklaces or crowns, or be allowed to get as long as possible. Leaves and sturdy blossoms can be threaded on soft, covered wires from a telephone cable to make bracelets. Large leaves strung together can become Indian headdresses. Two hollyhock blossoms can be stacked and joined through the center with a toothpick to make dolls with hollyhock-bud heads and daisy hats.

Children can place small sprigs of evergreen in a water-filled ring mold to make a table-top Christmas wreath. Use small pine cones for turkey bodies; tiny hemlock cones, painted red, for heads; insert bird feathers for tails.

Food Experiences

Make applesauce when apples are in season. Try drying raisins if grapes are abundant in your area. Children can learn to scrub and peel raw fruit or vegetables for snacks and prepare vegetables for soup. Any time flour or sugar are used in classroom cooking projects, mention the plant source.

Discuss the parts of plants that are being served for lunch. "Are we eating the leaf, the root, or the stem of the celery plant (the potato, the carrot)." Talk about the wheat seeds and the sugar plant stalks, or possibly roots, that went into the snack-time graham crackers.

Thinking Games

1. Play a simple guessing game in which children take turns describing mounted pictures of plants for others to guess. "I'm thinking of a plant that: we

eat for breakfast, makes something for bluejays to eat on the feeding tray," and so on. Seed catalogs are good sources for pictures. (Pictures printed directly on cardboard food boxes don't need further mounting.) Include a piece of plain paper, a mounted ice cream stick, and a cotton ball or fabric.

2. VEGETABLE SOUP. This is a cumulative memory game. "My mother made some vegetable soup, and in it she put. . . ." Each player recalls the vegetables already mentioned and adds a new one. Start a new pot of soup when the list gets too long for children to remember well. Read "Birthday Soup" from *Little Bear*, by Else Minarik.

Field Trips

1. We usually think of pleasant woods and meadows as ideal sites for plant life field trips. But the closest grocery store also has important plant learnings for children. Go there to see how much we depend upon plants for food. Visit the produce section; the shelves of dry staple foods (flour, pasta, sugar, legumes, cereals, and all the packaged mixes); the canned and frozen fruits and vegetables; and the baked goods. A natural foods shop (not a health food store that features vitamin preparations) is a fine place to see what whole grains look like, and to watch a small flour mill in operation. Flower shops and greenhouses can be fascinating, if children are welcomed by the owners.

2. INDOOR-OUTDOOR TREE WALKS. How many different kinds of trees grow within walking distance of your school? How can children tell that they are different? If leaves are too high to be examined closely before they fall, bark characteristics can provide identification clues. Let children make bark rubbings with old crayons on thick, flexible paper. The backs of vinyl-coated wallpaper samples are good for this. Compare the differences in bark textures for different species.

Now move indoors to complete your tree walk. Ask the children to tour the classroom looking for all the wood they can find in use there. Old buildings may have ceiling moldings and window and door frames of wood, so suggest looking up to find wood. Make a list of the found items. Pencils and paper should be on the list too.

3. HAVING A QUIET LOOK OUTDOORS. When the weather is fine, explore a nearby weedy patch. Minimize the scatter tendency of unconfined children by defining small observation spaces with six-foot loops of yarn. Before going outdoors decide on groups of three or four children to share a looking loop. Children can stretch out on the ground, radiating from the loop like the spokes of a wheel. Ask children to report what they see in their space. Later make a summary chart of the observations, including soil, rocks, and small creatures as well as plants. Tape samples to the chart.

4. WILD-FLOWER GATHERING. Check grassy areas near your schools in early spring for the presence of tiny wild flowers. Try to obtain permission for your children to pick tiny bouquets to take home. (Small groups at a time make it a happier occasion.) Show the children where they may hunt, then let them take their time to find spring beauties: chickweed, violets, or whatever the lawnmower

spares. Put the flowers in capsule vials of water. Label each with the child's name. Use them for table decorations, then wrap each child's flowers in a twist of waxed paper when it is time to go home.

Creative Movement

Curl up on the floor with the children to be seeds that have been planted in spring (or bulbs planted in fall if this was a class project). Move with the children to enact the growing story as you softly tell it. "Here we are waiting under the ground. The sunshine makes the soil warm; rain falls, and we begin to expand. The tiny plant inside grows bigger and pokes out of our seed cover. We send a root down to get water. Now our stem starts to push its way up . . . up . . . up to find the sunlight." Slowly describe the growth of the plant above the ground: leafing; budding; blooming; swaying in the breeze; feeling the sun and rain; losing petals; forming seeds; then slowly withering and scattering seeds for next year's plants.

Secondary Reinforcements

Keeping Concepts Alive

A row of potted plants on the classroom windowsills guarantees year-round attention to plant growth needs. Plant tending can occupy an honored position on the children's daily job chart. Younger children may need some help carrying the pitcher and deciding how much water to use. Older children can handle the task independently if pots are labeled with suitable watering advice. Comment on changes taking place, such as new buds, fading leaves, and unwanted insect tenants.

Classes in session during the regional growing season might be able to keep plant life concepts in focus by planting and maintaining a garden. Other classes could try portable gardens: plants started at school in the spring, moved to the home of a child or teacher for summer care, and returned to school for a fall harvest—with luck. Start pumpkin and sunflower seeds in good soil, using two-gallon plastic buckets with drainage holes cut in the bottom. Thin out all but one vigorous seedling. Give it full sunshine and plenty of water. The plants won't attain full growth, but the pumpkin can produce a vine with leaves, tendrils, blossoms, and possibly a fledgling pumpkin. The sunflower will develop a seed head and may grow taller than a five- or six-year-old. Slip a section of old hosiery or netting over the fading blossom to keep the birds from feasting on the seeds too soon.

If long-term growing projects cannot be worked out, perhaps you can duplicate the efforts of one very fine teacher of three-year-olds. Each fall she scouts the countryside to find a whole, dried cornstalk complete with ears of corn. It creates a fall harvest mood in her room, and provides an awesome lesson for the children who seem dwarfed by the giant plant that grew from a single kernel of corn. Later, shelling the corn becomes an absorbing task for the children. They feed some kernels to the birds, and save some to germinate in spring.

Other plant life experiences sometimes come about inadvertently. Capitalize on them. For example, an aging Jack-O-Lantern might develop a moldy spot. Instead of quietly discarding it, keep it in the room, as long as odor permits, to observe the changes. Then add it to a compost pile so that it can contribute soil enrichment for next year's plants.

Relating New Concepts to Existing Concepts

1. SOIL COMPOSITION RELATIONSHIPS. Repeat the experience of pulverizing shale to form powdery clay. Try growing an extra seedling in it. Compare its growth with seedlings growing in true soil that also contains bits of decayed plants and animal matter. This idea could lead to starting a compost pile or bag in the fall. Let the children rake available leaves and grass clippings into a large plastic trash bag. When it is approximately half full, add a soup can full of fertilizer or powdered lime; a can of water; and a few shovelsful of dirt. Close the bag and leave it outdoors where it won't be forgotten during the winter. It will need to be turned, shaken, and opened several times for some air. Although the completeness of the change that may occur by spring is not predictable, bacterial growth within the bag environment will have interacted with the materials to promote decay into compost (humus) to enrich the soil.

2. PLANTS THAT HELP CRUMBLE ROCKS. Look in shady areas for greenish-gray patches of lichen growing on rocks. Lichen are fungi and algae that live together as a single unit. Together they make acids that slowly dissolve the rock surface.

Other plants sometimes grow in rock crevices, and their roots may break off pieces of rock. Perhaps there is a section of concrete sidewalk near your school that has been cracked or pushed up by strong tree roots. Watch for them as you take walks with children. Stop to look at them. Recall with the children that slowly crumbling rocks become part of the soil that plants grow in.

3. AIR/WATER CYCLE. Use the term *evaporation* when plants are being watered. Some of the water will be taken up by the roots of the plants, the rest will evaporate.

If you make a terrarium, talk about how rarely it will need to be watered. Bring out the idea that the water taken up by the air in the closed terrarium will change into large drops on the cool glass sides. If you make the terrarium before the children have tried the evaporation and condensation experiences, postpone the discussion.

Parent Involvement

Children may take care of keeping their parents well informed as to the progress of their seedling experiences. Parents can be asked to save eggshells for the project. Their help will be needed in providing a good growing location and in overseeing the care of the seedling that is sent home. Dittoed plant care tips could be fastened to the container. Include a few lines about other aspects of the projects which can help parents become informed listeners of their children.

References

Bendick, Jeanne. *All Around You.* New York: McGraw-Hill, 1951. General nature study book has sections on plant life in child-like text. Better used as reference than story because illustrations are too few to hold the attention of young children.

Cooper, Elizabeth K. *Science in Your Own Back Yard.* New York: Harcourt, Brace, 1960. Well organized, practical information about the close-at-hand natural world. Covers rocks and minerals, fossils, plant life, insects, and small invertebrates. Highly recommended.

Ferguson, Grace. *The How and Why Wonder Book of Wild Flowers.* New York: Wonder Books, 1962. Information in this inexpensive book includes directions for pressing flowers and terrarium construction.

Frazier, Beverly. *Nature Crafts and Projects.* San Francisco: Troubador Press, 1972. Interesting ideas in this inexpensive paperback pamphlet for using seeds, flowers, and cones.

Hussong, Clara. *Nature Hikes.* A Golden Exploring Earth Book. Racine, Wis.: Western Publishing, 1973. A variety of information is included in this very inexpensive book about animal and plant life.

Russell, Helen Ross. *Ten-Minute Field Trips: Using the School Grounds for Environmental Studies.* Chicago: J. G. Ferguson, 1973. Good nature study information geared to older city children. Ideas can be adapted to young children.

Saunders, John. *Nature Crafts Hobbies and Activities for Boys and Girls.* New York: Golden Press, 1958. Includes some leaf, seed, and kitchen cuttings projects.

Sholinsky, Jane. *Growing Plants From Fruits and Vegetables.* New York: Scholastic Book Services, 1974. A very inexpensive pamphlet with good instructions for growing plants indoors from cuttings and seeds.

Skelsey, Alice, and Huckaby, Gloria. *Growing Up Green.* New York: Workman Publishing, 1973. Excellent precepts for gardening and other plant life projects with children.

Zim, Herbert S., and Martin, Alexander. *Trees: A Guide to Familiar American Trees.* A Golden Nature Guide. New York: Golden Press, 1956. Inexpensive pocket and comprehensive guide book.

14

Animal Life

Animals of all sizes and conditions fascinate many children who are eager to watch, touch and care for creatures. Other children have limited tolerance for anything that creeps, crawls, or nips. The experiences suggested for this chapter can both expand the knowledge of the creature lovers, and soften the feelings of anxious children into moderate respect for the useful and beautiful small animals around us. These concepts will be explored:

THERE ARE MANY KINDS OF ANIMALS
ANIMALS MOVE IN DIFFERENT WAYS
EACH ANIMAL NEEDS ITS OWN KIND OF FOOD
MANY ANIMALS MAKE SHELTERS TO REAR YOUNG

The feasibility of the experiences will depend upon having specimens for observation. Greater flexibility in use is needed for this chapter than for others. It would be sheer luck for a spider and a teacher to meet precisely on the day set aside for spider study.

Buying, housing, and maintaining classroom pets can be expensive. However earthworms, spiders, and insects exist everywhere and can be easily obtained. The experiences that follow use insects, worms, fish, wild birds, and pictures to illustrate concepts. Suggestions for acquiring and understanding insects and ideas pertaining to borrowed pets are included.

Concept: There are Many Kinds of Animals

Introduce this topic with a question for children to think about: "What is an animal?" Responses about specific animals will flow easily. Then suggest that there are so many kinds of animals in the world that it would take days just to say their names. "Here is a shorter way to say what an animal is: *An animal is any living thing that is not a plant.*" How many animals can the children think of now? Their list can include people, spiders, earthworms, and insects. There are more than 800,000 species of insects alone! They all have some features in common.

1. What Is an Insect?

LEARNING OBJECTIVE: To discover ways in which insects are similar to each other.

MATERIALS:

Temporary cages (see page 193)

Live insects *

Preserved insect in plastic box or vial

Magnifying glasses

Paper

Crayons

GETTING READY:

Follow capture techniques on pages 192-193.

Keep live insect cages out of direct sunlight.

* Spiders are not insects. They have eight legs and are classified as arachnids. Caterpillars are insects. Although they appear to have more than six legs, only six are true, jointed ones.

SMALL GROUP ACTIVITY:

1. Ground rules for observation should be set: (a) Insects or other small animals stay in the cages. (b) Cages must be handled gently.
2. Suggest looking for things that identify members of the insect family: three body parts (head, thorax, abdomen); six legs; two feelers (antennae).
3. Encourage children to try drawing pictures of the insect they are watching.
4. Try to mention: (a) These are adult insects. First they were eggs, then larvae (wingless, worm-like) before changing to adult form. (b) Insects have no bones. They have stiff coverings protecting their soft bodies.
5. Release insects outdoors at the end of the day.

Capture Techniques

Locating Creatures

Start looking for specimens near your own doorstep. On warm nights check screen doors for insects that are attracted by light. Hunt for web-building spiders on windowframes and shrubs. Turn over rocks on the ground to find crickets, beetles, and such. Look in flower borders for ladybugs, bumblebees, grasshoppers, ants, and wandering spiders that chase their prey instead of catching them on webs. Examine weed clumps like Queen Anne's lace and wilkweed for caterpillars.

Catching Creatures

Cold-blooded animals do not move rapidly in cool parts of the day. A bumblebee is groggy and easy to catch early on a crisp fall morning. Scoop it up with an open jar, then quickly clap on the lid. Slip in a dewy sprig of the plant that the bee rested on, and recover the jar with a piece of nylon hosiery or netting, held with a rubber band. Bees may be easier to locate during warmer parts of the day but quicker to defend themselves! Try using bamboo toast tongs to catch an alert bee. Use tongs to pick up very spiky-looking caterpillars. Some cause skin rashes if touched.

Wandering ground spiders and grasshoppers may be caught by clapping an open jar over them. Both species seem to hop straight up inside the jar, making it easy to slip the lid under it.

Nets are preferred for the safe capture of butterflies and moths. Sweep the net over the insect; flip the bag to fold it over the catch. Remove the butterfly by gently holding two wings folded back together. Slip it into a waxed paper sandwich bag. Keep it out of the sun until it can be transferred to an observation terrarium or box.

Only two small spiders have a dangerous bite. Avoid:

The black widow: shiny black body, with bright red hourglass mark beneath the abdomen (back section). Young may have three red dots on top of the abdomen.

The brown recluse: Rare. Lives indoors in attics, closets, or other dark corners. Yellow to brownish color. Fiddle-shaped mark on top of front section (cephalothorax) in dark brown. The base of the fiddle is between the feelers, the neck of the fiddle runs toward the spider's abdomen.

Temporary Housing

There are several ways to make inexpensive cages for small creatures. *Small Pets From Woods and Fields,* by Margaret Buck, shows many of them. However it is good ecology teaching to release a specimen after a day in the classroom. Comment that the insect is needed outside for cleanup work or pest control, or to help flowers make seeds (see page 195). This also skirts the problem of providing live food for some small animals.

A simple temporary cage for small insects can be made by covering a clean plastic tumbler with a piece of nylon hosiery, stretched and held in place with a strip of tape. For larger insects, cut large windows in the sides of a cottage cheese carton, as shown in figure 21. Pull the foot half of an old nylon stocking over the carton, gathering the top tightly with a rubber band. Snap the carton lid over the gathering. Put in a bit of wet cotton for moisture. Keep cages on hand to use whenever children bring small creatures to share. (It can be difficult to sell some children on the cage idea. Joey, for one, was in favor of keeping his caterpillar on a leash of " 'gotch tape.")

FIGURE 21

One fascinating exception to the same-day-release rule is a mother spider. She does not feed during the period of egg-sac construction, nor during the weeks before the spiderlings emerge from the sac. The spiderlings also have a stored food supply for use after their birth.

Wolf spiders fasten egg sacs to their undersides. The babies migrate to the mother's back after emerging. There, they cling to knob-tipped hairs as passengers. A wolf spider and her young can survive for a week of observation in a plastic playing-card box, if moisture is provided.

A potential disappointment with spider watching is that the mother spider spins an egg sac whether the eggs have been fertilized by a male spider or not. If the eggs are infertile, the mother does not tear the sac open.

Preserving Specimens

Youngsters with a strong fear of insects may shrink from examining caged live insects. They may be able to approach a mounted insect that is sealed in a plastic box instead. Start a small collection of insects at opportune moments. Preserve them for children to inspect in school.

Do the preserving away from children. Soak a cotton ball in nail polish remover or carbon tetrachloride cleaning fluid. Drop it into a small, screw-top jar with the insect. Later glue the specimen to the bottom of a small plastic box. Tape the lid shut. The insect won't skid around inside the box when the children handle it.

Butterfly mounting is not difficult to do. Directions are given in most butterfly

INTERESTING, HELPFUL INSECTS

Insect	Function	Interesting Features
Ants	Scavengers who clean their surroundings. Newly discovered function: pollinators of flowers.	Social insects who live in colonies with separate jobs to perform; some nurse young, some just gather food.
Bees	Highly valued pollinators of plants. Producers of honey and beeswax.	Social insects who live in colonies with specialized jobs to perform.
Butterflies	Pollinators of plants. (Explain to children as helping the plants make seeds.)	Slender bodies Antennae have ball tips Fly by day Fold wings straight up when resting Usually form a chrysallis
Moths	Some are pollinators. Silk moths spin strong, lustrous fibers that are made into fabric.	Fat, furry bodies Feathery antennae Wings spread flat when resting Usually spin cocoons Fly at night
Beetles	Some kinds are scavengers who tidy up. Ladybug beetles are valued for pest control by gardeners. Some beetles destroy crops.	Many handsome varieties: striped, spotted, iridescent.
Crickets	Serve as food for other animals. They are destructive to some crops.	Only male crickets chirp. They raise and rub their hard wing covers to make vibrations.
Fireflies (*soft-bodied beetles*)	Appreciated for adding charm to summer nights.	Fireflies signal to one another with flashes of light.
Grasshoppers, Locusts	Destroy some crops but serve as food for other animals.	Wings barely visible when flying. Jump with hind pair of legs. Hearing area is in the abdomen.
Praying Mantis	So valuable for pest control that egg cases are sold to gardeners.	Almost 4" long, so body parts easily seen. Frightening to see them tearing other insects apart.
Wasps and Hornets	Some wasps pollinate fruit trees. Some eat destructive larvae.	Hornets and some wasps chew dead wood into paper to make nests for their young. Some wasps make nests from mud. Beautiful engineering.

study guide books. They also appear in *The Golden Book of Nature Crafts,* by John Saunders.

Insect Pests

Some insects do more harm than good to humans and plants. Among them are: flies, mosquitoes, cockroaches, black widow and brown recluse spiders, miller moths, and clothes moths. Many insects that sting to defend themselves will not bother people if they are not disturbed. Among them are: wasps, hornets, bees, and spiders.

2. How are Other Groups of Animals Alike?
(Classifying vertebrates and mammals)

LEARNING OBJECTIVE: To begin recognizing ways of grouping animals according to body structure and mode of reproduction.

Introduction: "Some kinds of animals have bones inside their bodies. Some have hard coverings outside their bodies instead of bones. Can you feel the bones inside your body? People are animals with bones inside. Are insects the same? Here is a game about animals that are alike in some ways."

MATERIALS:

Part 1:

Pictures of familiar animals

Two trays

Shells of any sort

Chicken bone

Part 2:

Piece of fur (such as rabbit-fur mitten, real fur toy animal, or raccoon cap)

Feathers or reptile-skin objects to represent non-mammals (or model animals)

2 trays

GETTING READY:

Collect animal pictures to mount on small cards (pictures printed on pet food cartons are already mounted)

SMALL GROUP ACTIVITY:

1. Identify bones and shells as inside bones, and outside coverings. Place on trays.
2. Give equal piles of pictures to children for classifying, "Put pictures of animals with inside bones on the bone tray, and those with outside covers on the shell tray."
3. Trade pictures among children, continue classifying as long as interest holds.
4. Change to Part 2 tray objects. "Another way animals can be alike is that some have fur or hair." Discuss tray objects as class symbols. Divide pictures among the children to reclassify according to these characteristics. Together look at fur-animal pictures. "Do these animals also have bones inside?"
5. Think about how animals feed their young. Mammals nurse their young. Go on to group pictures again according to mammal or non-mammal classification.

Variety store animal sticker
books are good sources.
Include pictures of:
shellfish, snail, turtle, fish,
worms, insects, reptiles,
familiar mammals.

Concept: Animals Move in Different Ways

1. How Does an Earthworm Move?

LEARNING OBJECTIVE: To observe and describe the ways in which different animals move.

Introduction: "Do you need six legs to walk on? If your body were bent over and close to the ground, would more legs help keep you balanced? What helps some insects and birds move through the air? Can you think of a very small animal that has no legs—one that only has muscles and tiny bristles to help him move? Perhaps we'll find some worms to watch when we go outdoors.

MATERIALS:

Shovels and a digging place

Produce trays

Light colored sand

Bucket, stick

Soil

Peat moss

Water

Newspapers

Plastic shoe box

Nylon net, rubber band

Dry oatmeal, coffee
grounds, or cornmeal

GETTING READY:

Check soil, where you have
permission to dig, for
presence of earthworms
before taking children.
If children can't do the
digging, bring worms and a
shovelful of soil to
school in a bucket. Cover

SMALL GROUP ACTIVITY:

1. Let children dig for earthworms, if possible.
2. Give them equal amounts of peat moss and soil to mix with a stick in the bucket. Add water to dampen well.
3. Spread a thin layer of sand on bottom of the shoe box. Cover with 3″ of mixed soil.
4. Sprinkle meal or coffee grounds on top, scratch in with the stick. Put all but two earthworms on the soil. Cover top with net, fastened with large rubber band.
5. Put two earthworms on trays to watch them move. (Bristles are retractable and hard to see. A wide, light band at mid-section is the egg case. The tail end is tapered, head end is rounded. They have no eyes.)
6. See page 199 for earthworm farm care. Check sides and bottom for signs of change. Dark soil streaks in the light sand show how earthworms mix soils.

with a plastic bag. See:
How To Hold an Earthworm,
in the following section.

Care of Earthworms

Earthworm Farm Care

Wrap black paper around the sides of the shoe box to encourage tunneling where
it can be easily seen. It will take a while for the earthworms to get used to the new
soil before they start tunneling. Remove the paper for short periods of time to
check for signs of activity.

Earthworms will not survive long in dry soil. Keep the farm away from a heat
source. Sprinkle the soil frequently to keep it damp. The box lid can be placed
loosely over the net to retain moisture, but some air must enter the box.

Work in a spoonful of dry food each week. Try adding bits of grass and leaves.
Tiny balls surrounding tunnel holes on the surface of the soil are the castings of
soil digested by the earthworms. This is one way that worms enrich the soil. They
also help water and air reach plant roots as they make their tunnels.

How to Hold an Earthworm

Youngsters credit adults with unlimited ability and courage. Measuring up to this
idealism can be hard for some of us when it means holding a child's cherished
earthworm. Bolster your courage for this eventuality with some understanding
about your tactile senses: compare the sensation of holding a slippery object in
the palm of the hand with that of holding the same object between the thumb and
forefinger. The palm of the hand has fewer nerve endings to convey tactile sensa-
tions. Therefore a placid worm that is loosely cupped in the palm of the hand can
scarcely be felt.

2. How Does a Fish Move?

LEARNING OBJECTIVE: To observe and describe the ways in which different animals move.

MATERIALS:

1 wide-mouth gallon jar

Aquarium gravel or lake sand

Rocks

Water plant—purchased or
from lake or stream

1 small goldfish or wild
fish from lake *

1 snail

SMALL GROUP ACTIVITY:

1. Look at the body of the fish. Discuss how it is
   different from the earthworm's body.
2. Recall the looping, sliding movements of worms.
   Compare with varied movements of the fish: it
   darts up, down, forward, backward, or rests.
3. Find 7 fins: 2 pair about where our arms and
   legs grow, topside, underside and tail fins. (Arm
   and leg position fins work fast to move fish
   forward and back, top and bottom fins give

Black paper

Newspaper

Water

GETTING READY:

Involve children in as many preparation steps as you can.

Let a gallon of water stand overnight in open containers (so chlorine can escape).

Wash local water plants carefully. Wash lake sand in a deep pan, by letting a slow stream of *hot* water fill pan. (Plants and gravel from a good pet store need not be washed.)

Put an inch of sand or gravel in jar. Put plant roots in sand, anchor with a rock.

balance, tail fins steer fish as it swings from side to side. Some fins look like fancy decorations, but they have delicate bones, and they work hard.)

4. Tap the tank lightly. Does the fish go faster? Does it move differenty to speed up? Watch closely.

To keep the fish as a class pet, put fish feeding on a rotating routine chart. Each day a different child feeds it a *pinch* of tropical fish food. No weekend feeding is needed. Keep the aquarium away from direct sunlight. Tape dark colored paper around the side closest to the window to cut down algae growth. Some light is needed. Syphon or dip out 1/3 of the water, replace with aerated water as needed.

Cover sand with folded
newspaper while pouring in
water. Remove paper.

Put fish in water.

* Excellent, comprehensive directions for starting and maintaining a wild fish aquarium are given in *Pets From The Pond,* by Margaret Waring Buck.

Concept: Each Animal Needs its own Kind of Food

Introduction: "Did you have a nice bowl of acorns and a plateful of grass with ladybugs for breakfast today? Why not? What did you have?" Help children recognize that each kind of animal needs its own kind of food in order to live. Read *Cow's Party,* by Marie Hall Ets. Discuss making a feeder to help winter birds get the kind of food they need. Plan to maintain the feeder until spring. Some birds may come to depend on that food supply and starve without it.

1. Can We Feed Winter Birds?

LEARNING OBJECTIVE: To develop concern for helping wild animals find food.

MATERIALS:

A.

Gallon milk carton or clean
plastic bleach jug

12″ stick

Scissors

Twine

Commercial wild bird seed,
plus seeds saved from
plant experiences

B.

Dried pine cones

String

Peanut butter

C.

Half-pint milk cartons,
tops off

String

Melted suet

SMALL GROUP ACTIVITY:

A. Cut out two sides of carton or jug, leaving two inch border near the bottom to hold seeds. Poke the stick through the feeder in border edges to form two perches. Pierce holes through the carton top for hanging twine, or wind twine around jug top and handle. Tie to a tree branch low enough for easy refilling.

B. Wind string around top scales of cones, make hanging loop. Let children stuff peanut butter between scales with spoon handles.

C. Melt suet away from children. Use a heavy, deep saucepan over low heat. When cool, divide into bowls. Let children mix it with seeds, then fill cartons with mixture.

Seeds

Spoons, bowl

D.	D. Let children lace two baskets together with yarn.
Pint plastic berry baskets	Add chunks of suet before last side is lashed
Yarn	together. Tie to tree trunks.
Suet	

Locate feeders out of the reach of squirrels or cats. Sprinkle seeds on the ground beneath feeders, when they are put out, to attract birds.

Concept: Many Animals Make Shelters to Rear their Young

---

1. Do Ants Care for their Young in Nests?

LEARNING OBJECTIVE: To become aware of the social nature of ants.

Introduction: "When you were a tiny baby, did your mother put you outdoors to find your own food? Why not? Many kinds of animals make shelters where they can take care of their babies. Perhaps we can see how ants do this." Discuss making an ant farm. If this cannot be done, try to observe an anthill outdoors. Gently poke into the hill with a stick. The children may be able to see nurse ants carrying eggs, larvae, and cocoons as they leave their disturbed nest.

MATERIALS:

Widemouth quart jar

Slim olive jar to fit in
the quart jar

Construction paper

Rubber bands

Piece of nylon hosiery

Bit of sponge

Flashlight

Jam or syrup

Newspapers, trowel, double
grocery bag

Ants, nest soil

GETTING READY:

SMALL GROUP ACTIVITY:

1. Prepare outdoors, if possible. Let children center closed olive jar inside the quart jar; fold and tuck newspaper into top of quart jar as a funnel.
2. Gently transfer ants and soil from bag to jar. Quickly stretch hosiery over jar top, slip on a rubber band. Let children wet the sponge and place a dab of jam on it. Quickly slip it into the jar and recover with hosiery.
3. Let children wrap black paper around the jar, fastening it with rubber bands or tape.
4. Let children keep the sponge damp by dropping water through the hosiery daily; replenish jam weekly.
5. In a few days let children remove paper for a few minutes to see what ants are doing. A flashlight may be helpful. Lift jar to check activity

Do this away from children the first time. You may be very *busy* for a while.

Locate and dig into nest of medium or large ants. Quickly scoop ants, larvae, eggs, cocoons, and soil into bag. Fasten top well. (Do not mix ants or soil from two nests.)

Keep bag in cool place till needed.

at the bottom of the jar. Rewrap jar after viewing. Try to see: food gatherers, nurses for young, nest cleaners, soldiers, and hump-backed queen.

2. Can We Help Nest-building Birds?

LEARNING OBJECTIVE: To develop a concern for helping wild birds provide shelter for rearing their young.

Introduction: "Do you think that a mother bird lays eggs on tree branches and leaves them to hatch by themselves? You're right. She works hard with the father bird to build a nest where she can keep the eggs warm, and keep the hatched babies safe and fed. When the babies are big enough to take care of themselves, the whole family leaves the nest and never uses it again. Let's take a close look at a nest." (Hunt for your nest when deciduous trees have lost their leaves. Look in dense shrubs, heavy vines, tree crotches, or under eaves. Call your county agricultural extension agent for suggestions on finding nests. Check for exhibits in a library or museum, if you cannot find one.)

MATERIALS:

Abandoned bird nest

Clear plastic shoe box

Tape

Plastic berry baskets

6″ pieces of yarn

Excelsior

Dried tall grass

SMALL GROUP ACTIVITY:

1. Let children examine the nest structure. Is it lined with special material? Why? Keep nest in the plastic shoe box, taped shut for easy handling and storage.
2. If another nest is available, let children gently pull it apart to see how hard the birds work, piece by piece, to build nests.
3. Let children prepare nest materials for birds that come to school feeders: pull apart clumps of excelsior, place loosely in berry baskets, and work some strands through the holes. Weave strands of yarn and long grass through bottom and side holes of other baskets.
4. Hang baskets near feeders.

READ: *No Roses For Harry,* by Gene Zion.

Animals in the Classroom

The Borrowed Pet

Much can be learned by children who help to provide the daily life requirements of a classroom pet. Many of those learnings can also be sampled during a short visit by a borrowed pet.

Before the pet arrives, discuss with the children safe ways to watch and care for it. For small pets accustomed to pens, make an observation box from a large carton. Cut windows in the sides and cover them with plastic wrap, if needed. Some pets are better off being held by their owners during the visit. Try to let children see the animals eating and drinking water. Help children find answers to questions about how the animal moves, gets its food, and protects itself. Does the pet have bones inside, or a hard outside covering? Does it have hair or fur; smooth or feather-covered skin? Does it nurse its young? Does it build a shelter for its young?

Recent animal visitors to our school included a pet boa constrictor who laced himself through the rungs of a chair, and a small pony who unexpectedly was led into the building by a mischievious owner.

Animal Rearing

Rearing butterflies or moths from caterpillars, chrysalid, or cocoon stages can be enthralling or disappointing. Try following the procedures described in *Terry and the Caterpillars*, by Milicent Selsam. Strong interest and luck are required for success. (Childcraft sells a Butterfly Garden with caterpillars.)

The same mixture of dedication and luck also contribute to a good outcome with an egg-incubating project. A commercial incubator is probably a better choice than improvised equipment for classroom use. Follow the instructions included with the incubator. Be sure that the fertile eggs have not been allowed to cool after being laid. Plan in advance for a home for the chick or duckling after it has hatched.

Are Classroom Pets Necessary?

Good teachers allow for individual differences in children's responses to animals. They do not assume that all children adore animals. Also, they do not insist that a fearful child make physical contact with animals.

Teachers should extend the same consideration to their own feelings about animals. While they should avoid expressing negative attitudes about animals to children, they need not feel obligated to undertake year-long care if they do not enjoy the experience. Neither should they feel inadequate if they prefer to skip the responsibility of animal care. The teacher's primary affective focus and primary responsibility are caring about and caring for children. Feeling similar warmth and commitment toward animals is an asset, but not a requirement.

Primary Reinforcements

Music (References found in Appendix 1)

Many traditional and contemporary children's songs compliment ongoing animal life study:

"Shoo Fly, Don't Bother Me" (5)
"The Eency Beency Spider" (1)
"Jig Along Home," by Woodie Guthrie (7)
   (Worms and grasshoppers are among the dancers.)
"The North Wind Doth Blow" (2)
"Three Little Ducklings"(10)
"Over In the Meadow" (2)
"You Can't Make a Turtle Come Out" by
   Malvina Reynolds (4)

Listen to: *Birds, Beasts, Bugs and Little Fishes,* sung by Pete Seeger. The songs were written by Ruth Seeger, in *Animal Folk Songs for Children* (6). Also listen to: "I Like the Animals In the Zoo," sung by Ella Jenkins on *Seasons For Singing.*

The song provides a good pattern for improvising about the animals that visit your room:

> "I like the grasshopper, in the jar.
> I like the grasshopper, it jumps far."

Animal horns were among the earliest forms of musical instruments. Conch shells are still used as horns in some parts of the world. One of the percussion instruments on our classroom music shelf is an unoccupied box turtle shell. The children enjoy playing it.

Math Experiences

Many commercial math materials incorporate animals:

1. Animal Match Ups: Puzzle cards with sets of animals designed to link with numerals.
2. Magnet Board Forms: Plastic ducks and rabbits are used in magnet counting sets.
3. Felt animal shapes are included in several flannel board counting sets.
4. "See-Quees" puzzles include the development from egg to butterfly; from egg to frog; and from nest building to robin egg hatching. The pictures are to be arranged in frames according to time sequence.

Use collections of small seashells as materials for counting, classifying, set making, or numeral game markers.

Keep a flannel board talley of small animals brought into your classroom or observed on walks. Mount pictures of the animals cut from magazines on sandpaper or flock-backed adhesive paper backing. Bring out the envelope of pictures for children to count when new observations are reported.

If your class tries an incubating project, make a chain of 21 large paperclips to represent the days of the incubation period. Remove a clip each day, and count the days left in the waiting period.

Stories and References about Insects, Spiders, and Earthworms

Bason, Lillian. *Spiders.* Washington, D.C.: National Geographic Society, Books for Young Explorers, 1974. Amazing photographs of spider engineering. Be sure that children understand that the photographs are larger than life size.

Caudill, Rebecca. *A Pocketful of Cricket.* New York: Holt, Rinehart and Winston, 1964. A cricket brought from home helps ease a boy's first days at school.

Conklin, Gladys. *I Like Caterpillars.* New York: Holiday House, 1958. Excellent text and illustrations.

———. *I Like Butterflies.* New York: Holiday House, 1960. Fine child-oriented text, nice illustrations.

————. *We Like Bugs*. New York: Holiday House, 1962. Accurate information, nice illustrations, and a child-like appreciation of fascinating insects.

Daly, Eileen. *Butterfly! A Story of Magic*. Racine, Wis.: Western Publishing, 1969. The story of a monarch's life cycle that incorporates excellent photographs with drawings. A supermarket paperback.

Friskey, Margaret. *Johnny and the Monarch*. Johnny's duck hatches a brood during the span of a butterfly's life cycle. Chicago: Childrens Press, 1961.

George, Jean Craighead. *All Upon a Stone*. New York: Thomas Y. Crowell, 1971. A day of adventure for a mole cricket among the animals and plants living on an old, worn stone (a microhabitat).

Goudey, Alice. *Butterfly Time*. New York: Charles Scribner's Sons, 1964. A nicely illustrated story, including a list of plants on which specific butterflies lay their eggs.

Graham, Margaret Bloy. *Be Nice to Spiders*. New York: Harper & Row, 1967. A fine story about a garden spider that improves life for the animals in a zoo. It promotes respect for spiders.

Hitte, Kathryn. *Boy, Was I Mad!* New York: Parents Magazine Press, 1969. A child almost forgets how mad he is when he becomes absorbed in watching ants that are living in a crack in the sidewalk.

Hogner, Dorothy Childs. *Earthworms*. New York: Thomas Y. Crowell, 1953. Comprehensive information.

————. *Spiders*. New York: Thomas Y. Crowell, 1955.

Lionni, Leo. *Inch by Inch*. New York: Ivan Obolensky, 1960. An imaginative story about worms and birds.

Lubell, Winifred and Cecil. *The Tall Grass Zoo*. Chicago: Rand McNally, 1960. Accurate, melodic text describing common insects and other small animals.

Mizumura, Kazue. *The Way of an Ant*. New York: Thomas Y. Crowell, 1970. A beautifully illustrated story about an ant that aspires to climb to the sky.

Podendorf, Illa. *The True Book of Insects*. Chicago: Childrens Press, 1954. Clear basic concepts, simplified text, and large illustrations make this a useful book for children.

————. *The True Book of Spiders*. Chicago: Childrens Press, 1962. The characteristics of spiders are well described.

Selsam, Milicent E. *Terry and the Caterpillars*. New York: Harper & Row, 1962. In this book Terry is a *girl* who collects caterpillars! Accurate information about nurturing caterpillars and caring for cocoons are blended into a good story.

Stevens, Carla. *Catch A Cricket*. New York: Young Scott Books, 1961. About the capture and care of insects and other companionable creatures. Excellent photographs amplify the good information in this book.

Wonder Starters. *Butterflies*. New York: Wonder Books, 1972. Presents factual information, other than metamorphosis, about butterflies. Paperback.

Stories and References about Animal Babies, Homes, and Hatching

Cohen, Miriam. *Best Friends*. New York: Macmillan Co., 1971. The friendship of Jim and Paul is cemented by their mutual rescue of the classroom incubation project.

Fisher, Aileen. *Like Nothing at All*. New York: Thomas Y. Crowell, 1962. A child learns how animals' protective coloration is suited to their habitat.

_____. *Best Little House*. New York: Thomas Y. Crowell, 1966. A child finds animal houses made of sand, mud, bubbles, paper, silk, leaves, and one of wood for a dog.

Flack, Marjorie, and Wiese, Kurt. *The Story About Ping*. Seafarer ed. New York: Viking Press, 1961. Ping, a duck, wanders away and returns to his houseboat home on the Yangtze River in China.

Kirk, Ruth. *Desert Life*. Garden City, N.Y.: Natural History Press, 1970. Excellent photographs show how plants and animals adapt to a difficult environment.

McCloskey, Robert. *Blueberries for Sal*. Seafarer ed. New York: Viking Press, 1968. Four sets of mothers and their offspring are part of this story: Sal and her mother, plus bear, quail, and crow families.

———. *Make Way For Ducklings*. Seafarer ed. New York: Viking Press, 1969. Finding a suitable home and raising a brood of ducklings occupy Mrs. Mallard's time.

Schloat, G. Warren. *The Wonderful Egg*. New York: Charles Scribner's Sons, 1952. A bit long for very young children.

Selsam, Milicent. *All About Eggs, and How They Change into Animals*. New York: William R. Scott, 1952.

———. *Egg to Chick*. New York: Harper & Row, 1970. Some information in this book is too sophisticated for young children.

———. *All Kinds of Babies and How They Grow*. New York: Scholastic Book Services, 1971.

Stories and References about Birds, Fish, Mollusks, and Amphibians

Castle, Jane. *Peep-Lo*. New York: Holiday House, 1959. A child finds plover eggs in its nest in the sand.

Davis, Alice V. *Timothy Turtle*. New York: Harcourt, Brace, 1940. Clear thinking solves a turtle's problem when misguided group effort fails.

Eberle, Irmengarde. *Robins On the Window Sill*. New York: Thomas Y. Crowell, 1958. Good information and fine photographs, but too long for young children.

Flack, Marjorie. *Tim Tadpole and the Great Bullfrog*. Garden City, N.Y.: Doubleday & Co., 1959. The tadpole tells his story of growing into a frog.

Freeman, Don. *Fly High, Fly Low*. New York: Viking Press, 1959. Exciting adventures of a city pigeon that nests in an electric sign letter.

Goudey, Alice. *Houses From the Sea*. New York: Charles Scribner's Sons, 1959. Both a story and a reference book with lovely illustrations by Adrienne Adams.

Huntington, Harriet. *Let's Go To the Brook*. Garden City, N.Y.: Doubleday & Co., 1952. Information and photographs about less obvious small animal life in and near the brook.

Koehler, Cynthia, and Koehler, Alvin. *The Wonder Book of Birds*. New York: Wonder Books, 1974. Paperback. Contains well organized, brief bits about birds.

Kumin, Maxine. *The Beach Before Breakfast*. New York: G. P. Putnam's Sons, 1964. A child sees shellfish and shore birds that will be familiar to coastal area children.

Lionni, Leon. *Swimmy*. New York: Pantheon Books, 1963. A survival problem is solved by a clever school of fish.

————. *Fish is Fish*. New York: Pantheon Books, 1970.

McCloskey, Robert. *One Morning in Maine*. New York: Viking Press, 1952. Clam digging and shore animal life are part of this classic story.

Scarry, Richard. *Great Big Air Book*. New York: Random House, 1971. Contains a delightful description of how birds fly.

Selsam, Milicent. *Plenty of Fish*. New York: Harper & Brothers, 1960. An enjoyable story that informs about meeting the life requirements of fish in an aquarium.

Ungerer, Tomi. *Crictor*. New York: Scholastic Book Services, 1970. An engaging adventure story about a boa constrictor.

Zion, Gene. *No Roses for Harry*. New York: Scholastic Book Services, 1971. Nesting birds and Harry's sweater come together.

Stories and References about Pets

Bridge, Linda McCarter. *Cats: Little Tigers in Your House*. Washington, D.C.: National Geographic Society, Books for Young Explorers, 1974. Charming report about two kittens' first two months of life. Beautiful photography.

Burch, Robert. *Joey's Cat*. New York: Viking Press, 1969. A pet-keeping problem is resolved by a middle class black family.

Ets, Marie Hall. *Play With Me*. New York: Viking Press, 1955. A girl discovers how to make friends with animals. Good to read before a pet visits the classroom.

Keats, Ezra Jack. *Pet Show*. New York: Macmillan Co., 1974.

Miles, Miska. *Nobody's Cat*. Boston: Little, Brown, 1969. Vivid illustrations clearly show a cat's ability to defend itself.

Ward, Lynd. *The Biggest Bear*. New York: Scholastic Book Services, 1975. A touching lesson about trying to domesticate a woods animal.

Stories and References about the Death of Pets

Brown, Margaret Wise. *The Dead Bird*. Eau Claire, Wis.: Hale, 1958. The sadness of death is softened by ceremony and remembrance.

Viorst, Judith. *The Tenth Good Thing About Barney*. Boston: Atheneum, 1971. The conclusion of this story may not be acceptable to some adults. Decide for yourself.

Stories and References about Animals' Food Needs

Ets, Marie Hall. *Cow's Party*. New York: Viking Press, 1958. The cow learns that not all animals eat the same kind of food.

Poems (References found in Appendix 1)

"The Little Land" from *A Child's Garden of Verses*, by Robert Louis Stevenson, records a charming perspective of insects projected by a diminutive sailor on a leaf boat.

Many other poets create delicate or amusing sketches of insects and somewhat larger animals. Poems are found in these collections:

Brown, Margaret Wise, *Nibble Nibble:*
    "A Child's Delight" (a firefly in a jar)
    "Bumble Bee"

Milne, E. E., *Now We Are Six:*
    "Forgiven" (an adult discovers a child's pet beetle in an unexpected place)

de Regniers, Moore, and White, *Poems Children Will Sit Still For:*
    "The Caterpillar" by Christina Rossetti
    "Firefly" by Elizabeth Maddox Roberts
    "For A Bird" by Mura Cohn Livingston
    "Tails" by Rowena Bennett
    "Little Snail" by Hilda Conkling
    "Mice" by Rose Fyleman

Thompson, Jean McKee, *Poems To Grow On:*
    "Spiders" by Aileen Fisher
    "Fuzzy Wuzzy, Creepy Crawly" by Lillian Schulz
    "Earth Worm" by Mary McBurney Green
    "Mrs. Brownish Beetle" by Aileen Fisher
    "Little Bug" by Rhoda W. Bacmeister
    "Robin in the Garden" by Grace Tabot Hallock
    "Baby Chick" by Aileen Fisher
    "Mrs. Peck-Pigeon" by Eleanor Farjeon
    "Cat" by Mary Britton Miller

Fingerplays

Many of the traditional fingerplays are about the characteristics of small animals. Crouch down with the children to enact Vachel Lindsay's poem, "The Little Turtle."

The following is an animal shelter fingerplay:

Here Is A Bunny

Here is a bunny	(First with two fingers raised)
With ears so funny	
And here is his hole in the ground.	(Left hand on hip, arm curved)
When a noise he hears	(Stretch "ear" fingers)
He pricks up his ears	
And jumps in his hole in the ground.	(Thrust fist through curved arm)

—Author unknown

Add to this fingerplay to include the movement of small animals observed by children in your classroom:

Small Animal Parade

A slow, slow snail Drags down the trail.	(Stretch and contract right hand, dragging along left arm.)
A looping earthworm Moves along with a squirm.	(Loop and waggle one finger.)
A spider runs past With eight legs so fast.	(Hands one on top of the other, tuck thumbs under, wiggle eight fingers.)
The grasshopper springs With six legs and wings.	(One hand crossed on top of other, thumbs and little fingers held under. Leap up and down.)
The green and white frog Leaps over a log.	(Right fist leaps over left arm.)
A seven-fin fish Swins by with a swish.	(Palms together, hands twist and turn, moving forward.)

Art Activities

1. EASEL PAINTING. One of the early shapes many children paint spontaneously is a loop with many strokes radiating from it. Often these are called spiders or bugs by the painter. Provide green and brown paint on insect-watching days and casually suggest that some children could have fun making paintings of the spider, grasshopper, caterpillar, or whatever creature is of current interest. Newsprint sheets may also be cut into large butterflies or bird shapes for children to paint at the easel.

2. PAPER CUTTING, SHAPING, AND PASTING. To help children start this type of activity, have paper strips of ½″ by 4″ , and several sizes of oval shapes—already cut for them. Show them that a strip can stand alone after being

FIGURE 22

folded into a Z shape, or that it becomes a spring after being accordian pleated. Suggest that such folds could become insect legs when pasted to body shapes. A single slash cut in an oval shape can be pasted over into a dart to create a three-dimensional shape from flat paper. Hang the resulting creatures by a thread from a tree branch for an appealing mobile decoration.

3. CRAYON AND PICTURE COLLAGE. Provide pictures of animals (for children to cut out or have them cut out already for those new at cutting), paste, construction paper, and crayons for crayon-enhanced collages. Animal pictures are not too easy to locate in the typical household magazines. Old children's magazines, free nature publications from your state Natural Resource Department, or animal stamps from the National Wildlife Federation are good sources.

4. LEATHER AND FEATHER COLLAGE. Scraps of leather from a crafts shop and assorted feathers make interesting collage material. Use durable paper and white glue for best adhesion. (Feathers might be unacceptable collage materials in classes where allergic reactions to feathers are a problem.) Feathers can be collected from poultry farms, or on late summer walks near lakes or wooded areas. Feathers can be washed before use in this way: (1) Soak in cold water several hours. (2) Wash in warm water and detergent, swishing and surging water through the feathers. (3) Spread single layers on newspapers near a sunny window (no breeze, please). Let the children smooth the dry feathers with their fingers.

5. ADDITIVE SCULPTURE ANIMALS. Pine cones make good bases for making animal forms. Turkeys can have rounded Scotch pine cone bodies, red painted balsam cone heads, and feather tails.

Use strips of molded paper egg cartons as caterpillar bodies. Offer tempera paint, fabric, paste, feathers, and snips of pipe cleaners for fanciful decorations.

6. EGG SHELL MOSAICS. Broken, dyed egg shells can be glued to paper for egg hatching project extensions. The younger the age group, the larger the shell bits should be for best management of materials.

Dramatic Play

1. FISHING. Add a dishpan full of water to indoor camping play. Tie a small magnet to a string. Attach to a stick. (Or use cork bobbers as suggested on page 54.) Cut simple fish shapes from pressed Styrofoam packaging sheets, attach a safety pin through it.

2. ANIMAL PUPPET PLAY. Put out animal hand puppets for children to animate. A small table turned on its side makes a good improvised stage.

3. DRAMATIZE ANIMAL STORIES. When a group of children is familiar with an animal story that involves "a cast of thousands," they enjoy acting out the story in an informal, simplified way. Assign roles to all the children, so that no one is left out, even if someone has to play the part of a tree in the forest. Good animal stories that meet the casting requirements are: *The Story of Ping, Timothy Turtle, Make Way For Ducklings, The Tortoise and The Hare,* and *Caps For Sale.* Help move the story along informally, as needed. "One day Timothy Turtle was sliding down his favorite mud bank, he slipped and landed on his back . . . (Maria, you

are pretending to be Timothy can you roll over on your back now? Good! You're waving your arms and legs just as he did!)" Assign areas in the room for different scenes. "Here's the island on the river where the Mallards build their nest, and the block area is the Public Garden where they swim." Use simple props if they help carry out the story. For example, arrange a few blocks in a boat outline as Ping's houseboat, for the duck relatives to crouch in.

Food Experiences

Children accept the idea that people eat fish and chicken, since the terms are customarily used at mealtimes. There seems little to be gained, however, from pressing the point that the hamburgers being served for lunch were once steer, that the ham in the casserole was once a pig. Concentrate instead on ideas that foster positive emotions: cows giving milk, hens giving eggs, or bees making honey for people to enjoy.

To confirm man's dependence upon other forms of animals for food, many cooking experiences are possible in the classroom: making butter (use fresh, not sterilized, cream), instant puddings, ice cream, custard, and egg nog.

Thinking Games

1. HABITAT CLASSIFICATION. Pin pictures of a tree, lake, and grassy meadow to a flannel board. Mount small pictures, or cut out simple felt shapes of an insect, fish, frog, turtle, snake, worm, spider, bird, and others. Let the children tell which picture "home" that the creature belongs near. Can some animals live in more than one kind of "home"?

2. I'M THINKING OF AN ANIMAL. Offer simple descriptions for children to guess, like: "I'm thinking of an animal that has no eyes, no legs, no arms; it has a mouth and a long body. What could it be?" Children who are experienced enough to take turns guessing will enjoy describing small mounted pictures drawn from a bag.

Creative Movement

It's easy to draw children into the fun of acting out animal characteristics. Creative movement suggestions may also strengthen children's recall of the life cycles of animals that undergo metamorphosis. Slowly and dramatically read animal poems aloud for children to interpret with you. Good poems to try include the following found in *Poems To Grow On*, by Jean McKee Thompson (see Appendix 1):

"Cat" by Mary Britton Miller
"Mrs. Peck-Pigeon" by Eleanor Farjeon
"Baby Chick" by Aileen Fisher
"Fuzzy Wuzzy, Creepy Crawly" by Lillian Schulz
"Earth Worm" by Mary McBurney Green

Clare Cherry suggests many animal movement stimuli in her book, *Creative Movement for the Developing Child*. The RCA Dance-A-Story record, *The Duck Story*, by Anne Lief Barlin may be available from lending libraries, or from Ginn and Company. The script and music appear in the book, *The Magic of Music*, by Lorraine Watters and others. It guides children to depict the story of a duckling who hatches, gets lost in new surroundings, and is rescued.

For an organized indoor play activity, children can be invited, one by one, to travel across the floor like the animal of his or her choice. (Groups of young children wait turns more patiently if they are sitting on the floor before and after their turn to travel.) One quick thinking pair of five-year-olds brightened our day when they piggy-backed to crawl together as an eight-legged spider.

Field Trips

The list of potential problems and hazards that might be part of an outdoor animal observation hike could rule out this kind of field trip for a large group of young children. It can also be very disappointing when the objects of the trip do not display themselves. Try instead to pause for watching time whenever you encounter small animals while outdoors with your children: ants at work in a sidewalk crack nest, limp worms washed out of their tunnels after a hard rain, or squirrels and birds gathering food.

Other field trip possibilities are to a farm, zoo, pet shop, or animal shelter. The state conservation department will have information about the location of animal preserves, hatcheries, or parks with programs by naturalists. They may also have free or inexpensive leaflets about animals.

Do not forget the grocery store as an animal study resource. Animals provide indirectly for our many dairy products, eggs, and honey.

Secondary Reinforcements

Keeping Concepts Alive

A teacher vividly reinforces concepts about the usefulness of insects by reacting calmly to an intruding bee or wasp. Remind children that insects of this sort sting only when disturbed. Open the windows from the top so that the insect can eventually fly out. Offer an observation jar to a shrieking child who is about to squash an uninvited spider. Do not undo what you have previously taught about the creature's place in the web of life by joining the chase with a can of insecticide. There is no need to be solicitous toward roaches, flies, or mosquitoes. If you must eliminate them in front of children, mention that they are pests to people, but good food for birds and toads.

Another reinforcement of respect for living creatures may occur if a classroom pet dies, or a dead bird is found on the playground. Let the children be aware of the death, and take part in a gentle burial. Say that the animal's useful life has ended. Try to read one of the stories about the death of animals that coincides with your views of death (page 209).

Relating New Concepts to Existing Concepts

The interrelationships and mutual dependencies of plants, animals, soil, water, and air are awesome and complex for adults to contemplate. Children make beginning steps toward these understandings through small, specific instances. For example, a child may observe a bird pecking at tree bark and wonder aloud if the bird is hurting the tree. An adult can clarify the bird's immediate purpose, and expand the idea of mutual dependency. "Yes, it does look a bit like the bird is hurting the tree. Really, it is getting its food, and helping the tree at the same time. The bird is catching tiny insects that are eating the tree. Can you think of a way that the tree can help the bird?"

A child may question the fitness of animals eating other animals, plants, and seeds for sustenance. One can appreciate the child's concern. Then suggest that each living thing can make many more seeds or eggs than are needed to make a young plant or animal like itself. If all the seeds grew into plants and all the eggs became animals, there would not be enough room in the world for all the living things. Some of the plants and animals need to be used in this way to keep the proper amount of each kind growing well.

Sound concepts can be linked to the study of animal life. Compare the high pitch of the wren's song with the low pitch of a dove's coo. Feel the vibrations of a purring cat. Think of the swelling air pockets that make a frog's loud croak possible. Recall the vibrating wing covers that can be seen when the male cricket sings. Relate air concepts to the life requirements of animals (see page 24).

Parent Involvement

Inform parents early in the school year that children are encouraged to bring in captured insects. You may never have to track down a specimen by yourself, after the first few planned experiences, in order to have a well stocked seasonal menagerie.

A knowledgeable parent might be willing to set up a classroom aquarium, make a pet cage, or arrange to bring in and show a family pet. His child's social standing with the group usually blossoms as a secondary benefit.

Remind parents about animal exhibits in nearby museums, or local events involving animals that families could see on outings. "Your children can see newborn lambs if you drive past the Rogers' farm on Hastings Road." Shopping centers may have a chick incubator exhibit near Easter. Most areas have resources for families to explore.

References

SMALL ANIMAL PETS; GENERAL ANIMAL STUDY

Bendick, Jeanne. *All Around You.* New York: McGraw-Hill, 1951. Includes information about animal classification.

Borror, Donald J., and White, Richard E. *A Field Guide to the Insects of America North of Mexico.* Boston: Houghton Mifflin, 1970.

Brown, Vinson. *How to Make a Miniature Zoo.* Boston: Little, Brown, 1957. Catching, caging, and caring for insects and other small animals.

Buck, Margaret Waring. *Small Pets From Woods and Fields.* Nashville: Abingdon Press, 1960. An excellent guide to catching, feeding, and housing insects and spiders; amphibians; reptiles; and small mammals. Terrarium and vivarium construction is well described.

Cooper, Elizabeth. *Science in Your Own Back Yard.* New York: Harcourt, Brace, 1958. Excellent information about insects, worms, snails, spiders, birds and familiar small vertebrates.

Dobrin, Arnold. *Gerbils.* New York: Lothrop, Lee and Shepard, 1970. Everything about gerbil care.

Green, Ivah. *Animals Under Your Feet.* Scranton, Pa.: Laurel Press, 1958. Factually based stories for children.

Greenberg, Sylvia, and Raskin, Edith. *Home-Made Zoo.* New York: David McKay, 1952. Complete pet-care information given for snakes, salamanders, fish, frogs, turtles, guinea pigs, mice, hamsters, and birds.

Levi, Herbert W. and Levi, Lorna R. *A Guide to Spiders and Their Kin.* A Golden Nature Guide. New York: Golden Press, 1969.

Mitchell, Robert and Zim, Herbert. *Butterflies and Moths.* A Golden Nature Guide. New York: Golden Press, 1964.

Russell, Helen Ross. *Ten-Minute Field Trips: Using the School Grounds for Environmental Studies.* Chicago: J. G. Ferguson, 1973. Practical and comprehensive nature study approach for elementary grades.

Saunders, John. *The Golden Book of Nature Crafts.* New York: Golden Press, 1968. Excellent pictures of plant and animal treasures which may be collected.

Siverly, R. E. *Rearing Insects in Schools.* Dubuque, Iowa: W. C. Brown, 1962.

Wyler, Rose. *Exploring Earth Science.* Racine, Wis.: Western Publishing, 1973. Paperback. Good, brief bits of information about animal classification, habitat, feeding, hibernation, and reproduction.

Zim, Herbert. *Golden Hamsters.* New York: William Morrow, 1951. Describes hamster care.

INSECTS

Farb, Peter. *The Story of Butterflies and Other Insects.* Irvington-on-Hudson, N.Y.: Harvey House, 1959. Includes suggestions on finding cocoons and butterfly rearing.

Lane, Ferdinand. *All About the Insect World.* New York: Random House, 1954.

Mitchell, Robert, and Zim, Herbert. *Butterflies and Moths.* New York: Golden Press, 1964. A Golden Nature Guide. Paperback.

Rood, Ronald. *The How and Why Wonder Book of Butterflies and Moths.* Columbus: Charles E. Merrill, 1963. By special arrangement with Wonder Books.

Selsam, Milicent. *Questions and Answers About Ants.* New York: Scholastic Book Services, 1967. Fascinating information about ant life. Includes good observation ideas. Paperback.

Swain, Su Zan. *Insects In Their World.* Garden City, N.Y.: Garden City Books, 1955. Good illustrations; collecting and preserving information.

Zim, Herbert. *Insects: A Guide To Familiar American Insects.* New York: Golden Press, 1956. Succinct information and accurate illustrations. Paperback.

Appendix 1

References for Music, Records, Poetry, and Creative Movement

MUSIC

(1) Berg, Richard et al. *Music For Young Americans, Kindergarten*. New York: American Book Company, 1959.

(2) Bertail, Inez. *Complete Nursery Song Book*. New York: Lothrop, Lee & Shepard, 1967.

(3) Boardman, Eunice, and Landis, Beth. *Exploring Music: Kindergarten*. New York: Holt, Rinehart and Winston, 1969.

(4) Boardman, Eunice, and Landis, Beth. *Exploring Music: I*. New York: Holt, Rinehart and Winston, 1969.

(5) Boni, Margaret Bradford. *Favorite American Song*. New York: Simon & Schuster, 1956.

(6) Dykema, Peter et al. *Happy Singing*. Boston: C. C. Burchinal, 1957.

(7) Landeck, Beatrice, and Crook, Elizabeth. *Wake Up and Sing*. New York: Edward Marks Music Corporation, William Morrow & Co., 1969.

(8) Landeck, Beatrice. *Songs To Grow On*. New York: William Sloane Associates, 1950.

(9) Seeger, Ruth Crawford. *Animal Folk Songs for Children*. Garden City, N.Y.: Doubleday & Co., 1950.

(10) Sur, William et al. *This Is Music*. Boston: Allyn & Bacon, 1965.

(11) Watters, Lorrain et al. *The Magic of Music, K*. Boston: Ginn and Co., 1965.

RECORDS

Barlin, Anne Lief. Dance-A-Story *Balloons*. RCA Victor, LF104.

Glazer, Tom. Singing *Now We Know (Songs to Learn By)*. Columbia Records, CL670.

Jenkins, Ella. Singing *Seasons For Singing*. Folkways Records, #7656.

Seeger, Pete. Singing *Birds, Beasts, Bugs and Little Fishes*. Folkways Records, #FTS31504.

POETRY

Brown, Margaret Wise. *Nibble Nibble*. New York: Young Scott Books, 1959.

deRegniers, Beatrice Schenck; Moore, Eva; and White, Mary M. *Poems Children Will Sit Still For*. New York: Scholastic Book Services, 1973.

Milne, E. E. *Now We Are Six*. New York: E. P. Dutton, 1961.

Stevenson, Robert Lewis. *A Child's Garden of Verses*. New York: Airmont, 1969.

Thompson, Jean McKee. *Poems To Grow On*. Boston: Beacon Press, 1957.

CREATIVE MOVEMENT

Cherry, Clare. *Creative Movement for the Developing Child*. Palo Alto, Calif.: Fearon Publishers, 1968.

Appendix 2

Salvage Sources for Science Materials

Resourceful teachers know how to compensate for tight equipment budgets. They scout the community for discarded materials that can be put to use in their classrooms. Most of the materials and some of the equipment called for in this book were acquired in this way. As our society shifts from a throw-away orientation to one of more conservative use of materials, some of these items may become scarce. Depend upon personal ingenuity to devise even better substitutes for the obsolete materials. The following is a list of the current suppliers of the materials on our science shelves.

Clinic medical laboratory:
  Discarded test kit bottles with dropper tops, 1½″ to 2″ size (ask if sterilizing is advisable before using in school)
  Plastic prescription vials with caps
  Screw-top plastic bottles, 4-ounce to 1-pint size

Dress shop alterations department or drapery shop:
  empty thread spools

Electric motor repair shop:
  old magnets from motors

Grocery store:
  plastic berry baskets (available during fresh berry season)

Photography studio:
  color film cannisters, film spools, 30mm film cans, small plastic chemical bottles (wash carefully before reusing)

Retail shops of all sorts:
  Styrofoam packing chips, molded Styrofoam packing sheets, plastic bubble packing papers

Shoe store:
  shoe boxes (our science supplies are stored in 26 shoe boxes)

Telephone installation crews:
  short pieces of telephone cable containing copper wires insulated in nice colors

Tire store:
old inner tube

Many parents are willing to support science activities by saving materials or lending equipment. A list of appreciated materials might include these:

Aluminum foil pans
Bottle caps
Broken hand-wound clock
Broomsticks
Coffee cans, with plastic lids
Cottage cheese cartons
Disposable plastic tumblers
Fabric scraps
Frozen juice cans
Garden hose lengths (clear)
Ice cube trays, molded plastic
Lids from cocoa tins
Margarine tubs
Meat trays (Styrofoam or clear plastic)
Mesh onion or potato bags
Metal ends from biscuit tubes
Milkshake container lids (plastic)
Mirrors (pocket)
Newspapers
Plastic prescription vials, screw-top bottles
Muffin pans
Paper bags
Pulleys
Small, rigid suitcase
Washers (metal)
Seed catalogs
Vitamin drop bottle (plastic)
Tobacco tins with clamp-on lids

Families may be willing to lend:

Acrobat balance toy
Cookie press (screw-type)
Bicycle tire pump
Camper's step pump (bellows type)

Kitchen scale

Postage scale, or calorie-count scale

Old-fashioned piano stool

1½ volt dry cell (#6). (If not available, consider purchasing "D" flashlight battery holders from the SEE catalog to take the place of the more expensive dry cell. Purchase "D" batteries locally.)

Reasonably priced, sturdy science equipment for classroom use is sold by mail from:

Selective Educational Equipment (SEE), Inc.
3 Bridge Street
Newton, Massachusetts 02195

Write for their *Science and Things* catalog.

Index

Air concepts, related to: gravity, 83; seed propagation, 39; sound, 39, 118; water, 39

Alexenberg, Melvin, 131

Aliki, 155

Animal life concepts, related to: air, 215; plant life, 215; sound, 118, 215

Ant farm, to make, 203

Aquarium, to prepare, 200

Art activities, related to: air, 36; animal life, 211; electricity, 144; gravity, 79; light, 130; magnetism, 68; plant life, 183; rocks and minerals, 159; simple machines, 97; sound, 116; water, 54

Attention, 3; focusing of, 14, 15

Barlin, Anne Lief, 38, 214

Bottle organ, to make, 111

Bradbury, Ray, 121

Branley, Franklyn, 62, 109

Bright, Robert, 50

Bruner, Jerome, 4, 5, 20

Buck, Margaret Waring, 210

Cherry, Clare, 38, 81, 214

Creative movement, related to: air, 38; animal life, 213; gravity, 81; light, 131; plant life, 187; rocks and minerals, 161; simple machines, 100; sound, 117; water, 56

Crystal garden, 156

Curiosity: in children, 6; in teachers, 8

Dramatic play, related to: air, 37; animal life, 212; electricity, 145; gravity, 80; light, 130; magnetism, 69; plant life, 184; rocks and minerals, 160; simple machines, 98; sound, 116; water, 54

Earthworm farm, to make, 190

Education Development Center, 19

Electricity concepts, related to magnetism, 146

Elementary science study, 19

Erikson, Erik, 8, 20

Ets, Marie Hall, 201

Fear, reducing of about: animals, 204; darkness, 121, 128; insects, 194, 214; lightning, 135; shadows, 128; sounds, 105, 115, 118

Field trips, related to: air, 38; animal life, 214; electricity, 145; gravity, 81; light, see Parents, involvement; magnetism, see Parents, involvement; plant life, 185; rocks and minerals, 160; simple machines, 99; sound, 117; water, see Parents, involvement

Fingerplays, related to: air, 36; animal life, 210; electricity, 143; plant life,

Fingerplays *(Continued)*
182; simple machines, 97; sound, 115; water, 54
Flack, Marjorie, 44
Flavell, J.H., 20
Food experiences, related to: air, 37; animal life, 213; electricity, 145; gravity, 81; plant life, 171, 176, 184; rocks and minerals, 160; simple machines, 99; water, 55
Freeman, Mae, 81

Gagné, Robert, 3, 21
Gears, 93
Glazer, Tom, 35, 118, 123, 125, 127, 171
Glider, to make, 30
Gouday, Alice, 125
Gravity concepts, related to: air, 83; simple machines, 101; water, 52, 83

Hawkinson, J., 113
Hoban, Russell, 121
Holl, Adelaide, 126
Holt, John, 20
Howell, Ruth, 165
Hunt, J. McVicker, 20

Insects: catching, 193; characteristics, chart of, 195; preserving, 194
Intellectual development, 7, 8
Interest, fluctuating, 14

Jensen, A.R., 3, 6

Kagan, Jerome, 3, 6
Keats, Ezra J., 48, 107
Krockmal, A., 178

Landeck, Beatrice, 94, 114
Landreth, Catherine, 20
Light concepts, related to: surface tension, 132
Lionni, Leo, 129

McCloskey, Robert, 101
Magnetism concepts, related to: air, 70; electricity, 146; simple machines, 101; water, 70
Math experiences, related to: air, 34; animal life, 206; gravity, 78; magne-

Math experiences *(Continued)*
tism, 66; plant life, 180; rocks and minerals, 157; simple machines, 96; sound, 114; water, 52
Miles, Miska, 169
Milgrom, Harry, 75
Minarik, Else, 81, 185
Montessori, Maria, 8, 20, 117
Music, related to: air, 34; animal life, 205; electricity, 142; friction, 94; gravity, 78; light, 128; magnetism, 67; plant life, 179; rocks and minerals, 157; simple machines, 94; sound, 113; water, 52

Notkin, Jerome, 89, 131

Parachute, to make, 32
Parents: as teaching partners, 11; involvement with science learnings, 38, 58, 70, 83, 101, 118, 132, 146, 162, 188, 215
Periscope, 130
Pets in the classroom, 204
Piaget, Jean, 3, 7, 15
Pitcher, Evelyn, 20
Plant care, 174
Plant life concepts, related to: air/water cycle, 188; rocks and minerals, 188; water, 58
Podendorf, Illa, 58
Poems, related to: air, 36; animal life, 209; electricity, 143; gravity, 79; light, 129; plant life, 182; rocks and minerals, 159; sound, 115; water, 53
Primary reinforcements, purpose of, 4
Problem solving, 8
Pulleys, 93

Razran, G., 3, 6
Rey, A.A., 54, 81
Rocks and minerals concepts, related to: plant life, 162; water, 47
Rogers, Fred, 16

Safety, 25, 58, 88, 101, 108, 138, 139, 142, 179, 193
Saunders, John, 196
Scarry, Richard, 75, 94
Science and Children, 19
Science experiences, adapting for: disad-

Science experiences *(Continued)*
vantaged children, 17; early elementary classes, 18; younger children, 17
Science teaching: incidental approach to, 13; purposeful approach to, 9
Secondary reinforcements, purpose of, 5
Security, promoting feelings of, 6, 58, 73, 148
Self-concept enhancement: mastery, 5, 8, 123; self-esteem, 101; strength, 28, 88, 94, 101
Selsam, Milicent, 58, 128, 157, 204
Sesame Street, 16
Simon, Seymour, 46
Simple machine concepts, related to: buoyancy, 101; gravity, 101; magnetism, 101;
Sound concepts, related to: air, 39, 107, 111, 112, 114; animal life, 118; friction, 118; water, 108, 111, 114
Stories and references for children, related to: air, 34; animal life, 206–9; electricity, 142; gravity, 79; light, 128;

Stories and references *(Continued)*
magnetism, 67; plant life, 180–82; rocks and minerals, 158; simple machines, 96; sound, 114; water, 52
Syphon, to make, 58

Thinking games, related to: air, 38; animal life, 213; electricity, 145; gravity, 81; light, 132; magnetism, 69; plant life, 184; simple machines, 99; sound, 117; water, 55

Vaughn, Eleanor, 62, 109

Water chimes, to make, 111
Water concepts, related to: air, 39, 47, 49, 57; gravity, 52, 83; simple machines, 101; sound, 108, 111, 114
Weather, 30, 39, 45, 47, 48, 49, 52, 57
Webber, Irma, 171

Zion, Gene, 203